"Organizations knowing the cost of everything and the customer value of nothing will not survive. John Seddon has thrown a lifeline to those who are inspired enough to seize it."
—Stephen Parry, Head of Strategy and Change, Fujitsu Services

"Seldom in our lifetimes does a person advocate a journey that only promises the opportunity to feel completely and utterly uncomfortable and wrong. Destroying the working paradigm takes a massive act of conviction from management, admitting that you have been wrong (for years) takes an equally massive act of bravery. Putting the two together feels fundamentally insane but to create real moments of change in today's business world takes leaps of faith. In this book John Seddon provides a key to the wise and the brave that can unlock their people, their customers and their profits. Do you have the faith, bravery and conviction to use it?"
—Bruce MacLellan, Director, Customer Contact, Capital One

"John Seddon describes the real world. In the real world people make the work work—if managers know how to let them."
—Alan Hughes, Chief Executive, First Direct

"Another masterpiece by John Seddon. This book inspired me to get out in my business and do things. It is practical, relevant and challenging."
—David Rixon, Chief Executive, Giles Foods

"Taiichi Ohno's system (the Toyota Production System) was an innovation in manufacturing. He proved how better quality and lower cost can be attained at the same time. In plain language, John Seddon shows how to successfully translate these ideas to service organizations."
—Takaji Nishizawa, consultant in world class manufacturing

"UK productivity continues to improve at a pedestrian pace. The target culture in the public sector is destroying the very service ethos that it is meant to foster. When will UK plc and the government wake up and embrace the road to sustainable continuous improvement that John Seddon espouses?"
—David Mead, Group Operations Director, AON

Freedom from Command & Control

Rethinking Management for Lean Service

John Seddon

Productivity Press
NEW YORK, NEW YORK

Most Productivity Press books are available at quantity discounts when purchased in bulk. For more information contact our Customer Service Department (888-319-5852). Address all other inquiries to:

Productivity Press
444 South Avenue South, 7th floor
New York, NY 10016
United States of America
Telephone: 212-686-5900
Fax: 212-686-5411
E-mail: info@productivitypress.com
Library of Congress Cataloging-in-Publication Data

Seddon, John.
     Freedom from command & control : rethinking management for
  lean service / John Seddon.
        p. cm.
     ISBN 1-56327-327-6 (alk. paper)
     1. Industrial management.   2. Industrial management—
  Employee participation.   3. Organizational effectiveness.
  4. Organizational change.   5. Industrial efficiency.   6. Customer
  relations.   I. Title: Freedom from command and control.
  II. Title.
  HD31.S3663   2005
  658.3′152—dc22

                                                    2005015339

09 08 07 06 05   5 4 3

For
Flora, Jodie and Angela

Contents

Acknowledgement

The material in this book could not have been developed without Vanguard clients and consultants. It has been immensely enjoyable to have been learning as we have been working.

INTRODUCTION

There is a better way

Command and control is failing us. There is a better way to design and manage work—a better way to make the work work—but it remains unknown to the vast majority of managers. The better way has a completely different rationale to command and control, and that, perhaps, is the reason it remains unknown. It is difficult to understand a different logic. People interpret what they hear from within their current frame of reference, so that what they 'hear' is not necessarily what is meant—it is the frame of reference from which they 'understand' that gets in the way of understanding. It is correspondingly hard to change norms through debate, easier to change them through action.

WHAT'S WRONG WITH COMMAND-AND-CONTROL MANAGEMENT

Our organizational norms are based on command-and-control thinking. We think of our organizations as top-down hierarchies; we separate decision making from work; we expect managers to make decisions with measures like budgets, standards, targets, activity and so on. We teach managers that their job is to manage people and budgets. These are the principles and practices that constitute command-and-control management.

Doubts about the effects of the command-and-control philosophy of management are now common. People discuss the problems caused by the top-down imposition of targets in our public services. The same conversations were had in the private sector years ago, but the prevailing culture meant these thoughts were treated as subversive; the well-known problems became accepted as things that needed to be discouraged and/or managed. But problems such as these cannot be solved or managed away within the prevailing view. To do so leads us merely to 'doing the wrong thing righter.'[1] We need to determine what is the right thing to do—to treat the causes rather than the symp-toms. We should realize that these problems are signals for us to call into question some quite fundamental beliefs.

In recognition of the fact that command and control is fail-ing, we promote solutions which themselves do not represent a change in paradigm. For example, the recent popularity of 'coaching' is a response to the perceived problems with com-mand and control; it is a palliative, not a solution. It is under-standable that 'coaching' should appeal. Command and control implies 'dictating,' so it follows that managers should dictate less and consult and develop more. But the problem is not that com-mand and control is insufficiently people-centered; it is that command and control represents a flawed logic about how we should design and manage work. It might be the normal way to do so, but it is not the best way. Involving workers more is not a remedy for a faulty paradigm. To 'delegate' a paradigm through coaching, empowerment or an employee involvement program will not lead to improvement if the very method implicit in the paradigm is flawed. W. Edwards Deming[2] described command and control as an organizational prison; he reminded us that as we invented it, we could and should reinvent it.

The problem is, however, that command and control seems to work, after a fashion. Because we are inside it, we do not see the enormous waste of time, effort and money it imposes. We shrug off its obvious imperfections as normal—'that's just the way it is.' There is, therefore, little cause to question whether it could be bettered. Moreover, command and control is ubiquitous. Its associated norms are rarely, if ever, challenged.

"We are going to win and the industrial west is going to lose out; there's not much you can do about it because the reasons for fail-ure are within yourselves. Your firms are built on the Taylor model.[3] Even worse, so are your heads. With your bosses doing the thinking while workers wield the screwdrivers, you're con-vinced deep down that is the right way to run a business. For the essence of management is getting the ideas out of the heads of the bosses and into the heads of labor. We are beyond your mindset. Business, we know, is now so complex and difficult, the survival of firms so hazardous in an environment increasingly unpredictable, competitive and fraught with danger, that their

continued existence depends on the day-to-day mobilization of every ounce of intelligence."—Konosuke Matsushita[4]

The separation of decision making from work, the cornerstone of command-and-control thinking, has its roots in Taylorism (scientific management), and was developed through the work of Henry Ford (mass production) and Alfred Sloan ('management by the numbers'). The issue is not that command and control was without value, for it solved problems for each of these management pioneers in new ways. But we have not continued to learn; the basic precepts of command and control are unquestioned although the underlying paradigm has outlived its usefulness. Managers share and do not doubt assumptions that govern the way we run our organizations. The problem is a problem of culture; it is a problem of management thinking.

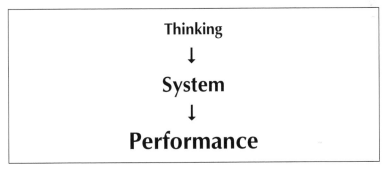

Figure P1: Thinking governs performance

There is a story of a Japanese guru working with a board of management on what to do to improve their organization's performance. He drew up a flip-chart list of recommendations on which the first one was, 'The board should resign.' He got their attention. The point he wanted to make was that unless you change the way you think, your system will not change and therefore, its performance won't change either. The question is: 'What thinking needs to change?'

THE BETTER WAY—A DIFFERENT LOGIC

The better way is to manage the organization as a system.[5] As figure P2 illustrates, it is a way of thinking about the design and management of work that is diametrically opposed to command and control.

Command and control thinking		Systems thinking
Top-down, hierarchy	**Perspective**	Outside-in, system
Functional	**Design**	Demand, value and flow
Separated from work	**Decision-making**	Integrated with work
Output, targets, standards: related to budget	**Measurement**	Capability, variation: related to purpose
Contractual	**Attitude to customers**	What matters?
Contractual	**Attitude to suppliers**	Cooperative
Manage people and budgets	**Role of management**	Act on the system
Control	**Ethos**	Learning
Reactive, projects	**Change**	Adaptive, integral
Extrinsic	**Motivation**	Intrinsic

Figure P2: Command-and-control versus systems thinking

Throughout the book, I shall illustrate how command-and-control thinking represents a logic governing how work is designed and managed. At the heart of this logic is the separation of decision making from work. You will see for yourself that the consequences are high cost and poor service; poor service costs more than good service, because it takes longer and is more expensive to carry out and correct work that is badly designed. Top-down functional hierarchies add to this cost by damaging the way with which customers are dealt.

Some examples are so alarming that you might think I am making them up—managers surely could not be so irrational. Yet every example is from today's enterprises. It is not the managers' fault. The astonishingly adverse consequences can be traced back to the way managers manage—the way they think about the design and management of work. It is only when they learn to take a different view that they can 'see' the irrationality and its consequences, things that previously were invisible. You may wonder how management could get so far away from the plot.

Management must return to being inextricably linked with operations. The job of management is to make the work 'work' better. You may be thinking, How could it be otherwise? All I can tell you is, it is. Over the last century we have developed a way of managing that is detached, remote and the primary cause of poor economic performance. Of course, many managers find it hard to believe this to be true because they are actively engaged in managing their operations. But command-and-control management keeps managers out of touch with their operations; the means of management's current engagement ensures its remoteness. Managers may believe they are in touch with their operations, yet they are anything but.

A central tenet of the traditional command-and-control mentality is management by the numbers; this is the basis and means for decision making. The numbers are largely financial and activity-related (what people do), which may or may not be of value to understanding and improving the system. With a proclaimed interest in 'shareholder value,' senior managers sit astride a system that they make more unstable and suboptimal through financial interference. Almost without thinking about it, the purpose of the organization becomes 'make the budget.' As with any target, in the pursuit of this purpose managers actually make performance worse—by 'managing costs,' for example, they create (more) costs. If only they knew. In pursuit of economies of scale, managers of service organizations build factories to handle work and worsen service, but they remain unaware of the extent of the damage, because their measures, being activity- rather than purpose-related, keep them blind. Top-down imposition of targets and other edicts results in 'cheating.' Dysfunctional behavior is ubiquitous and systemic, not because people are wicked but because the requirement to serve the hierarchy competes with the requirements to serve customers. People's ingenuity is engaged in survival, not improvement.

When managers learn to take a systems view, starting outside-in (that is, from the customer's, rather than the organization's, point of view), they can see the waste caused by the current organization design, the opportunities for improvement and the means to realize them. Taking a systems view always provides a compelling case for change and it leads managers to see the value of designing and managing work in a different way. The systems approach is to design against customer demand (the things customers want from you) instead of in functional hierarchies (the convenience of the organization). To design against demand removes the abundant waste inherent in the current design. As waste is removed, capacity increases, lessening costs and providing scope for growth. The case material will illustrate that (and how) the systems alternative works. But the better way represents a challenge to current management conventions. Measures and roles need to change to make the systems solution work. You have to be prepared to change the system, the way work is designed and managed; especially the way measures are used in management.

Only when managers see for themselves the dysfunctional consequences of their current measures do they engage in devising measures that will be more beneficial. In the systems solution, measures are derived from purpose (not the budget), and are used by the people who do the work to understand and improve it. To use measures this way is to put back together the elements of decision making and work that Taylor took apart. It encourages people to bring their brains to work, as Matsushita counseled.

The benefits are significant. The systems approach creates an adaptive organization. As demand changes, people change what they do—something that is impossible to accomplish in a command-and-control design. It puts people back where they belong: managing relationships with customers. Managers' roles change from working in the hierarchy to acting on the system.

Deming used to ask, 'Doesn't anybody care about profit?' for it comes down to that. The better way leads to better profits. But it is even better than that. The better way leads to improved morale and lower turnover of personnel. It leads to better service—how else could customers be persuaded to stick around for longer and continue to support the enterprise? The problem is, the better way is based on an entirely different way of thinking about the design and management of work. Any challenge to the prevailing norms is bound to be treated with skepticism at best, and cynicism at worst.

HOW THIS BOOK IS ORGANIZED

From Deming I learned about the work of Taiichi Ohno, the first person to realize the profound benefits of managing the organization as a system. I want to take the reader on much the same journey, so the book starts with Ohno's work in manufacturing. My main interest has been the application of these ideas to service organizations, so Chapter 2 begins with the simplest system, the service center. The issues raised by the application of these ideas, even in something as simple as a service center, are significant. The most significant, and one most managers struggle with, is measurement, so I devote two chapters (3 and 4) to issues of measurement. Chapter 5 puts it all together using 'break–fix' systems as examples. Chapter 6 talks about leadership—and has nothing on vision and values, and a lot on how to get in touch with the way the work works; in short, how to lead. Chapter 7 is all about being customer-driven and, en route, I discuss whether Customer Relationship Management (CRM)—a current fad— will provide sustainable solutions. This leads me to Chapter 8: 'Do these hold water?' I hope, by then, the reader will have grasped the fundamentals of the systems approach and thus will appreciate my criticisms of management fads. We would have fewer fads if we had more knowledge. In Chapter 9, 'Watch out for the toolheads,' I explore the current fad, lean manufacturing tools, and illustrate the mistake of applying these tools in service organizations. Ohno taught us that we should not codify method (create tools); instead, we should focus on thinking. Which brings me to the Conclusion, an appeal to return to valuing knowledge in operations, the essential prerequisite to creating an adaptive service system.

Although I use some public sector examples in the book, I return to the public sector in the Appendix: 'The better way to improve public services.' British government ministers have adopted the tenets of command-and-control management in their pursuit of public sector improvement with disastrous unintended consequences. There is an urgent need to review policy and practice.

Throughout the book, I've included many examples and case studies, which are highlighted in italics. These are intended to show you the real-world application of the principles I describe.

My hope is that this book will provide readers with the desire to increase their awareness and, more important, behave in ways that further their understanding of how to act on their organizations for improvement. The challenge is to be prepared to change the way you think. The reward is to discover a better way of managing. That can only be good for yourself, your management colleagues, all those employed by the enterprise and for society in general.

CHAPTER 1

Once upon a time in manufacturing

More than 50 years ago, something occurred at Toyota and a small number of other Japanese manufacturers that has still to make its impact in the broader organizational world. Taiichi Ohno[6] developed a radically different approach to the design and management of work. He inspired others with his results.

The number of man-hours it takes to make a Lexus is less than the man-hours used in reworking a top-of-the-line German luxury car at the end of the production line, after it has been made.[7]

The research that reported this incredible result was published 10 years ago. People say the Germans are catching up. But would you imagine that Toyota has stopped improving over the last decade? How much further is it likely to have gone? And how much easier is it for the company to continue to progress when its supply chain is inculcated with the same philosophy? How difficult is it for a traditional mass-production motor manufacturer to switch from managing function to managing flow? We have seen many manufacturers make extensive use of quality tools and problem-solving teams, but have they changed their systems?

Toyota has not achieved its exemplary status (about to overtake Ford as the second-largest motor manufacturer in the world, its market value is greater than that of General Motors, Ford and Daimler-Chrysler put together) by managing in the way that might be considered normal—setting targets and driving people to meet them. Instead of top-down command-and-control management, Toyota has learned how to use local control—control at the point where the work is done. The philosophy is fundamentally different. It represents a seismic shift in organizational culture. The attitude is no longer 'make these numbers,' but 'learn and improve.' To Western minds, 'learn and improve' is a problem. It is not very macho. It is 'soft.' It requires openness, enquiry and cooperation—all things our organizations claim as values, but rarely practice. They are hard to practice because they run counter to the underlying hierarchical philosophy.

To a command-and-control manager, the change in locus of control looks like anarchy. Nothing could be further from the truth. Paradoxically, 'learn and improve' gives more control, not less. Equally paradoxical, as I shall demonstrate, command-and-control methods not only afford little real control, they are a major cause of business escaping it. By causing managers to lose sight of their customers, they can ultimately contribute to putting the organization out of business altogether.

SO WHAT HAPPENED IN TOYOTA?

Thomas Johnson and Anders Broms[8] tell a story about a meeting between the executives of Ford and Toyota in 1982. It is reported that when the Americans visited Japan to find out how Toyota could produce better quality at lower cost, they were astonished to receive the response, 'We learned it from you.' Before building manufacturing facilities in Japan, the Japanese had studied American plants. In particular, Ohno spent time at Ford's Highland Park[9] plant. Built during World War I, Highland Park produced 15 million model-T Fords by 1927 with remarkable efficiency. Highland Park was the original mass-production system. Production costs were cut through standardization—it was the era of 'any color as long as it's black.' Henry Ford halved the costs of making a car and doubled his workers' wages. His system was a genuine landmark of modern management.

When Ohno studied the plant, what he instantly perceived was flow—simple, standardized and unchanging. As each car rolled off the line, it represented to him a 'heartbeat' that dictated how everything moved (was 'pulled') through the system. Ohno put that principle to work throughout the Toyota Production System. Today the customer order triggers flow; nothing is made without an order and the customer receives the car within days.

Remarkable: low cost and high quality. But the Americans did not 'see' flow; in their way of thinking, work was 'pushed' by the schedule rather than 'pulled' by the customer. They thought of the management task as increasing speed and volume. As each increased, costs fell. Ohno, on the other hand, saw the management task as improving flow.

Although each way of thinking sets out to achieve the same goal, better quality and lower costs, the limitations of the American paradigm became apparent when the market changed. Customers began to want variety. The problem was how to meet that demand at mass-production prices. The Americans and Japanese addressed this problem quite differently.

THE AMERICAN APPROACH TO THE 'VARIETY' PROBLEM

The American approach was to mass-produce in batches to maintain economies of scale. To do this they needed to create what Johnson and Broms call 'an information factory.' I prefer the label 'management factory' and shall use it here. Although there is a lot of information (and often of the wrong sort) in management, there is also a lot of behavior, so 'management factory' is in my view a better term. The management factory manages inventories, scheduling, planning, reporting and so on. It sets the budgets and targets. It is a place that works with information that is abstracted from work. Because of that it can have a phenomenally negative impact on the sustainability of the enterprise.

People who do the work become cogs in the machine. Decisions about work times, scheduling, parts and so on are removed from the work and are used to control the work and the worker. But the 'control' is illusory. Production in this environment is unlikely to match customer demand because there will always be problems of availability of the goods customers want to purchase.

In the early 1990s I was working with a new telephone sales operation selling computers—at that time a radical move. I found significant lost opportunity in the shape of unfulfilled customer demand. With the client we worked our way up the hierarchy to the place where decisions were made concerning inventory—that is, what we could sell. En route we saw that

> *the planning numbers were translated from products into money and back again. What was driving the system was production. When we presented our data and showed the lack of fit between what was being produced and the nature of demand, we were told: 'Read my lips: we make, you sell.'*

The direct sales operation was no more than an outlet or channel for the manufactured products. It was never thought of as a means to build relationships with customers, giving them what they need.

The 'make-and-sell' model creates waste. Its most obvious manifestation is inventory evident in fields all over Europe— unsold cars waiting for a market. The responsibility shifts to the people in marketing who must provide special offers, resulting in lower margins. To work this way amounts to make it, keep it and then give someone something to encourage them to buy it. The better way is sell it, make it, take the money.

In January 2002 I received this e-mail from a fellow systems thinker:

> *My brother-in-law works for a UK car manufacturer. He has just purchased a car for my sister. She ordered a base car with a factory-fitted sunroof; what she received was a car with factory-fitted sunroof and full electrics (windows, doors, mirrors and power steering). The reason is that the only cars they have available with a factory-fitted sunroof are cars that are due out to the market in four months time, which will have the higher specification. The questions I posed to my brother-in-law were: How much cost have they given away to my sister? What is the cost of storing all these cars? And how did they plan to sell the two things (electrics and sunroof) together? 'Marketing' was the answer: 'We'll do a special deal on this car in May.'*
>
> *I said that this was just adding another cost in chasing demand that wasn't there. He started to open his eyes. 'How would you do it another way?' was his question. My answer: I would only build cars that people wanted to buy.*

In the same month I learned that one of the 'big three' motor manufacturers was reluctant to remove the 'revenue-out-the-door' metric (i.e., what is made as opposed to what is sold) by which it measured the performance of its factories. Unless it does, it will never escape its current predicament—despite paying huge sums to recruit some Toyota-trained *sensei*[10] to work there. According to my informant, top management did not believe that the financial analysts would understand the move. Inventory of course appears on the balance sheet—but even bankers can be persuaded of the folly of that idea.

Ohno once remarked that manufacturing should be thought of as a simple supermarket. As a customer 'pulls' a product off the shelf, a little factory behind the shelf makes another and puts it in the vacated space. Sounds crazy? Maybe, but the fact is that working this way gives you less inventory, less time, less waste of other sorts and, most of all, good customer service.

So it comes down to a choice: use marketing to stimulate demand for what we have made, or build relationships with customers to deliver what customers want—push versus pull.

THE JAPANESE APPROACH TO THE 'VARIETY' PROBLEM

Ohno's solution to the variety problem was to put variety in the line. The same assembly line needed to be able to produce different models. His priority was therefore to determine what the people who did the work required to handle the variety, to do what was needed as each (different) car moved through the line. The result was the development of a system that managed flow, using the people within the work flow as the principal agents. This simple act, integrating decision making with the work, produced a wholly different management infrastructure and a new *lingua franca* for management. The purpose of the system is to produce against demand—to make the car only after receiving the order.

In Ohno's philosophy, each person's work is connected to the needs of customers, as opposed to arbitrary and counterproductive measures of activity. In command-and-control organizations it is usually the case that the measures used are derived from the budget—for example, the requirement to make so many items a week or month to fit periodic sales targets. But this introduces variation, making production performance worse and less stable. The result of production variation is variation in ability to service customers, variation in costs and, ultimately, variation in the probability of the system's ability to stay in business for the long term. Moreover, connecting work to arbitrary measures creates the need to have additional people processing information—scheduling work, reporting on work, making demands on those who do the work. Separation of decision making from the work is the defining rationale for the management factory. The Toyota Production System has no such management factory.

By removing the need for the management factory, organizations can make immediate and sustainable cuts in their operating expenses. The bonus is that they also achieve an immediate reduction in variation. But to remove the management factory without replacing it could cause the whole enterprise to fall. Before it can be dismantled, managers have to establish the better alternative. For this reason, we need to have a clear understanding of what the Toyota solution entails.

If the American solution exemplifies economies of scale, the Japanese solution represents economies of flow. The system is designed to produce to order, so the focus is on flow rather than function. All the information needed to do the work is integrated with the work itself, not in separate systems. The consequence is that variety can now be managed in the same process. This increases interest in the work for those who do it; it changes the locus of control, from external to internal, and, consequently, has a positive impact on motivation.

WHAT OHNO SAW

Ohno did not view low cost as attributable to scale, throughput, speed and cost targets. Instead, he saw a pattern permeating every part of the system, as though the work were 'joined up.' He recognized that work should flow continuously through each part of the system at the same rate that finished units flowed off the line. He could see that if every step in a flow operated at the same rate, then any moment in any step should consume only those resources required to advance a customer order one step closer to completion. In that way, costs would be as low as they could be. He saw that optimizing flow would lead to low costs because you only do what you need.

To tackle the variety problem, Ohno saw the need for the worker to design and control the steps so that he or she would be able to perform different operations according to what is needed. In this way, he concluded, variety could be achieved at no greater cost than if all units were identical. As we shall see, this is a profoundly important issue for the design of service organizations, for they exhibit much greater variety: the customer is involved as a co-producer in what is 'made.' In service organizations, the *only* way to solve the variety problem is to 'put variety in the line.'

There is another story told about Ohno.[11] He had returned from America having studied motor manufacturing, and his job was to create a plant to make cars in Japan. Toyota couldn't afford the number of pressing machines the Americans had; in fact it could only afford one. So his first task was to cut down changeover times—the amount of time it takes to change a machine from doing one thing to doing another. In a matter of months, he had cut the time from the American standard, 10 days, to 10 minutes. Then he had a counterintuitive moment—his costs went down. He, like others, assumed that smaller batch sizes would mean higher costs. But he realized that his costs had gone down because he had less inventory. Moreover, if something was wrong it would be seen at once and corrected; it did not appear much further down the line having consumed more resource. The time any parts spent in his system was shorter. There was less time between the order and delivery. Ohno realized that costs must be viewed end-to-end, and that time was predictive of costs. If he had focused on functional or 'unit' costs, as the Americans did, he might never have discovered the importance of managing and improving flow: the end-to-end work from receipt of the customer's order to receipt of the customer's money.

Having learned that the key to achieving efficient variety of output was to reduce individual changeover times, Ohno saw that he had to make the changeover times conform to the rate at which finished products flowed out of the factory. He theorized that if every changeover time was less than the time interval between units flowing off the line, then it would be possible for every unit coming off the line to be different; yet still the unit costs would be nearly identical to those if all units were the same.

It is extraordinary that these advances in management theory should have taken place in motor manufacturing, one of business's most complex organization forms. In service organizations, similar benefits can be achieved in a much shorter time, for little is physically 'made.' On the other hand, service organizations also have another crucial, countervailing difference—the inherent variety of demand. Customers make customer-shaped demands; if the systems cannot absorb this variety, costs will rise.

In manufacturing you can 'get away with' command and control (at a cost) because, after all, the products you make are standard; there are economies of scale. To adopt the same scale-economies approach for a service organization, however, is to court failure. When applied to service organizations, the traditional command-and-control design responds to the variety of customer demands by establishing procedures, standard forms, functions, levels, specialized 'factories' and the like to deal with them. The consequence is enormous amounts of waste. To eliminate the waste, you need to dismantle the functional structures and 'put variety in the line.'

Managers imagine this will take time. It is partly because of how they think about change. It is also because of what it implies for their past identity and effort. In the name of 'service,' many of our organizations have been built as mass-production factories subjected to detailed programs of activity directed by managers. Often, this is a significant investment in human and financial resources. To undo or redirect this effort represents a significant challenge.

Maximizing the ability to handle variety is central to improving service and reducing costs. The systems approach employs the ingenuity of workers in managing and improving the system. It is intelligent use of intelligent people; it is adaptability designed in, enabling the organization to respond effectively to customer demands. Workers are connected with customers in self-organizing relationships—diversity of flow is the hallmark of good service design. In managing flow, the work itself is the information, and this in turn comprises the information required to direct operations in the work.

People are good at handling variety; computers are not. As managers develop the systems approach, they learn to use computers for the things they are good at and *to the contrary* avoid using computers for things that people are good at. The consequences are fewer computer systems and more control. I shall return to some of the problems we are having with computer systems in Chapter 8. But, in essence, their value lies in supporting those who deliver service; today, too often they hinder. Computers have become the cement for command-and-control management. It is an unquestioned assumption that managers should have and set targets and then create control systems—incentives, performance appraisals, budget reporting and computers to keep track of them all—to ensure the targets are met. In Toyota, these practices simply do not exist. To make our service organizations work better, they need to be taken out.

ECONOMIES OF FLOW

By the early 1980s, Toyota was producing output at the rate needed to satisfy demand—as Ford had done in 1925—but with the difference that Toyota also produced variety. The Toyota Production System (TPS) used smaller machines and each step was performed at a slower rate. The Toyota system exemplifies economies of flow, a quantum leap beyond economies of scale. The concepts associated with economies of scale have governed managerial thinking for the last century or more, whether in the macro sense—mergers, structure and so on—or the micro sense—the design of work functions and methods. Economies of flow represent a challenge to current beliefs. It is a challenge of such scale that this—the challenge to current beliefs—becomes the most important hurdle for managers to get over, for as I shall show, the ideas themselves are simple, logical and practical. However, they are different and unfamiliar; as a consequence they are often perceived as a threat. They are certainly counter-intuitive to the 'command-and-control' mind-set.

The focus of this book is the translation of the principles behind the Toyota Production System for service organizations. The TPS provides a means to manage the work of making cars; it needs to be translated to apply the same ideas to understanding and managing customer service, a completely different kind of work.

> *The good news—for those of us working in service organizations—is that we don't make cars. The TPS has taken over fifty years of patient development, led by the late Ohno and now by many of his students. Because service organizations*

9

don't 'make' anything, the work that fulfills a customer demand can be easily redesigned. Change can be rapid: 50 days rather than 50 years. But why should it be redesigned? Because the current system of management is flawed, creating waste and suboptimizing service. In our service organizations costs are high and service is poor. As we have noted, the problem is that managers cannot 'see' the real costs, because their means of management acts like a blindfold.

I shall show how command-and-control management has created service organizations that are full of waste, offer poor service, depress the morale of those who work in them and are beset with management factories that not only do not contribute to improving the work, but actually make it worse. The management principles that have guided the development of these organizations are logical—but it's the wrong logic. The better way has a different logic. To explain the better logic I shall start with the simplest organizational form—the customer service center.

CHAPTER 2

The customer service center as a system

The advent of customer service centers was triggered by the availability of new technology. Automated call routing led to the creation of the command-and-control system's sleekest, most modern avatar, the call center—the office environment built as a mass-production factory. Just as we saw in manufacturing in the last century, mass-production offices have led to the alienation of workers, high staff turnover and low morale. In manufacturing, it caused poor product quality and industrial strife. In call centers, it produces poor customer service and high turnover of staff. In many call centers, 30 or 40 percent annual staff turnover is the norm. Today, because the customer can make contact through a variety of media—Internet, fax, phone—the call center has transmuted into the service center. But nothing of substance has changed.

Service centers can be rapidly transformed by a systems approach. When such a transformation occurs, it triggers an immediate improvement in performance and morale. You might think everyone would be doing it. They probably would if the ideas did not represent the complete antithesis to current management philosophy. In this chapter, I unpick that philosophy and introduce the systems alternative—the better way. I shall start with planning for a service center.

HOW DO ORGANIZATIONS PLAN FOR A SERVICE CENTER?

To plan resources, managers typically start from call data such as volumes and duration. They ask: How many calls will there be, how long do they take to handle, and on that basis, how much resource (people) do we need to answer them?

11

With the aim of cutting high branch staff costs, the organization and methods personnel of a UK bank measured the volume and duration of phone calls into the bank's branches. This 'sized' the work. They then routed all the calls to three purpose-built new call centers and made the surplus branch staff redundant. However, because of higher than anticipated demand, managers were soon obliged to add a fourth call center and then a fifth. At this point, the chief executive started to express concern about costs. Rationalizing the reason for the unanticipated volume of calls, managers claimed customers must be making more use of the service because they were enjoying it. They compared their experience to that of the advent of the M25 motorway. Just as this road had experienced unexpected volumes of traffic when it opened, their call centers were attracting unanticipated demand.

However, managers knew nothing about the nature of this demand. When I became involved, I listened to calls, discussing with the agents what I was learning. There are two broad types of demand on any service center—value demand, the calls we want, and failure demand, the calls we don't want. Value demand is what the service center exists to serve; it represents the demands customers make for things they want, things that are of value to them. Failure demand is created by the organization not working properly. I define it as follows:

Failure demand is demand caused by a failure to do something or do something right for the customer.

A failure to do something—turn up, call back, send something that is anticipated and so on—causes the customer to make a further demand on the system. A failure to do something right—not solve a problem, send out forms that customers have difficulties with and so on—similarly creates demand that represents extra work. Failure demand is under the organization's control and it is a major form of suboptimization. In the case of the bank, failure demand was running at 46 percent of the total. Now I knew how it had got to five call centers.

The majority of these (failure) demands had been caused by separating 'phone work' from other work.

It is a fundamental mistake in call center design and management to treat all demand as units of production. In service centers, managers are swimming in data about call volumes, time to answer, abandon rates, work accomplished by hours of the day, days of the week and by each agent. The underlying assumption is that customer service is a product that can be 'mass-produced' in a factory with standard times and standard procedures.

The planning tools used by managers of service centers were first developed many years ago to enable them to calculate how many operators to employ in telephone exchanges. At that time, operators handled all phone calls. There was little variation in customer demand—most customers simply needed connecting to the number of their choice—and the data could hence be used to plan robustly, taking into account waiting and call-handling time. Today, using the same tools, managers of service centers are preoccupied with 'service levels'—the percentage of calls answered in a standard time (usually 20 seconds)—the number of agents they have and the amount of work they do. Of course, it matters in any service center that the phone is answered, but to worry about these things and, what is worse, to turn these ideas into the means of management, invites disaster. They are worrying about the wrong thing.

The major difference between the environment in which the planning tools were developed and the work of a modern service center is the variety of demand. Treating all demand as 'units of production' prevents managers from 'seeing' demand in a way that would help them to meet it better. Failure demand represents a significant cost. Removing it has an enormous impact on the economics of a system.

The greatest leverage it is possible to have on a service center system is to alter the characteristics of demand.

The single greatest lever is the eradication of failure demand. Is there an economic prize associated with the removal of failure demand? Consider the following statistics. In the financial services sector I have found failure demand running from 20 to 45 percent of demand, in police forces, telecommunications and local authorities as high as 50 to 80 percent. Consider the cost associated with such levels of waste—for that is what it is. In service organizations, failure demand is often the greatest source of waste. Imagine the productivity improvements that follow its removal. The bank could get rid of two of its five call centers overnight.

A correspondent wrote to me:

I listened to calls in our call center. I reckoned there to be something between 30 and 40 percent failure demand. I put this to the call-center manager. He said that this was to be expected; it was the industry norm.

Rationalization is the greatest enemy of learning. If Ohno had had such a complacent attitude, he would never have created the Toyota Production System. Of course there is no industry 'norm.' It would be a sad joke if such a norm were researched and reported. I could have told him I know of systems similar to his that were both better and worse, but what value is there in arbitrary comparison? The only sensible thing to do is act. Failure demand is caused by the way we work; it is entirely under our control. The only goal required is perfection—zero failure demand. It should not require much consideration; it simply requires systematic action.

TAKING ACTION ON THE SYSTEM

The first step in reducing or eliminating failure demand is to establish whether it is predictable. To do this, you need to understand the 'type and frequency' of demand. Type: What are the reasons for customers calling from their point of view, and what does this tell us about which processes have failed? Frequency: how many of each type do we have, and do these recur over time? The latter helps us understand predictability, which is crucial. If failure demand is predictable, you can and should act to remove the causes. If it is unpredictable, the best thing to do may be nothing. Things will always go wrong; you need to sort out what is going wrong predictably.

I have been writing about this simple phenomenon for many years. I hear from many managers who are aware of the enormous potential for working on removing failure demand but are frustrated because the causes of failure demand lie outside their control. In that case, the only courses of action are writing reports and attending meetings across the functional hierarchy, probably the most predictable means of preventing learning and change. In the short term, action requires leadership from a senior manager, someone to whom the hierarchy 'looks up to.' The longer-term requirement is a change to the whole system. Roles and measures have to change from managing through the hierarchy to managing flow—managing the work end-to-end. The management factory needs to be removed as roles and measures are redefined.

But this does not mean the 'production' measures—volume of calls, time to answer, abandon rate and so on—are of no value. Service center managers do need to plan how many people they need to handle the volume of work, but they should not use these measures to manage. They are after the event. It might appear to make sense to use planning data to manage, but it focuses management on the wrong thing. The solution is to separate planning from operational management. The means for improvement lie in understanding demand from the customers' point of view. As you remove failure demand, production measures will show improvement. Paradoxically, the production improvement will come from managing flow, not production.

Unfortunately, most service centers are managed solely on production data, measuring activity rather than anything relating to purpose. Service centers appear as costs in top management's accounts. This is why managers are attracted by the idea of outsourcing. They hand over calls to an agency, whether in the same country or, more recently, in low-wage countries abroad, and pay per call for the service. The result is often simply to outsource waste. These managers are paying someone else to deal with their failure demand. Moreover, moving calls elsewhere makes understanding what is going on all the more difficult—out of sight, out of mind. Should we praise such leaders for operating in a global economy or embarrass them for missing the obvious? Once again, they can see cost but they cannot see flow. They are oblivious to the real costs because their measures keep them blind.

Some service center managers do try to determine the reasons for a customer call, but most often they do so in an 'internal'—'what we do with it'—perspective. When I look at 'call coding,' as it is often described, I find the codes make no distinction between value and failure demand. Worse, call coding is often 'compulsory'—it is a forced part of the 'wrap' procedure (the work an agent has to do following a call). This only encourages agents to put in any code that will move calls on—they don't want to get 'bad wrap' data, as too much time in wrap will mean the agent will get paid attention to. In short, I have yet to find good information about the nature of demand in service centers. Yet it is the first thing to establish on an assignment. When I arrive in a service center, I generally find managers know everything about volumes and activity, but little or nothing about the real nature of the work.

Consultants behave in similar fashion. In one organization, a major consulting firm was conducting an analysis of call demand. I asked how much failure demand it had found. The answer: none. The consultants did not think that way. Instead, they analyzed demand through a 'marketing' filter, being concerned with what the calls revealed about customers and the products they had bought, rather than what the calls really meant from the customers' point of view. In fact, failure demand was running at a predictable 65 percent of call volume. Clearly customers were experiencing a number of problems, all of which were under the organization's control. The consultants had persuaded the managers that knowing more about the customers would enable managers to promote more products and services to them. I would have recommended that they make their current service amazing for their customers. To promote more services to customers who are calling because they are annoyed may just make them angrier. If action had been taken to remove the causes of failure demand, service would have improved and customers would then be more likely to come back. The consultants thought 'push,' I prefer to think 'pull.'

Being blind to the nature of demand also means losing opportunities to design the work to meet it—to give good service at the lowest cost. In cases of high failure demand, you need fast recovery—solving the customers' problems—while you also urgently invest in eradicating the causes of the customers' problems. With value demand, you need to deliver what the customer wants efficiently. To do this means working on the work flow, from the customer demand through to its completion. The traditional service center manager has no information about flow. Instead, he will be using data about activities, standards and costs. Perversely, this leads the manager to put the 'best' people in places where customers will find it hardest to get to them. The 'production' logic is, 'I can't have my most able people taking the easy calls.' So managers create levels and specialist functions to receive calls from those who filter at the 'front end.' The manager will have no idea how much rework, duplication, errors and time is built into the system and, in turn, how much failure demand these procedures create. To repeat, the real costs of production are end-to-end. Managing with the wrong means creates more costs, yet managers congratulate themselves on managing costs. The consequences are invisible to them. They cannot 'see.'

ACTING ON VALUE AND FAILURE DEMAND

You act in different ways for each type of demand.

In the case of failure demand, you act to remove the causes. The impact can be seen immediately on measures of productivity and customer service. With value demand, you act by designing to meet it in the most efficient way. You want customers to 'pull value' from the organization. If you design the work to do the 'value work'—what matters to the customer—and only the value work, costs will fall as service improves, something that most call center managers find counterintuitive, for their whole world is based on production assumptions, equating service with cost.

In the mid-1990s, I worked with an IT company's help desk. It was a traditional design. Managers measured the volume of demand and the workers' activity ('production') to do resource planning. Agents were monitored for their call activity; experts were right at the back of the flow. The engineers—the people who do the work—studied the nature of demand on the system. They discovered that they were using the same process to handle a wide variety of demands. By tracking each of the major types of demand through the system they could see waste and its causes. For the first time, they established a true end-to-end measure of the time it took to identify and fix a problem from the customers' point of view. It was stable and averaged six days.

The engineers took action. The experts moved to the front of the flow. They had learned from meeting customers to find out what mattered to them that the customers were experts too. They realized the quickest way to establish the value work in any call was to have the two experts talk to each other.

Many managers will now be thinking, 'But what about the cost?' Remember, cost is end-to-end. End-to-end, there was a large amount of duplication and rework in the functional design.

In the new set-up, the experts either closed the call by solving the problem or passed it to someone who had the best skill-set for resolution. It was a one-stop or one-pass philosophy. As a result, capacity (productivity) quadrupled, and end-to-end fix time fell to an average of less than a day. Morale went up, to boot. The engineers worked to solve problems such as how best to pass work and to whom, how to track the type and frequency of demand, and work with it intelligently. Being clever people, they developed IT tools to aid their efforts.

I should warn you against interpreting the case study by drawing the general conclusion that we should always 'put experts at the front.' It is the nature of demand that will tell you about the requirements for expertise. The customer demand dictates the value work; the value work dictates the expertise required. In this case the complexity of demand dictated an 'expert' response at the front end.

Acting on demand creates the greatest leverage on a service center. Performance improves enormously. Perhaps the greater priority is to restore morale. Happy people make better workers. In service centers, people are unhappy because they are monitored to death, and the way measures are used destroys their morale. These people are best placed to understand and act on demand—it gives meaning to their work and is a cornerstone in destroying the sweatshop culture. The nature of demand is just one thing managers of service centers cannot 'see.' Let's step back and build a picture of the typical service center organization to learn more about what managers *do* see.

ACTING ON THE WORK, NOT THE WORKERS

The sweatshop culture has been created by the production logic where the focus of management is on how to 'get them to do it'—take the requisite number of calls. This is to act on the worker, not the work. When we look at the typical service center (Figure 2.1), we see a hierarchical design based on the measures discussed above.

Figure 2.1: The service center hierarchy

Managers monitor their measures to manage resource against demand volumes. Top management will often be heard to say things like, 'If only we could reduce our average call length by 30 seconds, we could improve our bottom line by. . . .' This is to focus diametrically on the wrong thing. Of course, top management has no other view than cost data. The service center could be experiencing 70 percent failure demand, but management is focused on 'taking the calls,' not improving the system.

The service center manager sees his or her job as setting and monitoring work standards, productivity and procedures. It is an uncritically inherited assumption of traditional management thinking that people are the primary causes of poor or good performance, rather than the system in which they work. As a consequence, management becomes concerned with working on the people. Paradoxically, managing productivity in this way undermines productivity because the major causes of variation in performance are in the system—the way the work works. As the manager is preoccupied with meeting his service standards, team leaders become preoccupied with making sure people do 'as they should'—according to the plan. People are set targets or work standards. They are derived from the plan, not the work.

Let us suppose I work for you in a service center, and you have set a work standard of 100 calls a day. Yesterday I took 120 calls, today I took 80 (see Figure 2.2). What happens to me?

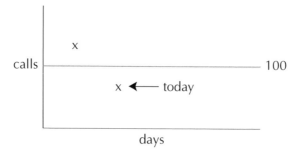

Figure 2.2: John's calls per day

In most service centers, this means I'd get paid attention to. In harsh cultures another term for this is bullying. In many service centers there are now policies about treating staff well, so the manager would turn up and 'coach'[12] rather than bully. But is this of any real difference? It is, most often, a mistake even to turn up. If you look at my performance over time, you might find I could do as few as 75 and as many as 125 calls in a day (Figure 2.3). But the reason for the variation is not me—the same me comes to work every day—the variation is in the system.

Figure 2.3: John's capability chart

Figure 2.3 shows my capability—what I am achieving and how predictable my performance is. If you were my manager you could now predict that I will handle between 75 and 125 calls a day, unless something changes. My capability is measured by taking time-series data: the calls I can handle every day, plotted over time. The statistical variation in my daily measures sets the upper and lower limits[13]—what can be expected as 'just as likely' results. It is not worthy of note that I might do as few as 75 calls or as many as 125; both results can be expected in this system.

There is always variation in anything that we do. In a call center, variation will be caused by the nature of the call, the mood of the customer, complexity of the product, design of the procedures, availability of information, knowledge of the service agent and so on. There will be many causes. To improve performance we need to understand and act on these causes. This is an easy exercise to run in any service center. Put the current performance measures in a capability chart, explain to people that the chart shows variation and ask what they think, from their experience, the causes of variation might be. Then, having brainstormed the causes, return to the list and ask: Which of these are attributable to the system—the way the work works—and which are attributable to agents? It is always as Deming and others taught: 95 percent or more of variation in performance is in the system. By working on the agents, service center managers are working on the remaining five percent—a staggering waste of management resource.

When I explain this to service center managers, there is usually someone who claims they do not react to a single data point but wait for a 'trend' to show in agent data before taking action. I always ask: 'Do you have measures that are plotted as time-series data'? The only way to determine what is going on, whether a difference is a 'real' difference or a blip, is to plot data in a capability chart. This tells you how much 'noise' (common cause variation) you have. Other than Vanguard clients, I know of no service center using measures in this way. Generally, you find managers 'eyeballing' tabular data to make decisions about 'trends.' You should never eyeball data, because you cannot reliably distinguish signals from noise[14] without plotting the data in a capability chart.

If service center workers' behavior is subject to variation, the extent and nature of that variation must be established before any action can be contemplated, otherwise managers will make the situation worse. Managers (and service agents) need to know whether variation in performance is attributable to agents or the system. Current approaches to people management in call centers ignore this important question. The 'sweatshop' sobriquet is a direct result. To hold the worker accountable for performance, when in fact it is governed by the system, causes stress. Because managers hold them accountable, service center workers often believe, as their managers do, that they are wholly responsible for their performance. When they have a bad day they leave work feeling guilty, ashamed and responsible. The organization has conditioned them to the prevailing philosophy; any agent who questions the philosophy is labelled as difficult or making excuses.

When, as will be inevitable, they risk becoming losers, agents 'cheat'—they do anything they need to do to make their numbers. People's ingenuity is engaged in surviving, rather than improving performance: a tragic waste of human talent. Agents close a call before the customer is finished, and sometimes before the customer has started; they tell customers to call back, they reroute difficult calls, in short they do all they can to avoid missing work targets or standards. Knowing that they do these things to survive exacerbates their feelings of demoralization. These are not bad people; they work in a bad system. The human costs of demoralization are incalculable. The immediately obvious costs are in recruitment and training, because these conditions create high staff turnover. But the real costs are higher—poor service and high costs are associated with customer dissatisfaction and staff dissatisfaction.

When managers first see agent data in a capability chart they express either disbelief or panic. Their attention is always drawn to the lower limit—they are terrified at the prospect that one day or one week all service agents would take 75 calls (using the example above). However, one would not expect a series of observations at the lower or, for that matter, the higher limit of the chart. The chart simply illustrates the extent of variation in numbers of calls per day that can be expected in the normal course of events. All, however, would be distributed around the mean.

The better way to think about managing people is to lead them in understanding and acting on the system. Rather than engaging their ingenuity against the system, it channels service agents' ingenuity into contributing, learning and improving. Just as service agents are best placed to understand and work to demand, they are best placed to address the question: What are the causes of variation? Causes of variation identified as within the team's control can and should be acted on by the team.

Causes of variation identified as beyond the team's control can and should be acted on by the manager. The measures help both managers and agents learn to 'see' the waste and causes of waste in their work.

Management's focus changes from managing people—ensuring that people do as they 'should'—to managing the system—understanding and improving how well the work flows, end-to-end, to fulfill the customers' demands. They establish a collaborative relationship with the agents, for they are working on the same problems (for a change). It is to move from managing the 5 percent to managing the 95 percent.

This is a revolutionary leap away from the current preoccupation with managing people. It is a step that managers are only prepared to take when they have first learned that their organization's performance is governed by the system and not the people. Once managers make this conceptual leap, they stop wasting time doing people management ('one-to-ones'); the impact on productivity is enormous.

In a financial services organization, systems thinking was piloted in one service center. Following the analysis of the 'what and why' of current performance as a system, it became clear how performance was being governed by the system, not the agents. All activity and sales targets were removed and replaced with capability measures. In this way, any real differences between agents were clear—managers were no longer treating noise (common cause variation) as signals. The focus for the agents moved from 'make these numbers' to 'serve the customer.'

One key measure in many financial services organizations is sales. Agents are typically targeted with up-selling and cross-selling products to customers who call in. Following the transformation and the removal of sales targets, sales became more stable in the pilot site. Sales did not go up or down, they just became more stable.

Before the change, managers, especially senior managers, had been concerned about the impact of the change on sales. Managers believed agents 'made sales.' Having invested heavily in sales training, they didn't want anything to happen that would cause a drop in sales. However, analysis showed that sales were being driven by two different things—demand and flow. In other words, the more customers call up to buy, the more sales we make; and the better we can make the sales fulfillment work (flow), the more sales we make again. Despite the knowledge provided by the analysis, senior managers remained nervous—they were wedded to the view that it was the agents that made the difference.[15]

So the teams went back to do more analysis. They took the last 100 purchasers and listened to the phone call where the transaction occurred. In more than 90 percent of cases the customer had bought—the product was not 'sold' by the agent. In the minority of cases where the agent had sold a product, most represented a loss of revenue to the organization. Typically, agents were making sales by restructuring the customers' finances.

Targeting and incentivizing sales was therefore irrelevant and, worse, counterproductive. Such findings are hard for managers to take on board. Managers enthusiastically invest in sales training in the belief that sales are made by agents. In truth, agents are no different to someone gambling at a fairground to pluck ducks out of a water carousel—that is, when they get a demand for a product, they service it ('sell' it). Sales were being neither won nor lost in the service center; they were primarily dependent on demand and secondarily on flow—what happened after the first point of contact. The volume of sales lost through poor flow in financial services organizations is often scarcely believable. But once again it is something managers usually cannot 'see.' I shall move on to managing flow in a moment, but first I shall redraw the picture of the service center, this time considering the things we need to manage to improve the system.

THE SERVICE CENTER AS A SYSTEM

The service center manager is still concerned with the center's ability to take calls, but these measures are now in capability charts. This fosters questions about causes of variation and avoids the mistake of treating noise as signals. Team leaders can now do as their job title suggests—lead. Variation between agents will be one source of learning for improvement; again, by using capabil-

Manager
Focus: creation of value for customers
Measures: demand and flow; service capability—predictability of:
• demand
• response
• failure
Role: leads action on the system

Team leader
Focus: creation of value for customers
Measures: achievement of purpose, demand and flow; variation in service agent performance
Role: leads agents in action on the system: act on causes of variation within the team's control; act on causes of variation beyond the team's control

Type and frequency of demand

Agent
Focus: creation of value for customers
Measures: achievement of purpose, variation in service agent performance; type and frequency of demand

Figure 2.4: Managing the system for improvement

ity measures, the team leaders avoid treating noise as a signal. As seen in Figure 2.4, team leaders and agents are attuned to the nature of demand—a major cause of variation. Fortunately, there are no computer packages capable of analyzing the type and frequency of demand. I say fortunately because the removal of measures to computer systems is often the beginning of the command-and-control disease, removing measures from the work. Demand can only be analyzed and understood by the people who do the work. It becomes a central part of what they do.

ACTING ON FLOW

If attention to demand is the greatest point of leverage on performance of a service center system, the next greatest is acting on flow. In service centers, there are many customer demands that cannot be handled at the point of transaction. Sales are just one type. These demands have to be sent to other departments or functions for information collecting, decisions, fulfilment or whatever. When you study these flows, you find a series of reasons customers might give up before they have achieved their original purpose. There is duplication, unnecessary procedures or bureaucracy, lost time and so on. Many things can make it difficult for customers to get what they want. In some organizations, one marvels at customers' preparedness to hang on, to get the service they require. Because they are full of waste, these systems carry high costs, the greatest cost being lost opportunity.

In financial services organizations, it is not unusual to find extremely low conversion rates for product sales. Part of the problem is 'dirty' input—for example, because service center agents are targeted on passing sales leads to other departments, they pass on whatever comes their way, just to make their targets. The result is that many such potential 'customers' are highly unlikely to buy. Generally, the bigger problem is the way the flow has been designed. Typically, managers have opted for 'economies of scale,' building factories for processing standard units of work. Customer demands are channeled into a standardized bureaucracy. Managers cannot 'see' the waste. Of course, managers are unable to ignore some of the resulting problems, but in my experience they generally act in ways that make them worse. For example, they will introduce inspection to catch those who are getting it wrong or cheating. More cost, more waste. And, moreover, it doesn't solve the problem; agents just get smarter at surviving in or beating the system. I have learned that as soon as you introduce controls on human behavior, you lose the game, particularly when those controls are at odds with the work.

However, the same talent that cheats the system can equally well be engaged in improving it. Improving flow starts with designing against demand. It reduces cost because you learn how to do only the value work. As costs fall, service improves and, consequently, in the case of financial services, sales improve.

Let's take a different example:

A new telecommunications provider was in trouble. Customers were so unhappy they were calling the chief executive. He called me for help. The work started in the service center— the eyes and ears of an organization, if it is prepared to use it as such. An analysis of demand showed very high levels of failure demand of two major types—progress-chasing and order fulfilment. Managers had established the following procedure for dealing with calls: Every call necessitated bringing up the customer record on the IT system and notes being made of the customer's request and actions taken. If the need could be met within three minutes, it should be done. If it seemed likely to take longer than three minutes, agents had to raise a 'task' on a separate 'work flow' IT system, duplicating much of the work already done on the customer record. The 'task' then had to be sent to the relevant department for action. Such tasks would wait in electronic queues. When this work was studied 'outside-in' (from the customer's point of view), looking at demand and flow, it became clear that enormous resources were being spent on 'non-value' work. Moreover, the batching, sorting, queuing and counting ('managing') of work was causing errors and failures to meet commitments made to customers. In turn, this was causing failure demand from customers—calls to chase progress, complain, raise a query and so on. The management's preoccupation with cost, which was behind the 'three-minute' edict, was actually causing much more cost. Some of the costs associated with waste were measurable; the costs of the impact on customers were much greater and incalculable.

In this case, managers were persuaded to throw the 'procedures' away. Instead, call center agents worked to the principle of 'handling everything that came in through to completion.' Those in other departments who had the expertise to solve customer problems were brought on to the call center floor. Thus, training became 'pull'—what was needed to resolve customer demands was learned immediately. The agents perfectly understood the logic because they had been involved in the analysis of demand. The consequence was rapid learning for the agents and a rapid improvement in customer service. For the first few days it was chaotic. In two weeks the call center came under control and reached a steady state. The volume of calls had dropped, because of reduced failure demand, and customers (these were business-to-business customers who had frequent contact) commented on the change. Of greatest surprise was the impact on average call handling times—which remained unchanged.

> *Managers discovered for themselves that learning to do the value work, and only that, reduced overall resource utilization and did not increase it in the service center. None would have predicted such a result, for it goes against the grain of a productivity mind-set.*
>
> *The order fulfilment problem required more investigation. When the flow was analyzed, it became apparent that no one knew how it worked end-to-end. It had been designed piecemeal by managers with heavy reliance on information technology. The analysis revealed no less than 26 handovers, eight inspections and a high probability that new customers would have a problem with their first order. To say it was broken is an understatement. The flow was redesigned.*
>
> *The first action—handling all calls at the point of transaction—took about three weeks to stabilize. For order fulfilment it took two weeks to establish a new clean flow and a further five weeks to move all the orders into the new flow.*

Just as Ohno had 'counterintuitive' moments when he first developed the Toyota system, we had one here. One would imagine that if the agents in the service center were working to solve all problems at the point of transaction by 'pulling' advice from the experts, call handling time would increase. Yet after the first week, call handling time stabilized at the same as pre-intervention levels. How could this be so? Agents were learning how to do the 'value' work—the work required to solve a customer problem. They were, quite literally, being trained against demand. But more than that, they were preventing repeat calls, irate customers from becoming angrier and unsolved issues becoming more complicated. In short, they were removing waste from the system.

The primary cause of failure demand—the order fulfilment process—was redesigned by studying what it took to do just the value work as a clean flow. Nothing was allowed to move forward 'dirty.' Forms that captured only the required information needed to be complete, information had to be exactly and only that required to ensure clean flow of work. To assess progress, agents needed measures. They needed to understand the time it took to fulfil an order accurately and the types and frequencies of failures to achieve that purpose.

So we can add some more elements to our picture of the service center as a system (Figure 2.5).

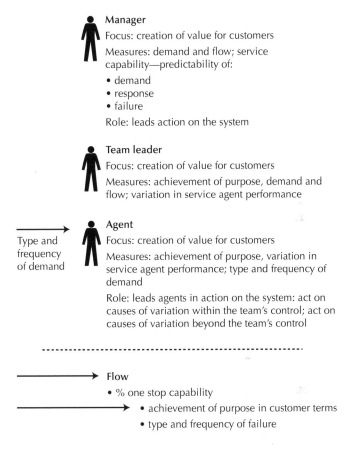

Manager
Focus: creation of value for customers
Measures: demand and flow; service capability—predictability of:
• demand
• response
• failure
Role: leads action on the system

Team leader
Focus: creation of value for customers
Measures: achievement of purpose, demand and flow; variation in service agent performance

Type and frequency of demand

Agent
Focus: creation of value for customers
Measures: achievement of purpose, variation in service agent performance; type and frequency of demand
Role: leads agents in action on the system: act on causes of variation within the team's control; act on causes of variation beyond the team's control

Flow
• % one stop capability
• achievement of purpose in customer terms
• type and frequency of failure

Figure 2.5: The service center as a system

It is important to know the service center's capability to handle calls on a 'one-stop' basis. Of course, this fits with the agent's work on the nature of demand and leads to questions about what needs to be done to handle more calls at the point of transaction. Any calls that need to go beyond the service center enter 'flows' that should be measured for their capability. In the above case, we were interested in the capability of new order fulfilment—so we must measure end-to-end time and the type and frequency of failures (things that go wrong). In the financial services case, we were interested in sales. Measures of flow are always end-to-end. If a flow starts in the service center, the measure must be used there to facilitate the work on understanding and improvement.

As measures change, so do roles. The work of management is to act on the system. I have discussed two broad examples of this: acting on causes of variation beyond the agent's control and acting on flow to improve capability. There are other very significant changes managers need to make. When you look at the complete service system, you find an array of management activities whose intent is to 'manage' the service agent: things such as quality control, incentive programs, sales prompts, absence management and so on are all part of the current (production) system and need to be designed out. I shall return to the customer service system in Chapter 6 to explore these aspects more fully.

This chapter has illustrated the application of systems thinking to the simplest organizational form—the service center—and en route I have introduced the importance of measurement. More needs to be said about measurement, so the next chapter will expand on the importance of measuring the right things. But first, I shall describe a complete case study to consolidate the ideas introduced thus far.

Case Study: How the System Fails When Sales Agents Are Besieged by Billing Inquiries

In the mid-1980s, I was asked to take a look at a newly formed telecommunications company. I started in the office closest to my home, in Milton Keynes (about 55 miles northwest of London), where I found the finance function. In finance was credit control—something that was customer-facing, so I began there (understanding a system always begins 'outside-in'). It soon became apparent that many customers were calling in because of problems with their bills. Not only that: they were frequently abandoning their calls because they couldn't get through. The first step was to establish the volume of abandoned calls and their stability.[16] This took a little time: because the data was not in use, I had to work with the staff to get it. We found that the abandon rate was stable and running at about 40 percent of all calls coming in. Thinking, 'How must this feel to the customer?' I asked to look at a bill and found another number promoted on it: the number for what was called 'customer services' in Manchester, England.

On a hunch, I drove to Manchester and, sure enough, found the service agents to be receiving billing queries, which, according to them, 'should have been handled by the finance office in Milton Keynes.' The senior managers in Manchester knew nothing about this. First-level managers were aware of what, in their view, was a 'problem' and had instituted a procedure to deal with it: service agents had to write down the customer details and query on a form; these forms were batched and sent back to the Milton Keynes office for credit control to deal with. I took a measure of how long this process took, predictably, from the customer's point of view. The answer was six days. What do you suppose customers did during those six days? They called in again. How did I find that out? By asking the service agents and credit controllers. Senior managers were quite unaware of what was going on.

While I was in the Manchester office, I asked myself, 'What is the purpose of this organization and how well is it achieving its purpose?' Despite being called customer services, it was, in fact, a sales organization, responding to incoming customer calls generated by marketing campaigns. I asked, 'Of all the people who call, how many do we sign up as customers?' No one could say. It took about three weeks effort to gather the data needed. The answer was 1 in 22. This measure had been taken over time and established as stable through the use of a capability chart. Was this good or bad? The answer is both. It was good that we now knew and could predict what would happen in the future. It was bad that it was so few.

What did the senior managers in the Manchester office 'know'? They could tell you about time taken to answer the phone, total work volumes, work states (backlogs), work activity and 'productivity'—calls per agent in volume and time taken, total revenue, staff satisfaction. Their world was one of resource planning and management. But they were oblivious to flow.

Having established the organization's performance against purpose, I looked at two things that affected sales capability: marketing processes and the fulfilment process.

To understand more about marketing, I sat with sales agents to listen to customers calling in. It soon became apparent that marketing was using postcodes for campaigns, in the hope of building the customer base in major towns and cities—those that were part of their network. Postcodes, for example for Reading, included villages that surrounded the town but were not connectable to the network. Prospective customers, having been encouraged to ask for the service, were turned away. What do you suppose they talked about with their friends? What are the costs associated with this sort of error?

What is the cause of the error? Thinking function, not flow. Just as customer services measured time to answer the phone, marketing measured spend (Figure 2.6). Any work to understand effectiveness was conducted at such a high level that the data was effectively meaningless.

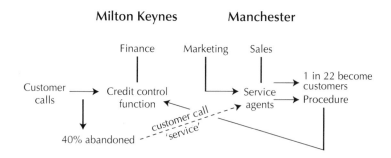

Figure 2.6: Telecommunications organization (part of) as a system

The fulfilment of orders was understood by 'being a customer' a number of times and learning what happened in what sequence, from initial contact to signing up. The exercise was repeated until the experience could be predicted for any prospective customer beginning with a call to customer services. To summarize what was learned: the organization's 'response' to customer 'demand' was (in effect), 'Hold on, there are four hurdles to get over; two are quite complex and another takes us a lot of time. But if you manage us for a month or more, you will become one of our customers.'

WHAT THIS CASE STUDY REVEALS: WORKING WITH FLOW IMPROVES PERFORMANCE—AND CUSTOMER SATISFACTION

The same phenomenon can be seen in some of the recent e-commerce companies, with the obvious difference that customers are less likely to 'manage' an organization in the e-commerce environment; they are only one click away from going elsewhere.

Think about this case for yourself. If you were the manager of this system, and you knew:

- The type and frequency of calls to credit control, why customers call in from their point of view
- The volume and predictability of abandoned calls
- The fact that it predictably takes six days to deal with a customer who calls the Manchester office with a billing query
- The fact that, predictably, only 1 in 22 of all those who call the Manchester office in response to a campaign become customers
- The nature of the transactions between the organization and the customer that make up the sales fulfilment process...
  ... Do you think you could improve performance?

The answer, of course, is Yes. This is to work with flow rather than function. To do this effectively requires different roles and different measures.

The above case is now around 20 years old. Nothing much has changed in the meantime. The same phenomena can be found in today's organizations. It is as though our organizations are inured to learning; their very systems prevent it. Yet these ideas will catch on, because they work. Money talks, eventually.

Command and control—the template for economies of scale—builds in 'tolerance of waste.' In manufacturing, this means managers set limited goals for themselves. They think in terms of 'acceptable' standards, 'acceptable' defects, 'acceptable' inventories and a narrow range of 'standardized' products. Beyond the waste attributable to methods in the manufacturing process, the design and management of the organization is the primary cause of waste. In service organizations, this is immediately apparent when one looks, as we did in the above example, 'outside-in.' Economics of scale and its management principle, command and control, leads to methods for the design and management of work that build in suboptimization.

By contrast, economies of flow and its management principles—systems thinking—provide the means for optimization.

Managing flow means managers can set their sights on 'perfection'—continuing improvement of standards, reductions in waste and defects, zero or negative inventories and abundant product variety. No lean producer has reached perfection; even the Toyota Production System has scope for improvement. The point is that the methods for managing flow give managers the *means* to work towards perfection.

What might 'perfection' consist of in the above example?

- No 'failure' calls to the Milton Keynes office;
- All 'value' calls to the Milton Keynes office being handled at the first point of contact;
- Every prospect calling the Manchester office being converted to a customer;
- No waste—prospects who could never become customers—being caused by marketing.

Is this view of perfection farfetched? No: it is simply far away from management's current preoccupations. Working towards perfection can only have a beneficial impact on the bottom line. But to work in this way, managers must identify and use different measures, ones that work *for*, rather than *against*, achievement of purpose.

CHAPTER 3

Redefining the purpose, measures and method of work

There is a systemic relationship between purpose (what we are here to do), measures (how we know how we are doing) and method (how we do it). In the example of the service center, command-and-control managers typically measure 'service level'—calls answered in so many seconds and agent activity. These measures not only obscure the means for improvement, they create de facto purposes that get in the way of the real ones: 'pick up the calls,' and 'make your activity targets.' At a stroke both agents' and managers' ingenuity is focused on how to survive; how to avoid being paid attention to. In the broadest sense, the purpose becomes 'make the plan.' It is dysfunctional, but managers do not know it. Although these ideas appear to work at one level, they hide the better alternative.

When the purpose is expressed as 'serve customers,' a completely different set of measures can be developed that help managers and agents to understand and improve performance. Instead of treating all demand as 'units of production,' demand is understood in customer terms, and action against value and failure demand improves productive capacity. Instead of management acting on the workers (inappropriately), both parties learn to act on the work, using measures that illustrate the organization's capability to respond. The consequence is liberation of method—by developing method, people learn how to work against and respond to customer demands. All parties work in an environment that has greater control over the work, this control being exercised through measures that relate to purpose. The relationship between purpose, measures and method is cultural. Most of our organizational cultures focus people's ingenuity on the wrong things.

To change the nature of measurement in our organizations is a major shift. It cannot be achieved by announcement—people who believe in the current measures need to learn for themselves what is wrong with them and then how to work with the better alternative. Managing with functional measures always causes suboptimization, because parts achieve their ends at the expense of the whole (see Figure 3.1).

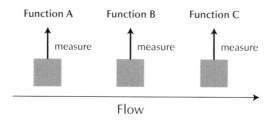

Figure 3.1: Managing functions damages flow

Recognizing suboptimization to be a problem, some managers seek to minimize the adverse consequences by managing them. But this does nothing to remove the cause of the problem or to seek a better way. In fact, it represents another form of waste. To manage work with functional measures might seem logical from a top-down perspective, but its weakness is that it tells you nothing about what is going on. It can only tell you what has happened, and then, only from a functional point of view. It says nothing about method, how the work actually 'works.' The measures themselves are easily distorted to suit reporting purposes.

Controlling work through functional measures can only be harmful to flow. All work goes through some kind of flow, so we would be better having measures of it. Managers worry about this idea because they assume it may threaten costs. They cannot see the costs associated with the waste caused by functional management. Only by managing costs end-to-end, associating costs with flow, can you reduce costs in a sustainable manner.

In the last chapter, I introduced the idea of capability measurement. Capability measures are measures of the work that tell you about the predictability of performance. In the service center, this means knowing about the predictability of demand, the predictability of agent performance, the predictability of work flows that go beyond the agent and so on. The point is simple: using these measures to understand and improve performance will improve the bottom line. In the current management philosophy, it is assumed that the bottom line can be influenced by using functional measures, targets and standards to direct perform-ance. In fact, the only thing that can reliably be predicted is that managing in this way will worsen performance. How can I be so sure? By their very nature, service demands contain high levels of variety. To tackle variety with command-and-control methods is to stifle the organization's ability to absorb it effectively. It is to make customers take the service you have designed, making agents stick to procedures and targets. This is not the same as focusing agents on serving customers. And it shows. Many serv-ice organizations effectively say to customers: 'If you want this, here is what you have to do to get it'—not exactly customer-friendly. The better able an organization is to absorb variety, the better the flow, hence the lower the costs and the better the serv-ice. Capability measurement is essential in understanding how well the system absorbs variety.

Case Study: Meeting Your Customer Service Standards Doesn't Mean Your Customers Are Getting Good Service

The following is an example I frequently use to introduce the dif-ferences between command-and-control and system measures:

A loss adjuster had a traditional organization design. People worked in functions within branches and the head office. The organization chart looked like the one shown in Figure 3.2.

I met the chief executive when I was speaking at a conference at which I had explained the folly of assuming 'the people were the problem.' He said he'd been considering doing something about low morale among administration staff, but having listened to me he thought perhaps he had not really got to the bottom of the problem.

I took a look at the organization. The work started in central claims—insurers would send losses to be adjusted—where staff were require to log the work into a computer system by lunchtime. From there it would be sent electronically to the appropriate branch, whose administrator would call the customer to make an appointment. The administrators worked to a service standard: the percentage of appointments made within one day of receipt of

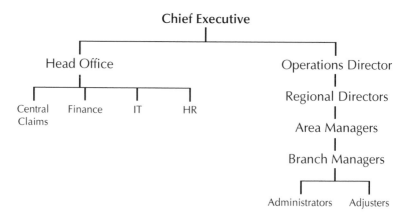

Figure 3.2: Loss adjuster's organization chart

the work. If they made a call and had to leave a message for the customer to call back, or had to send a letter because they could not make contact by telephone, these things 'counted' in the measurement of the standard. The one-day standard was being achieved at around 95 percent.

The loss adjusters were required to visit within four days and write a preliminary report to the insurer on the extent of the loss within seven days of receipt of the claim. Both these service standards were being met 95 percent of the time. At this stage, the adjuster would seek information about replacement costs, professional services (plumbing, building, etc.)—in short, solve the claimant's problem within the terms of the insurance contract. At the end of the process, there was another service standard—once the adjuster had announced the value of the loss to the customer, the customer should receive a check within seven days. Once again, the standard was being achieved at about 95 percent. From the service standards, it appeared that service was good. Procedures seemed clear and well understood. So why was there a morale problem in administration? To find out, we have to understand the organization as a system.

What is the purpose of this organization from the customers' point of view? To adjust losses. What matters to the customers when having their loss adjusted? Equity—is it fair? And time—how long does it take? The latter we can use immediately as an operational measure. Is there a measure of end-to-end time (from the customers' point of view) in this system? No, the service standards do not cover the time the adjuster spends adjusting. I took measures of end-to-end time from the customers' point of view and put them in a capability chart, shown in Figure 3.3.

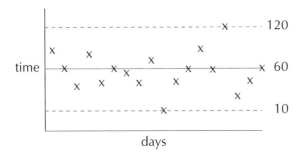

Figure 3.3: Loss adjuster's capability to adjust losses

The chart shows the system is stable with wide variation. You can expect the next loss coming in to this system to be adjusted within 10 to 120 days. Is this good or bad? It is bad, of course, when you compare the elapsed time to the 'value work'—the actual time it would take to adjust a loss.

It is a start, and therefore good, that you can now predict performance. As I discussed earlier, there is no point in spending management time arguing about cases that take, say, 100 days, or praising people for completing cases in 10. These are all from the same system. The good news is you can now predict that the next loss that comes in for adjusting will be adjusted in between 10 and 120 days.

Of course, that's not such great news when you compare it in your mind to the 'value' work. The value work would be: look at the contract and claim, look at how the insurer wants to receive reports, visit the customer's premises to assess the situation, determine replacement costs and write a check. How long do you think the value work would take if it were done end-to-end and cleanly? That, then, is the only benchmark you need, but at least you know.

The job of management is to find out what causes the variation.

To do that, you have to look at the work flow. This starts with demand—the type and frequency of demands (work coming in) from insurers. To keep this case simple, I shall deal with the high-volume, low-value work—domestic claims (the capability chart above was calculated for only this kind of claim). The work arrives in central claims early in the morning where it is sorted into 'easy' and 'hard' assignments by a supervisor. This is a 'production' assumption—'easy work' can be done by temps, experts should be limited to doing only those cases that need their expertise. The sorted piles are placed in a rack labelled with branch names. The branches are dealt with in order—if a branch was first yesterday, it is last today. Imagine what that does to flow.

At 9 AM, the temps and experts arrive. Their task is to take their respective piles ('easy' and 'hard') from the racks, log them on the IT system so that an electronic message can be sent to the branch, place the pile back in the rack, and take the next. The people in central claims have a manager who is preoccupied with the claims being put on the system by lunchtime. How else would the branch administrators meet their target to make the appointments? At 4 PM, a van takes the paperwork from the racks and out to the branches where it will be used to complete the work.

WHAT THIS CASE STUDY REVEALS: CHANGING THE WORK FLOW IMPROVES CUSTOMER SERVICE

You can probably guess what Ohno taught about the consequences of sorting, batching and queuing work. You get errors—the more of them the more you do it. In this case, errors will be compounded by another 'system condition'[17] to use Vanguard language—the managerial edict to 'get them on by lunchtime.' There are two schools of thought about how to react to the potential for errors. The first I sometimes describe as the 'retentive, cardigan-wearing, internally-focused, white-coat' school—I guess you can tell it's not the school I'm in. This is the ISO 9000 brigade, which would have you inspect the work against a standard and allocate blame where due. This is futile because errors are a consequence of design. I belong to the 'flow' school of understanding errors, which says that an error is only an error when you look at the impact further along the flow—somewhere it shows as 'dirty,' and rework, waiting or other forms of waste occur. There is no point in blaming the workers for this, because their work is governed by the system—the way work is designed and managed.

To understand what was happening in flow terms, we go to where the work arrived in the branches. Here we discovered that, all in, around 80 percent of the cases contained errors— wrong or missing post codes and addresses, missing information about the claim or the insurer, sent to the wrong branch, and so on. (This is the result of sorting, batching, queuing and then focusing on getting it out on time. It would be better to learn how to make it right for the next step in the flow.)

In the branches the problem was compounded. To meet their managers' preoccupation with 'production,' the loss adjusters were obliged to go out on four appointments a day, four days a week. Not surprisingly, under this pressure to meet activity- rather than purpose-related measures, the majority of visits resulted in not much progressing of the claim. Not very productive. The adjusting process was building inventory.

But it gets worse. The adjusters had taken to coming in on Saturday to catch up with their workload and to ensure that their preliminary reports reached the insurer within the seven-day standard. On Mondays, the administrators arrived to a pile of typing which, according to their work standard, they had to turn around within 24 hours. Mondays were the days most customers would call in—usually to chase progress (failure demand) and it is easy to see why. Now we know why the administrators were unhappy.

If you were an administrator, which day would you take off? Because this was a system problem, no amount of palliatives would help. The company had to redesign the system.

Branches used capability data to establish end-to-end time to adjust losses from the customers' point of view and set to work to identify and remove the causes of variation. Naturally, the major causes were in the work design, so that was the starting place. When work arrived at a branch, the first action was to 'make it clean,' that is, make it possible for the loss adjuster to close the case on the first visit. Making the work clean could and should involve customers, so they can 'see' the service process and their expectations can be managed. People are happy to cooperate if they know the purpose of the service provider is to sort them out. End-to-end time fell to an average of 20 days in a matter of weeks, despite the existence of a backlog.

Having achieved a step-change in performance by removing the waste created by the batching and sorting of the previous system, the company began the real work—identifying causes of variation within and across branches. As they were identified and acted on, time shortened and productivity improved further.

THE RESULT OF IMPROVED WORK FLOW: PRODUCTIVITY QUADRUPLED!

The result was a fourfold increase in productivity, with no additional employment. You might, quite justifiably, argue that the work would be better cleaned at the front end, in central claims. However, the objective of the intervention was to change the culture throughout the branches because the organization needed everyone to think and work this way. There were many things that required local initiatives and some things that required co-ordinated initiatives—the latter made sense to people who were thinking about their work from the same point of view, and this made them easier to implement.

In this case, managers had been using measures of work standards, service standards and productivity. To them, the service looked good. In truth, it was abysmal—not only bad from the customers' point of view, but costly, too. The measures in use caused managers to lose touch with how the work worked. In order to make the change, the managers had to be prepared to have their own implicit theories and practices put into the open and questioned, even criticized.

In ignoring variation, organizations subject their managers and workers to measures that demoralize them and drive them to behave in ways that add no value to the system. The focus on measures (output) over method is a primary cause of stress. Often, the consequence is high labor turnover. Henry Ford was not uncomfortable with the high labor turnover created by mass production. Today we see the same tolerance of high turnover in our service organizations. In service centers, 50 percent annual staff turnover is not uncommon. Ford famously doubled wages at the same time as cutting prices. Ironically, the rise in wages worked—it stemmed the turnover of employees, but only for a while, and then it worked against him; for the realization of a life-time of employment in such alienating conditions led to the creation of unions whose purpose was to control and protect jobs. The seeds were sown for inefficiency and lack of cooperation brought about by inflexibility and perceived inequity.

In many of our service centers, managers have cut the wages and sown their own version of inefficiency and inflexibility. Service centers are often designed to 'take the brain out of service.' Many of these places are run with controlled scripts, controlled procedures, arbitrary work standards and irrelevant targets, fostering dissent rather than cooperation. Variation inevitably increases, but managers remain unaware of the causes and in frustration intensify the controls, giving another twist to the vicious circle. I shall give examples of this in the next chapter.

Ohno observed that the American car plants he studied were full of waste ('*muda*' was his term) and he could see the causes. Senior managers set targets for 'goods shipped,' making the focus of everyone 'keep the plant moving.' Workers were aware that the rework department would fix anything that was not right, and the assembly workers—those who had the most important job—were treated as the least important. Schedulers, inspectors, foremen and so on were all held in higher esteem. It was no surprise to Ohno that workers cared little about quality. And so it is in most service organizations: Despite management's rhetoric to the contrary, people who serve customers are treated as the least important. Managers operate a system that damages their ability to serve the customer, treats them as inferior and encourages behavior that makes it worse. People do what they need to do to survive; it is hard to care about the customer in a system that does not encourage you to do so.

In service organizations, waste is much harder to 'see.' Ohno could see rework at the end of the line, he could see inventory, he could touch the dust on things. In service organizations it is hard to see rework, it is hard to see a work flow, and it is hard to see demand, especially when you use measures that are abstractions from these phenomena. Although I have 'seen' failure demand since the phenomenon first occurred to me in the late 1980s, it is something that is invisible to most service center managers. They 'see' the production figures, but because they usually have no idea of either the nature of demand or the way work flows, they are not in a position to reduce their costs and improve their service. The people—managers and workers alike—are locked into a dysfunctional system.

Ohno gave his teams complete responsibility for all of the operational requirements, not dividing the labor into specialities. He also gave them responsibility for the line. If something was wrong, they stopped the line so that it could be put right. He intuitively knew that 'clean flow' would improve production. In our service organizations we face the same challenge: to move the decisions about the design of work to where the work is done. To take responsibility, people need relevant measures, otherwise, how will they know how they are doing? Although taking current measures and expressing them in a different way can prevent managers from wasting time discussing differences that are not real, adopting different measures is much better. To improve flow you need measures of flow in the hands of the people who do the work.

Case Study: Finding the Causes of Poor Work Flow

A health care organization centralized its branch operations. The plan was to achieve economies of scale. Managers had used measures of productivity as their guide, but a systems approach revealed the following:

The actual time it took to settle a claim was between 15 and 50 days with an average of 32 days—stable but showing wide variation. Time to settle was a measure being used by management, but it used it to set targets (expressed as percentages of claims completed in two and three weeks). Expressing the same measure in a capability chart showed the system to be stable. There is no point in having a target if the system is stable. It is better to find the causes of variation and work to remove them. The systems approach showed that the principal causes of poor flow in claims handling were: 'dirty work,' work measurement and management activity. I shall explain each.

Dirty work: Claims arrived that could not be processed. Something 'up-stream'—the form and/or the transaction with the service center—meant the information was incomplete. Claims were also getting 'dirty' waiting around. When agents needed to access a case repeatedly, and as time became more drawn out, information was often forgotten or duplicated.

Work measurement: The claims agents were measured on how much 'work' they did. Work was seen in production terms. Because the work was presented to the agent on an IT work flow system, the work the agents did could be counted. Points were awarded for action on a case towards a daily activity target. To gain points, agents would take actions that might or might not have a bearing on the purpose of settling the claim. In fact, every unit of work arriving in claim was multiplied by the system into seven. For example, the agent would deal with (i.e., file) a cover letter sent in by the customer or write back to ask the customer for something that was missing. Each agent action would score a point on the agent's productivity statistics. The agent's purpose was to 'make points'—not at all the same thing as 'settle claims.'

Management activity: Managers saw their task as allocating resources to queues of work. By allocating lots of resources at work queues, they caused greater variation.[18] Whole queues would be on 'stop' or 'go.'

The systems approach exposed the *muda* (i.e., the waste). Now action could be taken for improvement. For example, action on 'unclean' demand (input) needed to be preceded by establishing which types of problems were predictable.

One major cause was the failure of agents in the service center to 'pre-authorize' the claim, hence ensuring the customers would claim correctly against their entitlements. Failure to do this led to high volumes of incorrect ('unclean') claims. There were a series of other causes of dirty input. While actions were being taken upstream on the causes, agents in the claims center were removed from the necessity to meet their work targets and instead worked against a measure of claims settlement— end-to-end time expressed in a capability chart. Their purpose was to settle claims, so they worked on how to make the work clean so that they could speed the flow.

In short, these actions increased capacity. It is as Ohno taught: capacity = work plus waste. To remove the waste and increase capacity, you have to see the organization as a system. You have to take an operational view of how the organization serves customers—to identify what happens to customers at the point of transaction; what demands they make and how the system responds to those demands. Managing flow means thinking of service as 'customers pulling value from the system.' If a customer's demand is met with a system that fulfils that demand, and only does that, the consequence is good service at the lowest cost.

WORKERS NEED TO BE IN CONTROL OF THEIR WORK

To manage clean flow workers need to have the expertise required by the nature of demand. They also need to be in control of their work, rather than being controlled by managers with measures of output, standards, activity and the like. These obviate good service design to the extent they are at odds with what matters to customers. It was Genichi Taguchi's work[19] that introduced me to these ideas. He challenged the idea of working to 'standards' or 'blueprints' in manufacturing, which meant 'working within tolerances' and showed that setting any (nominal) value and working to continually reduce variation around it resulted in better quality and lower cost. When manufacturing goods, working to standards or tolerances means tolerating variation. The consequence is always losses. Poor product quality means losses in terms of efficiency, customer satisfaction and, ultimately, revenue.

Taguchi explained his ideas with a diagram (see Figure 3.4). When making things, the further anything was from the 'nominal value,' the greater the economic loss to the system; in simple terms, the more things go wrong, break down, or take longer to deal with. Doing more than is required, for example through overspecification, is another potential loss.

Nominal Value

Think of any service you regularly encounter. If the organization understands and responds to what matters to you (your nominal

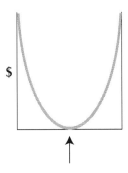

Figure 3.4: Costs of variation from the nominal value

value), you experience good service and the organization is likely to be delivering it in the most economic way. If, for any reason, the organization does not recognize and respond to what matters to you, your service experience is poorer and the organization consumes extra resources to resolve the situation. It may also cause you to go away. Unfortunately, because many service organizations are designed as though they were factories, service agents are told how they are to behave. When the prescriptions they work ignore the 'nominal value' of customers, as they most often do, suboptimization inevitably follows.

The starting place for making change under the systems approach is to look 'outside-in,' to know how your organization is perceived by your customers. The measures needed to understand and improve performance are concerned with:

- Demand—What are the types and frequency of demands that customers place on the system? What is the predictability of failure demands and value demands?
- Flow—What is the capability of the system to handle demands in one-stop transactions? Where a customer demand needs to go through a flow, what is the capability of that flow, measured in customer terms?

In both cases, we need to know the extent of variation in order to question its causes. It is a simple and powerful idea. By revealing variation, we invite questioning of its causes. By acting on the causes, we improve performance. None of this is possible with the traditional measurement methods; the numbers used encourage treating noise as signals (for more on this see the next chapter) and the only questions that are raised concern failures to meet budgets, something that encourages the wrong behavior.

Managers use the measures associated with command-and-control thinking to justify 'economies of scale.' By contrast, the measures associated with systems thinking illuminate the advantages of 'economies of flow.' This is a better way to design and manage work. Applying these different measures leads to less waste, less cost, greater control, more improvement and, just as important, a stronger sense of involvement among those who do the work.

BETTER MEASUREMENT PRINCIPLES AND PRACTICE

Instead of measures being used to command and control, the purpose of measures is to develop knowledge through action on the system.

Principle 1: The test of a good measure

The test of a good measure is: *Does this help in understanding and improving of performance?*

Measures derived from the command-and-control philosophy do not pass this test. Systems measures do. Compare, for example, targets and capability measures:

Targets are arbitrary, capability measures are not—they are derived from the work, not plucked from the air. Targets increase disorder in systems, capability measures lead people to act in ways that increase order and control. Targets focus people on the wrong things, the things they must do to survive within the system, not improvement. Capability measures encourage people to focus their ingenuity on how the work works. Targets have no value in understanding and improving performance; capability measures help both to understand and improve the work. Targets demotivate while capability measures motivate, because they put control and understanding in the right place: in the heads of the people who do the work.

Principle 2: Measures must relate to purpose

We should think about the purpose of an organization from the customers' point of view (Figure 3.5). Service organizations exist

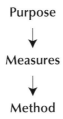

Figure 3.5: Fundamental principles of work design

to serve customers, so we need to know how well they achieve that aim as seen through the eyes of the recipient. The 'nominal value' is what matters to customers; whatever it is—speed, reliability, technical accuracy—dictates what should be measured. Using such measures affords people the freedom to experiment with method—how they go about accomplishing their purpose. This gives greater control than is achieved through traditional 'controls,' which are, in truth, in control of little.

Principle 3: Measures must be integrated with work

In other words, measures must be in the hands of people who do the work. This is a prerequisite for the development of knowledge and, hence, improvement.

LEADING AND LAGGING INDICATORS

The measures that are used in most organizations are 'lagging' or 'rear-view' measures—they tell you what you did. They measure daily, weekly or monthly output against the plan, or quarterly sales against this year's budget. They are derived from budgets and financial measures. Acting on lagging measures risks suboptimization of the system in ways that we are by now aware of. Not only do these measures hide waste, they cause it. The time consumed filling in budget forms and going to budgeting meetings is just one form of waste. When managers send targets down the hierarchy, they cause functions to achieve their measures at the expense of the organization's purpose. The mis-selling of financial services (naturally, the sales force is on commission) is a good example. There is a disincentive to outperform the targets, another form of suboptimization. The whole of the system is focused on satisfying management rather than customers, who are the source of the organization's sustainability.

Managers fear that a focus on customers risks increasing costs. Their preoccupation with cost management is coupled with the assumption that better service will cost more. When they learn to see their organization as a system, they discover for themselves that cost management actually increases costs and, by the same token, good service is in fact cheaper.

Managers do need accounts—they need to know the score. But to manage for improvement and sustainability they need different measures, measures that tell them about what is actually going on in the work. In service organizations, this means knowing about demand and flow. If costs are to be reported, they should always be reported end-to-end. But the more important measures to be used in managing the work are leading measures, for action on these will optimize the system. They are the subject of the next chapter.

CHAPTER 4

Better measures,
better thinking

I am always struck by people's unwillingness to question the
necessity of traditional organizational measures, especially targets. Targets are considered to be a normal part of organizational
life. People accept that targets have their difficulties, but they cannot countenance a world without them. In this chapter, I am
going to review the things I have discussed with managers, their
justifications for targets and question whether the justifications
stand up.

TARGETS ARE THE NORM

I overheard the following during breakfast in a hotel: 'I was told
I'm the only one who came out with the same numbers as when
he went in.' The man was proud to have won the budget game. It
made me reflect on a previous conversation with a top-level manager in the construction sector. He said: 'You go into the budget
review with six excuses or explanations, and if you get through by
using only two of them, you've got four left for next time.'

How much better would our organizations be if top management were focused on increasing knowledge—their own and others—of the way the work worked and how to make it better?
Naturally, they would claim they are, but in most cases the work of
management is predicated on measures that ensure they are dis-
engaged from the work. This provides the players with the scope
for creating excuses—the excuses just have to be plausible given
the prevailing logic. This is an unhealthy form of collaboration,
more divisive than cooperative.

We hesitate to question the existence of targets because they
are the norm. It is an unquestioned assumption that organizations must be managed by financial information from the

accounting system. As these budget-based measures cascade down the hierarchy, the successive levels of management and, finally, frontline workers, become engaged in 'making their numbers.' The budget or target becomes the purpose. Managers and workers know what they have to do to meet it and how they are going to be judged. To question the basis for a target, if it occurs to anyone to do so, might be seen as a sign of weakness.

Perhaps because managerial roles are created by the same logic, targets prevent managers from seeing the consequences of their actions. Their preoccupations are with the function they preside over, not the flow of work from and to the customer. In most organizations, the cycle of management activity is: plan the budget, cascade the plan and associated functional numbers, monitor performance against the plan. If everyone makes their numbers, the organization fulfills the plan, and all is well. Not so.

It was Alfred Sloan who coined the phrase 'management by the numbers.' For him, it solved a problem—in the 1930s, he could not tell which parts of the amorphous General Motors were making money. To find out, he introduced revenue and cost accounting to functions and sites. Sloan considered it unnecessary, even inappropriate, for senior managers to know much about the details of operations—how the work worked in operating divisions. If the numbers were bad, managers were replaced; if they were good, managers were promoted. Imagine the consequences (they are with us today): 'unlucky' managers out on the scrap heap; 'lucky' managers promoted to senior positions. Of course, it's not put like that. If managers are promoted, it is because they did something right—they employed the 'right' or best methods. But what did they do? Method is not talked about much in organizations. Many organizational cultures do not tolerate questioning of the current methods and their implicit assumptions.

Management by the numbers facilitated the spread of the command-and-control, hierarchical philosophy; it formed the 'rule book' for the relationship between operating and senior managers. Managers of subsidiaries, divisions and functions are given prescriptions for reporting and action by staff in senior or head office functions, with little room for debate about whether these things help or hinder. For the 'junior' players in the relationship to voice such concerns may be a career-limiting move.

Such prescriptions often go beyond the budget numbers; head office functions frequently demand a series of reports, 'scores' and standards to be implemented and reported. Should we assume they are helping the enterprise?

Over the last 50 years, the accounting profession[20] has ascended to the highest executive ranks. It is now normal to assume that chief executives could and perhaps should come from the accounting profession. The rise of the accounting profession has been coupled with the ability to get more and more detailed financial information through computers. Persuaded by the promise of ever greater control, managers have spent enormous sums on computers that can report detailed costs by function, level and activity. Control is, of course, an illusion, because costs are associated with flow, not function or activity. Numbers have achieved ascendancy over purpose. An idea that solved a problem for Alfred Sloan has become a disease within our organizations.

WHY DO MANAGERS VALUE TARGETS?

Sometimes when I am working with managers I stop and ask them to explain to me why we need or should have targets. I tell them I wonder if I've missed something. These are the arguments I hear in support of targets:

Targets 'motivate' people

They certainly do; they motivate people to do anything to be seen to achieve the target. Hence the cheating that is systemic in organizations. And to vilify the 'cheats,' as managers often do, is to blame the wrong people.

You cannot 'motivate' someone. Harvard Business Review has printed Frederick Hertzberg's classic 1968 article on motivation[21] four times to my knowledge, the last time in 2003. The essence of what he says is: you cannot. You can provide conditions in which employees are more likely to be motivated or demotivated, but it is a conceit to believe that managers can motivate people. It is stretching credulity to believe that a target, set in a hierarchical system, imposed by those above on those below, is something people would find motivational.

I can agree with the idea that *personal* targets—lose weight, run further, get another job, earn more money—could motivate individuals. But I only say 'could,' for of greater importance is that they have feedback systems (measurement) to track their progress. The same sense of personal ambition could potentially be applied to work, as something to which the individual has chosen to aspire. In a hierarchical system, however, a target is generally something that is imposed with authority by people who are detached from the work. It is unlikely to be based on knowledge. Probably derived from a financial plan, it is arbitrary.

Targets set direction

That's acceptable, provided there is no numerical expectation. Tellingly, managers often use this argument when they have failed to meet their targets.[22] But if you want to improve, it is more important to know the 'what and why' of current perform-ance as a system. 'What' tells you about achievement of purpose, and 'why,' self-evidently, tells you about the things that help or hinder achievement of purpose. Knowing about the 'what and why' of performance puts you in a position to act on the basis of knowledge for improvement. The best statements of direction would be those that are clear about the need to get down to just doing the value work—that which the customer pays for.

It comes down to how you set a target, managers argue: they are fine if you do set right. So, for example, they say:

Targets should be based on what is reasonable

But how can people know? They are bound to make judgments based on experience. Deming taught us not to rely on experi-ence, which is no substitute for knowledge. When you learn about the 'what and why' of performance, you discover how much suboptimization or waste there is in the system. The job in hand is to take it out. Should we have waste-reduction targets? No, it is sufficient to know less waste is better and get on with the job. Measures against purpose can be used to track improvement. Managers believe targets should be 'SMART' or pass the 'RAW' test.[23] Consider how you might have set targets for examples in this book. If the loss adjusters had known their service took from

10 to 120 days, what target should they have set? How would they have set it? In fact, before they obtained this knowledge, all their targets had been focused on service standards and activity measures—and they were hitting them at 95 percent. What would 'stretch' targets (however they are determined) have done to the system?

People should be involved in setting their targets

Can a target be made better if those who do the work help to set it? How would they know what is a reasonable target? What could they base their judgment on? If the parties have no reliable means for questioning and understanding performance, their assessments will by definition be arbitrary. In such a dynamic the weaker parties in the hierarchy will likely seek to minimize their risk and the stronger seek to push the boundaries. How could either know they are doing the right thing? How much is this discussion and its conclusion driven and limited by the manager's own targets?

I have often seen targets being set on the basis of forward projections of improvements on last year's costs. For example, if it cost x per unit to repair a product last year, the same cost less, say, 10 percent, is used as a target for the cost of repairs for this year. But what if the repair system were full of waste? The hidden costs would be carried forward. If the actual costs were shown in a capability chart, the variation would lead managers to ask about the causes. This would mean finding waste in the work flow and determining its causes. All parties would be in a position to improve things.

I often wonder how managers talk to each other when targets are issued. This is the conversation I envisage:

Senior manager: 'Here's your target.'

Junior manager: 'But what about method—how should I go about achieving it?'

Senior manager: 'That's what I pay you for, deciding how to achieve it. If you're any good you'll make your target.'

Junior manager: 'So that's how you determine which managers are good—those who achieve their targets?'

Senior manager: 'Of course. We want achievers in this organization.'

Junior manager: 'What you are saying is that you want people to achieve their targets. But what if people are doing things that ensure they meet their target, but which are not good for the organization as a whole?'

Senior manager: 'I expect people to be sensible. I expect them to work in the best interests of the company.'

Junior manager: 'But what if the targets force them to make their own numbers at the expense of someone else's?'

Senior manager: 'I expect my people to cooperate. If they don't, it's my job to knock their heads together.'

Junior manager: 'Well, that may be just fine if you know . . . but often you won't know that people are doing things just to "make target" because they cover them up.'

Senior manager: 'Give me their names.'

Junior manager: 'I couldn't do that . . . In any event, we were talking hypothetically. But listen for a moment. I have heard it said that we'd be better off with capability measures instead of targets—they tell you what's actually going on and help you get to a discussion about method, and that's what you want, isn't it?'

Senior manager: 'People can discuss all they like, as long as they achieve their targets.'

I can't imagine many senior managers disclosing their ignorance and asking what on earth a capability measure is and how it might point to method. I can imagine the preoccupation with who is to blame ('give me their names'). Many years ago, I was describing to a chief executive how his organization was suboptimized because of the way managers behaved with measures. He asked me three times for the culprits' names. On the third occasion I gave him one name—his.

WHAT MAKES A 'GOOD' TARGET?

Managers sense that there are problems with targets. They say things like, 'You can have too many targets. If everything is a target, then nothing is a target. You can have externally imposed targets that organizations don't feel that they own, and you can have targets that are not realistic.' I come back to the same point: how do you set a 'good' one? A target that is fair, sensible, reasonable and achievable—even, perhaps, a 'stretch'? No one has ever given me a method. I don't think there is one. It boils down to subjectivity and judgment. I prefer knowledge. Only capability measures should be used for managing. The discussion should focus on what can be predicted and what scope there is for improvement, which means working on understanding the nature and causes of variation. To set a target for improvement is fatuous.

Deming pointed out that if a system were unstable, it didn't have a capability, so a target was doubly arbitrary; if it were stable, it would reliably perform to its known capability, so a target was pointless. If, despite that, a target or standard is set at a level beyond the system or process capability, then people can only meet it—and avoid getting grief from their managers—by 'cheating' or some other form of distortion.

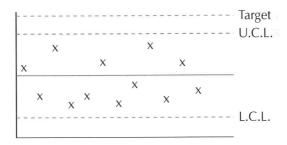

Figure 4.1: Target exceeds capability [UCL: upper control limit, LCL: lower control limit]

Capability measures (shown in Figure 4.1) tell you what a process or system is predictably achieving. The upper and lower control limits show what values can reasonably be expected, given the variation between the previous observations. So there is no point in taking action if a new value falls between the upper and lower control limits. To improve capability beyond its current state, to reduce variation or make a step-wise change in the level of performance, you have to act on the system. Showing the extent of current variation, the nature of the measure invites the user to study the system. To understand the causes of variation, managers and workers need to study flow—how the elements of the work work (or don't work) together. This is how to engage people's ingenuity in improving the system, rather than meeting, by fair means or foul, the requirements of arbitrary measures.

If a target or standard is set at a level that is below the process capability, there is no incentive to work for improvement; people slow down (Figure 4.2).

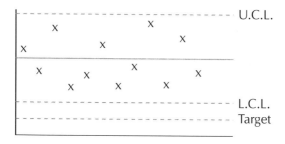

Figure 4.2: Target less than capability

In both of the above circumstances, the work ethic becomes 'make the target or standard,' do whatever it takes to avoid negative consequences (being 'paid attention to'). People find it hard to believe that managers might set a target below capability, but it often happens. It is an inevitable consequence of 'one-size-fits-all' thinking—imposing the same targets or standards on everybody.

If the target or standard is *within* the limits of 'natural' (i.e., system-induced) variation, some days workers will be 'winners'—they will meet or exceed the target—and some days they will be 'losers,' as shown in Figure 4.3.

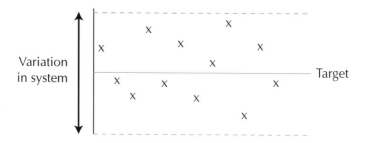

Figure 4.3: Some days you win, some days you lose

This is inevitable because their performance is governed by variation in the system. By focusing on the people rather than the system, managers cause psychological damage. The associated costs are incalculable.

Using measures of variation helps managers avoid the mistake of treating single measures as though they are different, when in fact they are 'the same'—a 'high' result on the above chart is as likely as a 'low' result. If they are within the control limits, they come from the same system. Only by taking data over time can you gain a true picture of what is happening. A capability measure helps managers distinguish 'signals' from 'noise.' A result outside the control limits would be a signal, as shown in Figure 4.4.

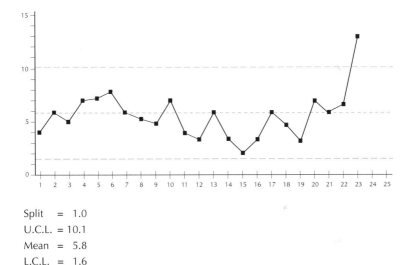

Split = 1.0
U.C.L. = 10.1
Mean = 5.8
L.C.L. = 1.6

Figure 4.4: A signal has occurred

The signal begs the question: What happened? Was there an external event that caused this result? Is there something different about the work that has caused this event? The capability chart will not answer these questions, but it will raise them. Often the best response to a signal is to wait and see what happens next. It may be just a one-off.

Compare how this presentation of data differs from the monthly reports that managers are used to. Such reports typically show data in a tabular form and invite month-on-month comparisons. This can mislead managers to believe they have a 'signal' when none exists. To make matters worse, acting on 'noise' typically increases variation, so worsening perform-ance. I shall give examples of this phenomenon at the end of the chapter.

A capability chart will also tell you when something has changed: see Figure 4.5.

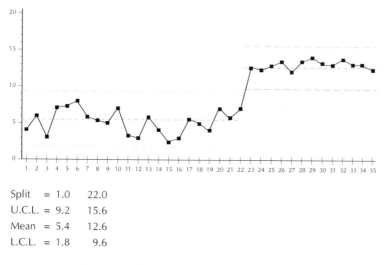

Split	= 1.0	22.0
U.C.L.	= 9.2	15.6
Mean	= 5.4	12.6
L.C.L.	= 1.8	9.6

Figure 4.5: The system or process has changed

Managers need to know that a change, for better or worse, is a real change and not just natural variation. Only capability measures will answer the question. Learning from variation is fundamental to performance improvement.

LEARNING FROM VARIATION

One way to begin is to take measures managers currently use and look at them in a different way—to find out whether there is any variation.

A roadside restaurant plotted its sales in a capability chart (Figure 4.6). They showed a pattern through the week—a high point on Saturdays and Sundays after a build-up through the week.

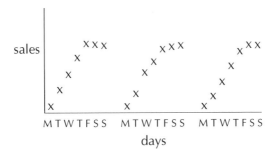

Figure 4.6: Daily sales in a roadside restaurant

Given the pattern, it made sense to run the data daily. Sure enough, days were stable. If you were running this restaurant on a Monday, you should expect to take between $200 and $400 (Figure 4.7).

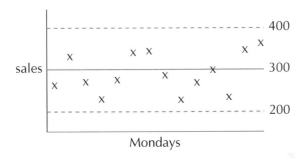

Figure 4.7: Monday's sales

Because they were used to seeing the data in tables, managers would hold an inquisition when the restaurant achieved a 'low' result, say around $200. The time wasted pointlessly discussing such results throughout the hierarchy was enormous. Because the system was stable, a better course was to focus on improving its performance. The best solution would be to attract more customers on a Monday. Local managers who learned this obvious truth used their ingenuity to do that. They achieved in weeks what their managers had been trying to do for years. The results showed a step increase in the chart, so they knew this was a genuine change for the better, not just 'noise' (variation).

When I point to the disillusionment and waste caused by targets, managers sometimes tell me these are just the consequences of not managing properly. I never get an answer to what 'managing properly' means. Instead, I find it easy to point to things that are currently being measured and 'managed' and question whether this represents 'proper' management. Their model of management is to 'control' through forms of specification, reporting and inspection using measures that are abstractions from the work.

DON'T MANAGE PRODUCTIVITY

Instead of focusing on purpose, managers become preoccupied with production. This is because their role has been conceptualized as 'resource management,' not work management. As we saw in the case of the loss adjusters, focusing on production as activity ('do four visits a day, four days a week') actually undermines production. This is a common phenomenon in service organizations. Engineers who fix computers, washing machines or air-conditioning units are given targets for the number of calls they should make. People's ingenuity is engaged in providing the hierarchy with what is asked for, not improving the work.

One of my earliest experiences in service improvement was in 1985 in a computer services organization. In those days, I used to talk about organizations being transparent—customers could 'see' what managers 'did.' If managers 'commanded' behavior that did not create value for customers, customers would 'see' the consequences. The director moved the focus of measurement away from the incidental—activity, standards, costs and the like—and towards purpose—what mattered to their customers. Managers spent time with customers understanding how and how well the services worked for them. As service improved, costs fell. The organization won an award; I learned a lot.

In another early case, I encouraged managers to remove activity targets because I knew they were of little value in understanding and improving the work and moreover were driving the wrong behavior. When the measures were turned off, people stopped working. I learned never to remove a measure without replacing it and helping people understand how to use the new measure.

The intent behind managing with measures of activity, standards and costs is to improve efficiency. The actual effects are to push costs up and to stifle pride among those who do the work. The manager as a 'resource manager' asks, 'How many people do I need to do this amount of work, and how should I motivate them to perform?' But this assumes no variation in the work: a major error. Whenever I walk into a service organization and find managers managing their people with activity measures, I know I can make a significant difference. Managing activity is to manage costs, and that, paradoxically, *causes* costs—always.

Managers measure and manage activity because they believe the amount of work workers can do needs to be planned and monitored against the plan. That is unquestionably true. But managers extend that idea to managing—controlling—workers' activity. In manufacturing, a vital distinction between world-class and traditional manufacturing operations is that the former use monitoring of activity to monitor the planning, whereas the latter use monitoring to monitor the worker.

In manufacturing operations, one would expect to find variation in activity times—but nothing like the extent we should expect in service operations. Service operations involve the customer in what is 'made,' so there is inherently much more variety in service than in manufacturing. Thus, to use production or activity measures in managing the people is only going to make things worse. The measures become constraints.

In many service organizations, we find that first-level managers (often called team leaders) have never done the job that they supervise. Senior managers have bought the idea that they need 'people managers' in the first line. These people managers can count. Hence the job gravitates to activity measurement and 'people' management. These team leaders do not gain the confidence of the people that they 'lead' because they are focused on activity measures and are unable to help the agent improve his or her work. Furthermore, because the team leaders know little about the work, the conversation with the agent centers on matters of morale and personality. 'Good people management' can be extremely demoralizing for the agent.

Activity measurement is just one of the management tools used to govern performance. Functional roles, service levels and procedures are others. The consequences become apparent to the customer—if you want '*x*,' you need to act this way to get it or you should expect to wait for the amount of time we have specified. The effect is to reduce the variety of the organization's responses. It is assumed that if we had no such tools the consequences would be anarchy. Yet it is plain to see that if in any way the management tools inhibit the organization's ability to respond to customers' demands, costs will rise.

A law of cost: In a command-and-control design, a service organization's costs rise in proportion to the variety of customer demands.

The assumption in the command-and-control design is that freedom must be subordinated to efficiency; the worker must be kept in control. In fact, efficiencies only come from freedom—the people who do the work must be able to decide the 'best' way to handle any particular customer demand to maximize efficiency. In turn, efficiency can only be achieved where one can predict the nature and volume of customer demands. It is only people who can do this work. It requires human intervention to provide good quality service: If the people who provide service are constrained in any way, service will suffer. Rather than being constrained by measures, the people who do the work should use measures and methods that enable *their* control of the work. What absorbs and controls variety? Variety.

CHANGING MEASURES, CHANGING THINKING

Improving performance means reducing variation. Rather than reduce variation, activity measures increase variation. They make the work worse. Of course managers may not 'see' this for themselves. The data they have may show everyone achieving the activity targets, but these data will not show the consequences of customers being less than helped—repeat calls, dissatisfaction and so on. Recall the exercise in understanding the causes of variation in agent performance in Chapter 2: concentrating on agent activity, managers are working on five percent of what governs the output of the system—an extraordinary waste of resource. They should be working on the 95 percent—the system itself. To work on that 95 percent, you need measures that describe what's happening in the system.

The measures associated with command-and-control thinking tell managers nothing about the system because they are based on a resource-management logic. This logic assumes that when capacity needs to be increased, it requires extra resources. But the better way to improve capacity is to remove waste; adding resource to a wasteful system just compounds inefficiency. Capability measures point to the variation in the system and encourage managers to find out what is happening in the work. When managers learn to manage flow, waste can be removed, increasing capacity in a sustainable way.

DROP TARGETS, INSTITUTE MEASURES DERIVED FROM THE WORK

The whole notion of targets is flawed. Their use in a hierarchical system engages people's ingenuity in managing the numbers instead of improving their methods. People's attention turns to being seen to meet the targets—fulfilling the bureaucratic requirements of reporting that which they have become 'accountable' for at the expense of achieving the organization's purpose. All this effort constitutes and causes waste—inefficiency, poor service and, worst of all, low morale.

Targets have now become prevalent in our schools, hospitals, local authorities, government agencies and police forces. Although government would no doubt want an effective dialogue about method, it behaves no differently from Sloan's concept of the senior manager—rating and ranking people by their numbers. Government officials, like Sloan's managers, must believe that this is sufficient to encourage a focus on method. However, the truth is, it focuses managers' attention on avoiding being ranked at the bottom—an entirely different motivation leading to entirely different behavior. Targets, standards, service levels, activity measures and budget are the common language of current management measures. Although these notions might be normal, they are counterproductive. They need to be replaced with a common language about how work works and how measures should support that purpose, not obviate it.

In time, command-and-control service organizations cease to adapt, and many do not survive. As we can now see, the cause is in the way they are designed and managed. To change this state of affairs, to succeed, we must first see organizations as systems and uncover the nature of their dynamics. The starting point is obtaining data about demand and flow, measures that tell you about the system's capability in responding to demand. The measures focus attention on the conditions that govern perform-ance and how they need to change to achieve both stability and adaptability. We need to reject the classical conceptualization of the organization. The top-down, hierarchical, functionally organ-ized phenomenon we would recognize as an organization might help us navigate our way around to answer the questions 'Who does what?' and 'Who is to blame?' but it does not help us dis-cover anything about how and how well the organization achieves its purpose.

The typical consequences of targets are: failure to achieve them, increased variability, more waste (errors and rework), higher costs, demoralization of the workforce and, ultimately, disrespect for management.

To change the system, we have to change management's thinking: see Figure 4.8.

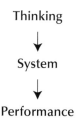

Figure 4.8: Thinking governs performance

The manager's job is to act on the system—that is what leadership consists of. Wherever command-and-control meas-ures have been thrown out and replaced by work-derived measures that are used by managers and workers alike to improve the work, quality and productivity have gone up sub-stantially, and people are happier on the job. Just as the role of first-level management changes to working on the work, so do all leadership roles. To have leadership at all levels in an organ-ization you need a common language for the work. Leaders have to 'see' the same things.

To become leaders, managers have to learn for themselves that their justifications for targets are invalid. Moreover, they have to learn that targets work against their intended purpose. Here is an example of the kinds of things managers learn:

In administrative ('back-office') service centers, agents are often measured by the work they do. Work is sorted into different electronic queues and each work queue has standard times. The standard times are translated into points, which cumulate to determine an agent's bonus. Two inevitable phenomena—the 'errors' introduced in sorting and the variation in the work—mean agents are effectively taking part in a lottery. Agents do everything in their power to maximize their points. They avoid or pass on difficult work, pass work back to customers or describe it as closed when it is not (from the customers' point of view). Equally, when redundant work comes in, they won't point out to management that it's pointless to put these items through handling, scanning, sorting and so on—why should they, when it wins them 'easy' points?

And it gets worse. When managing work held in queues, managers set targets for turnaround times. These are usually expressed as percentages of work to be completed in days (e.g., 80 percent in three days). Aside from the other problems I have just discussed, this leads managers to 'tamper.'[24] When volumes in queues become high, they move resource (people) to those queues. It seems logical from their point of view. But when you create capability charts of the true end-to-end time for all cases, you see that management's action has actually increased variation. In an effort to speed things up, they have slowed things down, increased variation and made the system more vulnerable to failure demand and other forms of waste.

In the capability chart shown in Figure 4.9, you can see when managers moved people to work different queues. When managers see such things for themselves they become alarmed. The data speaks for itself. Managers realize the consequences of their actions. They call into question the way they currently use measures. It is only when they get to this realization that managers drop standard times, activity measures (points) and turnaround targets. They appreciate the distortions created by the current measures and have confidence in replacing them with capability measures—true measures of capacity (how many things we do)

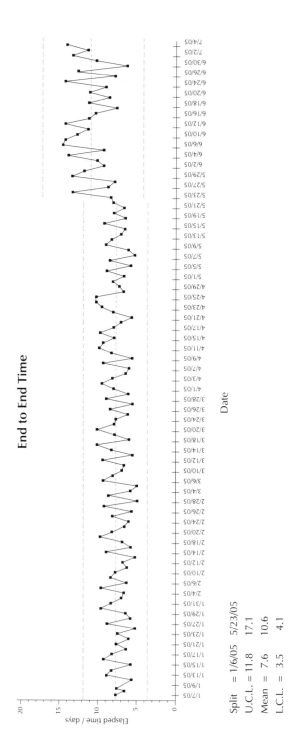

Figure 4.9: The consequences of tampering

and time (how long it takes to do all of the work from the customer's point of view).

MANAGING BY USING BOTH OPERATIONAL AND FINANCIAL MEASURES

The task for managers then becomes establishing the financial relationship between the system (operational) measures and budget (cost, revenue) measures. Managers know that changing the characteristics of demand and improving the way work is designed and managed will increase capacity. But they can never know exactly how much. Managers must determine the nature of the relationship between operational measures and financial measures by working with both sets of information, using one set to manage and the other to keep score.

CHAPTER 5

The 'break–fix' archetype

The case of the loss adjusters in Chapter 3 is an example of the 'break–fix' archetype. This archetype represents any system where a service begins with a customer in distress (something is 'broken') and ends with a resolution of the problem ('fixed'). It has a simple flow, shown in Figure 5.1.

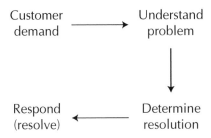

Figure 5.1: The 'break–fix' archetype

I shall begin with a complete case study of a 'break–fix' system, from analysis to redesign. The case is housing repairs, something that is relatively easily understood. I shall then show how these principles can be applied to other examples of 'break–fix' systems where it is not customers who make demands. This is to illustrate the generalizability of the systems approach to these kinds of organizations. The systems approach exposes what is wrong with the current design and provides the means to redesign for improvement—to design against demand instead of designing work in a top-down fashion. Finally, I shall summarize the kinds of organizational features we usually find in 'break–fix' systems—things that command-and-control thinkers use in a vain attempt to manage performance.

CASE STUDY #1: A 'BREAK–FIX' SYSTEM USED IN HOUSING REPAIRS

Local authorities and housing associations manage large stocks of housing. Inevitably, houses need repairing. The majority of housing organizations manage repairs with two measures, budget and time to repair. The latter has been mandated by the UK government as a 'Best Value Performance Indicator' (BVPI). The BVPIs have to be reported as percentages of repairs completed within certain times: emergency repairs in 24 hours; urgent repairs in seven days; and 'non-urgent' repairs in 28 days.

In most housing repair organizations, the repair work is controlled through a 'schedule of rates.' This is a comprehensive listing of repair types and their associated costs. These 'rates' are used either to pay subcontractors or pay bonuses to employees.

Taking a systems view of housing repairs: What's Wrong?

Taking a systems view of housing repairs, the first questions to ask are, 'What is the purpose' and 'How well are we achieving it?' The purpose from the customer's (tenant's) point of view is to do the repair properly and quickly. So to establish the organization's capability versus purpose, we need to measure end-to-end time from the tenants' point of view.

In Figure 5.2 are the results from one example.

The capability chart showed the average end-to-end time to be about 31 days, with the lower limit zero and the upper limit about 85 days. The chart also showed a number of 'special causes' or 'signals'—data points well above the upper control limit. These events were investigated to find out if they were different from others. The answer was no: the system was unstable and, as the chart shows, becoming more unstable with time. I shall return to this.

The team that built this chart could not use the data available in the organization, which was all in the form of percentages of achievement of the BVPIs. As a matter of interest, all the BVPIs were being achieved. To establish end-to-end time from the tenant's point of view, the team laboriously had to take each and every request for a repair and track it through to completion. What it found was a picture very different from the one painted

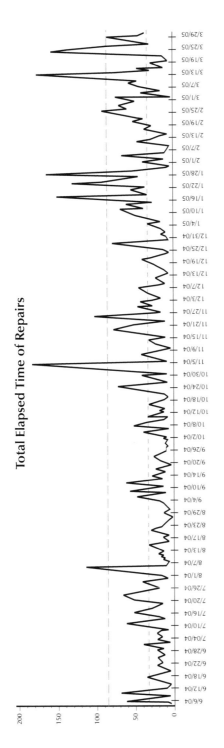

Figure 5.2: Housing repairs: end-to-end time for all repairs

by the BVPIs. It was not unusual, however—these things are to be found in all similar systems.

Firstly, targets were being achieved through 'cheating.' Jobs were closed and reopened even though they had not been completed, sometimes with 'justification'—for example, 'if tenants are out, we can't do the job so the measure shouldn't count.' Secondly, job classifications were changed to meet times—was this 'an emergency,' 'urgent' and so on. Thirdly, what was one repair from a customer's point of view (repair a window) might be four jobs for the system (glazing, carpentry, plastering, painting). Each would have a job sheet and be subject to the BVPI regime. The purpose of the system was to comply with targets; accordingly the de facto purpose had come to be 'open and close jobs,' not repair properties. People's ingenuity was focused on the wrong things.

The capability chart also shows that things were getting worse. Variation was increasing. The analysis team recalculated the control limits on the chart, choosing two places where they thought from visual inspection that the chart appeared to be moving to a different level, as shown in Figure 5.3.

By March 2002, the redrawn chart was showing an average capability of 51.4 days and an upper limit of 146.7—times were clearly lengthening. The chart led the team to ask the question: What happened at the two occasions when things clearly took a step change for the worse?

In October 2001, a new management structure was put in place. New supervisors, keen to be the best in terms of achieving their performance indicators, unknowingly destabilized the system. A month later, the organization introduced a call center, as mandated by UK government policy,[25] causing further destabilization. Again, no one had any idea of this until the capability measure invited the question.

How well was the system achieving its purpose? Not well at all. It was becoming increasingly unstable, and from the tenants' point of view it was taking longer and longer to complete repairs. At this point, managers might be seeking someone to blame. Yet the blame lies in the design and management of the work. It is of no value to blame supervisors and workers for 'cheating;' the measurement system drives that behavior—the hierarchy will judge the workers and supervisors alike on achievement of arbitrary measures. The call center workers cannot be blamed, for

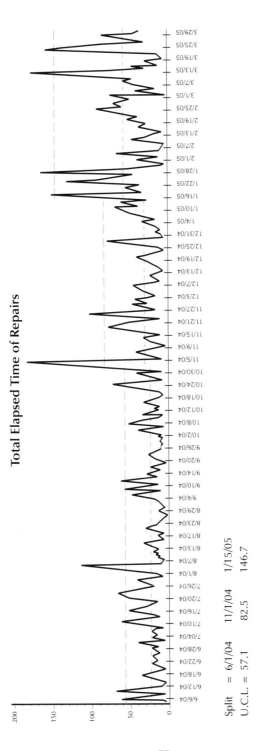

Figure 5.3: End-to-end time for all repairs, recalculating limits

they are only doing as directed by their managers. Of course the blame lies with management, but is it reasonable to blame managers for following the guidance of government and not knowing what they do not know? They may be guilty, but it is hardly their fault.

Determining *Why* the System Isn't Working

The team now knew about the 'what' of performance—how well the system achieved its purpose. The next step was to find out the 'why.' Figure 5.4 shows the basic flow of work in housing repairs.

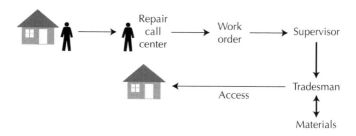

Figure 5.4: Housing repairs—basic flow

You might ask, What could go wrong? It seems quite logical: a tenant would call the call center to report a problem, the call-center worker would complete a work order, detailing the work to be done using the Schedule of Rates, and pass it to the supervisor, who would allocate it to a tradesman. The tradesman would get the necessary materials and complete the repair. To find out what is going on under the surface, however, you have to ask questions about demand and flow. As we saw with service centers, the best place to start is with demand—what is the nature of customer demands on the repair process?

Approximately 40 percent[26] of demands into the call center were 'failure demands'—demands caused by a failure to do something or do something right for the customer (for example, tenants chasing the progress of their repair or complaining that the repair had not been completed to their satisfaction). The remainder were 'value demands'—people requesting repairs to their properties. The failure demands clogged the system as the call-center workers located tradesmen or supervisors to find out what was happening, which often took time, and get back to the customer with an answer.

In this system, the call-center worker was effectively responsible for diagnosing the reported problem and determining its solution—that is to say, establishing the work to be done and deciding a specification from the 'schedule of rates,' which in turn determined how the tradesman was paid. The trouble was that in 90 percent of cases, the tradesmen disagreed with the work specified on the schedule of rates. Because of this, an administrative function, a cottage industry on its own, had been established to deal with these matters. The administrators would take returned works orders on which the tradesmen had altered the schedule-of-rates code and pass them to the supervisors to decide what was correct. Subsequent changes would be returned for further administration. None of this, of course, adds any value to doing the work—it is all waste.

Call center staff also arranged access to carry out the repair. At the same time, supervisors would allocate work according to value (earnings) to the tradesmen—and favoritism could play a part in allocating work. Tradesmen would schedule their work to maximize their earnings. As a consequence, tradesmen often had problems with gaining access and performing the repair. In addition, they would have to wait for up to an hour each morning, lining up to get their materials.

In summary, the real system picture looked as shown in Figure 5.5.

All of these problems had been created by design. Managers may believe that this organization would work just fine if everybody did as they should. But such thinking ignores the element of variety. To attempt to 'command and control' service delivery is the essential design problem. To design a service that works, you need to learn how to design against demand, to understand the nature and extent of variety in demand and optimize the way the system responds to it.

It is impossible for two parties who know little about the expertise of the tradesmen—the tenant and the call-center worker—to satisfactorily diagnose a repair. Turning the unsatisfactory diagnosis into a specification and linking that to pay are the conditions that lie at the heart of the system's failure. Waste

Housing repair

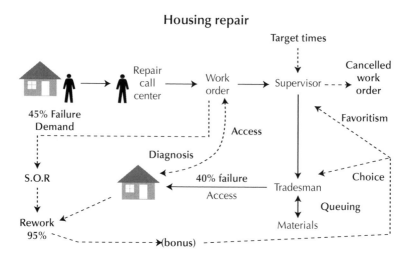

Figure 5.5: Housing repairs as a system

built into this system included revisiting the properties, reworking the schedule-of-rates paperwork, disputes over pay, doing more than was required in the repair hence wastage of materials and labor and so on.

Redesigning the Work

Having gained understanding about the 'what and why' of current performance, the people who did this work redesigned it. The first step in redesign is to clarify the value work. In this case, it can be described as: diagnosis, access and repair. The redesign was as follows:[27] the customer called the call center, which routed the call directly to a tradesman who was working on the estate (having learned that demand was predictable by geography, tradesmen could determine where to be located). The tradesman would arrange to visit the tenant, proceed to the location, and, if possible, complete the repair on the spot—now a good probability, because from analyzing demand, the tradesman knew what materials he was most likely to need. If for any reason he couldn't finish the job, the tradesman would arrange for a repair at an agreed date. Within weeks the end-to-end time for repairs plummeted. All the jobs were being completed in eight days. As well as transforming performance, the change transformed morale:

the people who were responsible for doing the work were also responsible for redesigning the system.

Alongside the reduction in repair times, there was less wastage of materials. Because jobs used materials as required, not according to the schedule of rates, there was no incentive to use extra materials. Seeing this, managers set about further reducing materials costs by working on the predictability of demand for materials by type and reducing the time they spent in the system.

Meanwhile, the tradesmen elected to be paid a salary rather than a bonus based on the schedule of rates, which they now recognized as one of the system conditions causing suboptimization. This, it should be noted, is an important point about intervention. If the exercise had begun with managers suggesting to workers that their payment system should change, it would never have got off the ground.

DESIGN AGAINST DEMAND

As with any system, the solution for a 'break–fix' system is to learn how to design against demand. Sometimes that demand comes not from customers or tenants but from the object providing the service. Utilities are a good example. Utility organizations have pipes, poles, boxes, sub-stations and the like, all of which need to be maintained. Although the stated purpose of such organizations might be expressed as 'preventing failure,' they usually work as 'break–fix' rather than preventative systems. As I shall demonstrate, this de facto purpose is one created by the way work is designed and managed.

To show how systems principles apply and broaden the discussion, I shall discuss experiences from a number of utilities. Rather than talk about the 'box,' pipe or utility, I shall use the generic noun: utility. This will also provide a modicum of anonymity for my clients.[28]

Managers of utility maintenance systems typically have no data about demand from their poles, pipes and boxes other than volumes of tasks; managers' roles are concerned with managing 'production levels' of workers. To do this, they usually manage people's activity—jobs per man per day and the like. Managers manage people (resources) against the work. This throws no light on the nature of demand, the value work that is thus implied and the work flow—how the work is currently being done.

CASE STUDY #2: IMPROVING THE PRODUCTIVITY OF UTILITY TESTERS

I shall start with a case where I was asked to consider how to improve the productivity of utility testers—people whose job it was to inspect utilities to ensure they were fit for purpose.

The job of a tester is to go to utilities as directed by a central function and test them according to a testing specification. This means conducting a series of checks on the utility's parts and digging around the utility to carry out a test below ground level. Managers were concerned with productivity—how many utilities were tested each day. The presenting problem was that some testers would do twice as many tests as others. Management wanted to know how to get everyone to the standard of the best.

Analyzing the Problem: Assessing What the Testers Did

When you work as a consultant, you sometimes have to work from the client's stated problem. My preference would have been to look first at the system, on the assumption that the system would be governing the testers' performance. But if the client wants to get the worst to be as good as the best, the place to start is with the testers, to find out why the groups differ. At the same time, we would consider the demands made by the utility and how the testers responded to them. So the Vanguard team went out with testers.

We chose a mix of high and low performers. We needed to spend enough time to gain a representative and reliable view of the work. In all, we witnessed about 100 utilities being tested. When we went out with low-performing testers, some of this group turned into high performers, suggesting to us that they had a significant problem with motivation. Others, to our surprise, did a couple of hours work and then quit. One called his accompanying Vanguard consultant to air his concern that we should not report him. It was obvious there was a significant problem of motivation amongst testers.

The temptation was to employ a performance management solution. The differences between the two groups were stable when run as capability charts, so there was little doubt that some people were shirking or slacking off.

But the problem went deeper. We discovered a culture of bartering between managers and testers—'I'll give you more tests if you give me . . . I'll go early today and give you one more tomorrow . . . .' Some testers were known to have refused to comply with the requirement to dig, the most difficult part of the job. A disciplinary meeting had been held, yet no action was taken. Naturally, this information had spread like wildfire. There were many other examples of what can only be described as very poor management. But we decided it was more than a labor-management problem. Having spent time watching the testing of 100 utilities, we came to the following conclusion:

The job, as currently designed, was pointless.

The frequency with which a tester could take constructive action was extremely low. Of course, the system wasn't designed for the tester to take action—it was designed for the tester to carry out the specification. Writing about what needs to be done rather than doing it is a soul-destroying job. Worse, the number of genuinely defective utilities, items that should be replaced to prevent catastrophic failure, was extremely low. The majority were labelled 'defective' because the specification dictated it, not because they were truly defective. For example, if a utility could not be climbed or was close to another structure, it had to be labelled defective, even if it was in perfect health.

Worse still, every utility had to be 'dug'—the hardest part of the job. Yet the knowledge gained from digging added no value to the testers' decision. Think of the impact on motivation of testing a utility to a specification, including a substantial amount of physical work, only to learn nothing more than you already know and being unable to do anything constructive to maintain the life of the equipment. Can you imagine digging out holes around utilities every day and finding that as few as one in 100 need replacement—but worse than that, knowing already which ones would show the result without having to dig? The purpose of the testers' job was to comply with procedures. It was demoralizing work.

We asked who wrote the procedures. No one was sure. The people who devised the procedures were long gone. People could only surmise who had written them and when. This is an important lesson about the consequences of separating decision-making from work. No doubt the procedures made sense to those who had originally specified them, but because they failed to put in place any means for people to question their relevance, the procedures remained static. These standards and procedures were unquestioned and unquestionable. Moreover, there was a bureaucracy to maintain them. In such systems, you find any challenge to the specification is met with a fear of what might happen if it were relaxed. Even when evidence is presented that shows the procedure is of no value and actually waste, 'just-in-case' thinking governs the decisions made.[29]

In so many cases of equipment maintenance, adherence to procedures and standards takes over as the de facto purpose of the system. The consequence is that these systems destroy knowledge, separating decision-making from work and then basing those decisions on abstractions from the work. The fundamental error is the separation of design from process.[30]

To put meaning back into the work, you have to ask: 'What is the purpose?' It should not be to work to a specification. The only value of a specification is in its ability to provide good method and that should always be open to question. To be able to question method, you need measures related to purpose—the only thing that will successfully mediate a discussion about the value of standards and procedures.

You could argue that the purpose of inspection was finding genuinely defective utilities. We discovered this represented about 1 percent of the testers' work. (Only in one area did the results differ, and this was the result of a combination of factors—age of utilities, ground conditions, etc. an assignable cause.) Yet the proportion labelled 'defective' varied between 10 and 90 percent of the work, the reflection, as noted, of issues such as hazards, inability to test, wrong depth or position. What is important is most of the foregoing were under the organization's control. This was a system that created its own waste.

Solving the Problem: Changing the Work so Performance Measures Relate to the Purpose of the Job

The organization's purpose ought to be to keep the utilities and the system it supports working. We asked if utilities ever fell down. We learned that the main cause was road traffic accidents, to which one feature made them vulnerable. When we followed the flow of work from notification of this (known) problem by a tester to resolution, we found it was taking an alarmingly long time, thus increasing the probability of a catastrophe. The 'fix' flow cut across functional and organizational boundaries involving handovers, inspections and controls of various kinds. When the end-to-end time was compared to the time taken to do the value work, the scope for improvement became stark. Although it would take less than an hour to remove the risk, it could take more than a year to take the necessary remedial action.

We asked if a utility had ever fallen down without being knocked down, through material failure, stopping the network from working. No one knew the answer. Managers showed us a management report on the number of utilities thought of as 'in danger of imminent collapse.' These data were based on the inspection regime described above and thus could be assumed to be unreliable. There was a backlog of 'defective' utilities waiting for replacement, but when managers themselves had studied the utilities removed from their sites, they could see most were being replaced unnecessarily.

So demoralization was designed in. Testers were concerned with 'being seen to follow the specification.' They ought to be concerned with 'how to keep the system working.' Measures should relate to purpose. Currently the de facto purpose is 'meet the productivity statistics.' This, paradoxically, undermines productivity—the testers were busy doing the wrong things, if they were busy at all. The purpose of the system ought to be to maximize availability of the network and extend the life of the utility. These should be the two primary measures used by both testers and managers. Additionally, as a corollary to maximizing availability, data about the type and frequency of failure should be collected. Predictable causes of failure could then be acted on in a preventative way.

There would also be a requirement for demand measurement—the type and frequency of demands from the utilities; in other words, the things that have to be done to maintain and prolong their life—and 'within process' measurement—the type and frequency of occurrences of things that stop or prevent the taking of action to solve problems presented by the utility. Over time, testers and managers would be able to make intelligent decisions about how to act to optimize the assets. The culture change that is implied would also have a significant beneficial impact on morale, as the testers would experience greater control, decision making and, in simple terms, meaning from the work they do. In effect, they would be self-managing. Managers would change their focus from managing people to acting on the system. The consequences would be more control, more learning and, most important of all, improvement.

CASE STUDY #3: IMPROVING THE PERFORMANCE OF A UTILITY NETWORK

I shall switch to a second example to make the case for this kind of change. It involved a network of utilities, buried in the ground, that are protected against corrosion by a small electric charge generated by ancillary equipment, also planted in the ground.

Analyzing the Problem: No Integration Among Functions

The job of the inspector was to take readings in specified places and report them on a form. Analysis revealed power values to be very unstable across the network. The method—inspect, report, remedy—was ineffective.

As in the previous case, the requirement for action ('fix') cut across functional boundaries, the immediacy of the need steadily diminishing as it travelled through the system. No less than six functions were involved in the fix, each working to its own specifications—not what you would call joined up. Not only did the flow contain enormous amounts of waste (rework, lost time, duplication of effort), perhaps inevitably the 'fix' specification was often wrong because it would be interpreted by people remote from the utility. They had their own perceptions of what to do, as governed by their roles. The consequences were mistakes and delays in fixing and a shortening of the lifespan of the utility.

Solving the Problem: Taking Action Rather than Just Reporting

A team of workers set about to redesign the inspectors' role. They visited every site where values were out of specification and determined the reasons why. They then added to their team all the expertise required to rectify the various situations. Once the power values had been stabilized, the team set about reducing variation further, ensuring the power created and used was optimized. They were proud of their achievement and knew how to work to maintain the purpose: optimal power all over the utility, all the time.

What changed? Previously, a requirement for maintenance action having been picked up by regular inspection would then wait for someone removed from the situation to specify a remedy. The operatives would then do what they were told, regardless of the impact on the utility. After redesign, the inspector's job was to maintain the power values. In simple terms, the job changed from 'turn up, take measures and report' to 'turn up, take measures and act.' The analysis had revealed the most frequent demands from the utility and the system had been designed to make the expertise required either available among the 'testers' or easy to 'pull' as required. Not only did this result in lower maintenance costs, it meant longer life for the utility.

In circumstances where specifications are kept separate from work, there are always contradictions and overspecification. Within the governing logic, this is natural: the specifiers being the brains of the system, their job is to second-guess every eventuality—in fact, an impossible endeavor. Imagine the impact on the worker of being fully aware of the contradictions and palpable waste from overspecification. The locus of control for the work should be moved to the tester who, on the basis of all available information, should make the judgment whether and how to test the utility. The tester should also be equipped to take or dictate all necessary actions to make the utility safe, prolong the life of the utility, and thus ensure the network is available.

CASE STUDY #4: IMPROVEMENT COMES FROM DESIGN AGAINST DEMAND

In a third example of utility maintenance, by changing the way work was designed and managed, maintenance engineers increased their productivity by 40 percent. It is a good illustration of the paradox that managing activity lowers productivity, whereas managing flow raises it.

In this case, the maintenance engineers were directed to their work each day by a dispatch function that worked to target response times: getting an engineer to the utility within a specified number of hours. As well as directing the engineers, dispatchers also decided whether to send anyone at all. The signals about a utility failure could come from a number of sources: the fault could be reported by cleaners, customers or maintenance engineers, or electronically by the utility itself. Note that the engineer's job was to report a fault, not just fix it; as is so often the case, the 'fix' did not 'count' unless it was first recorded centrally.

In the previous two examples, I showed how separating decision-making from work was at the heart of the problems experienced. In this case, we found the same phenomenon, but in a different form. To reduce the workload on dispatch, managers had bought a computer to automate dispatch decisions and improve efficiency. Signals from cleaners, customers and engineers were entered into the computer and a set of decision rules applied. In simple terms, it recommended things like 'ignore customer reports' (one shouldn't trust customers) and 'wait for a second signal in certain circumstances.'

It was obvious to me that this constituted interference with demand data. Rules often interfere with demand because they can't take into account the variety in the work and hence can lead to wrong decisions. I immediately recommended that the filtering should be turned off and all demand information passed directly to the engineers to decide the most appropriate course of action. Against my advice, this conclusion was presented to the senior management team. The managers thought I was crazy. They claimed the engineers would be 'swamped' with data, would not know how to act, and would fail to meet response times. They were wrong. When they did eventually route the data to the engineers, the flow improved and productivity went up.

To get to the solution took some time, not least because the senior management community were opposed to it—being presented with the solution had created resistance.[31] The first step was to engage the engineers in an analysis of their work. They did a diary check, analyzing their own calls in terms of value (a true signal), failure (to fix on first visit) and waste (repeat visits). Although the process was laborious (as is often the case, the computer systems specified by managers failed to capture data of this kind),[32] it resulted in attitudinal changes among engineers. For example, until that point, many engineers had been treating real and false signals alike; when they turned up at a utility that did not require repair, they just counted it as a job done instead of, as they should, treating it as waste—something to be eliminated.

It quickly became obvious to the engineers that they should work on their own geographical areas. Many of the recurring problems being predictable, knowledge of the utility, its location, and use, improved decision-making and gave engineers control of the work. As well as receiving information about demand from their own patch, engineers could view the adjacent areas and between themselves organize others to attend calls.

The engineers became more productive. Dispatchers used to schedule engineer calls to avoid 'blown response times.' This frequently meant engineers driving long distances, wasting substantial amounts of time. In the new design, engineers travelled less and were more productive. For example, a city-center engineer would go to the extremities of his patch less frequently because neighboring engineers were nearer and could field these calls more easily. As is so often the case, the engineers felt as if they were doing less work—which in a sense was true, because so much of it had previously been waste—whereas, in fact, in terms of value work, they were doing considerably more.

COMPUTER SERVICES

One of the most common 'break–fix' systems in which we have developed the systems solution is computer services. In the next case, which involved a desktop services (DTS) operation in Ireland, customers would call an interactive voice response system (IVR) and be given a series of choices with which to route their call. Having chosen, for example, whether the call was related to hardware, software, printer or monitor, the customer would be dealt with by the designated specialist group. The diagnosticians in each group had maximum times for dealing with calls. Problems with monitors being assumed to take less time to fix than servers, the monitors group had a maximum of 8 minutes to deal with calls, the server group 20 minutes. Having determined the problem and its resolution, diagnosticians would close the call with the customer and route their solution to a 'controller.' Controllers were ex-diagnosticians; they would sometimes change the action to be taken and were also responsible for sourcing spares and field engineers. Like diagnosticians, controllers and engineers were measured and managed with activity measures—in both cases, the number of calls they handled in a day.

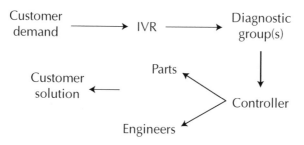

Figure 5.6: High-level flow: computer services

As seen in Figure 5.6, it was a classical command-and-control design. The measures hide the waste and are themselves a major cause of waste. When we studied this organization as a system, the following issues came to the surface:

- 25 percent of customer demands were progress chasing (failure demand). A choice on the IVR was 'seeking progress on an open call'—in other words, managers had institutionalized failure demand. A further 15 percent of demands were repeat calls, indicating that the original solution had not provided the right 'fix.'
- If customers routed themselves to the 'wrong' diagnostic group, they had to be put to the end of the line in the 'right' group, otherwise the call would not count in the group's statistics.
- Over half the calls were 'reworked' by controllers, changing parts to be sent to site or instructions to the engineers. Controllers justified this by claiming that their decisions were based on experience (they were more experienced than diagnosticians) and they had better knowledge about the availability or appropriateness of parts (which could save costs).
- Engineers were only able to resolve customers' problems 40 percent of the time. Often they needed to call the

diagnosticians to reconcile views of the problem and its resolution—it looked different to the engineer on site. Engineers would often swap a part as directed by the diagnostician even when they could see this would not solve the problem. It would look to the customer as though something were being done and it meant less trouble for the engineer (returning parts to stores required extensive paperwork).

- In short, only 30 percent of the work flowed cleanly from start to finish with no rework or other form of waste.

The primary 'system condition' driving behavior was the measurement of the work of the diagnosticians. The measures in use drove diagnosticians to 'do something' with a call, even (as often) where they had inadequate information. Often customers were internal 'help desks' in the clients' organization; their view of what was wrong was already one removed from the end-user.

An analysis of demand in customer terms showed that there were four primary customer demands: 'give me an engineer with a part to fix my problem,' 'help me solve the problem over the phone,' 'send me a part,' and 'give me information.' These types of demands existed across all product groups. In conjunction with the client we decided to begin the process of redesigning the work with a 'clean room,'[33] where customer demands would be dealt with one at a time, end to end, with the object of learning how to make the work flow cleanly. Having detailed knowledge of the type and frequency of customer demands informed the choice of participants in the clean room, which included engineers and diagnosticians. At this stage, the time taken to deal with a call was irrelevant; the key was to learn how to create clean flow.

In the first few jobs the clean room handled, diagnosis time was anything up to two hours. Not surprisingly, managers expressed concern; their mental model—treating the time in diagnosis as a cost of 'production'—meant they extrapolated this 'result' to the whole system. What they could not 'see' was that more time in diagnosis resulted in cleaner flow and thus less waste. Moreover, as time went on and solutions were found for predictable problems, diagnosis times shrank. The team in the clean room found their priority to be determining the right flow (against the primary demands outlined above) for any particular demand.

The results are shown in Figure 5.7.

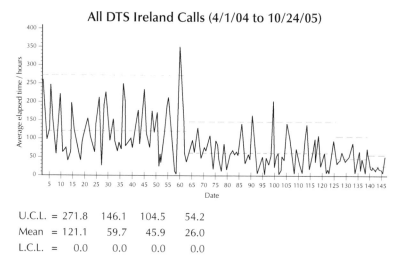

U.C.L. = 271.8   146.1   104.5   54.2
Mean = 121.1   59.7   45.9   26.0
L.C.L. =   0.0   0.0   0.0   0.0

Figure 5.7: Results from redesign

The capability chart shows a succession of step-wise improvements over time as the team learned to redesign the work against demand. As with the other cases, as flow improved, capacity increased, enabling more demand to be handled by the same system.

REDESIGNING MANAGEMENT ROLES

As the work of the clean room expanded to include more and more demand (and more and more personnel[34]), managers' roles shifted from managing resource through activity measures to managing the primary end-to-end flows. Each flow had data about achievement of purpose in customer terms, and it became management's role to identify and act on causes of waste in the flows. Additionally, managers were assigned to manage support flows—the most important ones being logistics (for getting parts to customers) and manufacturing (to help manufacturers design out known problems).

As was the case for all of the foregoing 'break–fix' examples, management roles changed from managing people to acting on the system. Much as with desktop computer services, managers in the housing repairs case worked on improving the way materials ('parts') moved through the system. The key concerns with parts or materials are type and time: what types of demands are there for parts and how much time is there between bringing the part into our system and using it. By working on cutting time by type, managers cut costs. Managing parts with cost data (as is usually the case) causes costs to rise.

In the utility examples, managers switched their roles from managing the activity of their engineers or testers to managing aspects of the system that were beyond their people's control. This included not only the supply of parts, but the supply and location of utilities: they established data on the life of utilities to begin the process of moving the organization away from a 'break–fix' design and towards a preventative design.

COMMON PROBLEMS IN 'BREAK–FIX' SYSTEMS

There are common design problems in 'break–fix' systems. Remember the basic design, shown in Figure 5.8.

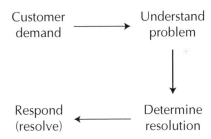

Figure 5.8: The 'break–fix' archetype

Command-and-control management typically does the following things, each of which is counterproductive.

Customer demand

- Treat all demand as units of production, ignoring failure demand—often the largest form of waste.
- Use interactive voice response (IVR—'press one for this, two for that') to route the call. This is attractive to

managers because it passes some of the costs of production to the customer. IVR 'works' when you can determine
why customers call—from their point of view—or where
you sell it as part of a service (although some customers
still hate it). But when these conditions do not prevail,
you find customers route themselves wrongly (silly customers) and drop out, resulting in lost opportunity.

- At the first point of contact, introduce a 'validation' step—
agents are told to ensure that the customer has a contract
and is entitled to the service. This is acceptable if made
easy, but sometimes entirely unnecessary. For example,
when callers have your unique equipment you would
want to provide service to them even if they do not have a
contract. Providing service gives you the opportunity to
move the customer on to a contract or send an invoice. If
people who hold your unique equipment are not customers, you would want them to be. Often the validation
process interrupts the service flow, for example when the
validation requires an up-to-date customer database. If
validation is necessary, it should either be mistake-
proofed, so it never fails, or be completed off-line. It
should not impede the service flow. In many cases, I have
seen validation employed to weed out non-customers,
making it difficult for genuine customers to get service.

Understand problem, determine resolution and respond

I lump these together because all these steps can suffer from the
same design problems.

'Proceduralize' ('dumb down'). This is done in diagnosis with
scripts and computer-driven diagnostic screens. Such work 'aids'
are generally designed with no real understanding of the type
and frequency of customer demand and hence often suboptimize
the flow of a call, worsening service, turning off customers and
adding to costs.

Locate expertise required to understand the problem in 'levels' or departments 'behind' the first point of contact. The rationale is to minimize costs. But cost is end-to-end. If there is no
justification for locating such expertise in the front line, for example because of low frequency of demand, the expertise should

nevertheless operate on a 'pull' basis to increase the competence of those in the front line. If the customer experience is to go through successive levels, service worsens and costs rise. Most customers don't mind being passed once if it is to the right place. Beyond that we try their patience. The solution is to allow customer demand to dictate the expertise required at the first point of transaction.

Measure people's productivity—how many 'pieces of work' they do. Activity measures always suboptimize flow, as do service standards and targets.

Use procedures, standards or other devices to control the behavior of those who do the work. As we have seen, this becomes a de facto purpose: 'do things right,' which is not the same as doing the right thing. Nor is it as motivational. People who work in 'break–fix' systems want to fix breaks and customers of 'break–fix' systems want their break fixed. If they experience that and only that (no waste, no rework, a satisfactory solution to the problem), they are likely to be happy and remain loyal. A cynic might say that these days they are likely to be amazed.

Try to give 'important' customers a better service. I say 'try,' because all the efforts I have seen consume more resource. They may justify the extra cost by pointing to the value of the customers, but to redesign against demand is the only sure way to improve service and reduce costs.

One way into a 'break–fix' system is to study how often it actually works in respect of purpose: how often breaks are fixed at the point of transaction. This cannot be learned from management reports; it needs to be learned by experiencing it where the transaction occurs. When you spend your time in those places, you find out how well the service works for customers. You also start to appreciate the waste: rework, doing too much work, duplicating work and so on. The extent, nature and costs of this waste are normally hidden from managers by the measures they use. Instead, the current measures are another cause of suboptimization. These are the things you learn when you study your organization as a system. It is not something that can be delegated; it is the defining mark of a good leader. So now I turn to leadership.

CHAPTER 6

Learning to see, learning to lead

It may surprise you to learn that there is no agreed definition of leadership in the management literature. It is a little like the problem of defining intelligence: We all think we know what we mean by it and hence we avoid a rigorous definition. Just as intelligence ends up being what the tests measure, leadership ends up being what the various theorists postulate it to be. Because of this, we now have generally accepted leadership myths: the leader should have a vision, subscribe to values, be a coach and so on. But do these things make a difference? Do they make leaders?

In my experience, adherence to such beliefs can be dysfunctional. In 'living the credo,' managers can stifle their organizations. Any behavior that is viewed by another as 'against the credo' becomes the subject of attention. As people debate the rightness or wrongness of each other's behavior, the organization can fall over a cliff. It is easy to see how the many leadership trainers, writers and philosophers get away with it. If you were to challenge their ideas, you might be accused of believing the opposite: are you saying a leader should have no vision? Do you believe a leader should be a dictator rather than a coach? Should a leader have no values?

The ideas about leadership in the management literature would have us believe there are leadership traits, there are leaders who are 'great,' leaders who enable their people, have a need for achievement, behave according to the situation or maturity of their followers, have a certain style and interpersonal skills and so on. In the many courses on leadership, managers will be told that to lead they need to be trustworthy, charismatic, visionary, and obsessed with goals. They must challenge assumptions, behave as a model, walk the talk, empower their people and so on. But what do we know about the reality of leadership? What must leaders and followers believe or know in order to influence one another?

Cast your mind back to the plight of the administrators in the loss adjusters case (Chapter 3). If you were an administrator, at work on a Monday morning under pressure to complete a pile of reports that adjusters had left on your desk from Saturday and having to deal with phone calls from unhappy customers, and the leader turned up to communicate his or her vision and values statements, how would you respond? I think the second word is 'off.' Suppose, however, the leader turned up and said: 'I have been studying the way the work works and am amazed at what I have learned. Our service standards do not actually reflect what happens for our customers. It actually takes a long time to adjust losses from the customers' point of view. The causes are in the way the work is designed and managed; the consequences for you are plainly ridiculous. I am going to change the system and I want you to be involved in this.' I think the administrators would be much more inclined to follow.

Leadership, in my view, is about influencing. Without followers there can be no leaders. What would cause someone to follow another? I think it is an acceptance by the follower that the idea of the leader will produce meaningful change that is in the interests of all parties. Anyone can demonstrate leadership. It is not associated with hierarchy.

> I bumped into a new employee at one of my clients. He told me he was very happy to work there and likened it to his previous job where he was working with Japanese managers: 'They came down to the floor every day, working with people to improve things. If you had knowledge—if you were interested in learning—they talked to you. If you were not engaged they just ignored you.'

Workers and managers were engaged in improvement; both parties were influencing each other. Both were showing leadership. Leadership or influence is based on knowledge: You need to be able to 'see' and you need to be able to describe a view of things that others find compelling enough to follow.

When you take a view of your organization as a system, it can be striking just how much current measures, procedures, process design and other features of the system effectively create a 'de facto purpose' that is counterproductive. As I have already shown, measuring activity often results in people doing what they have to do to achieve their measures, rather than accomplish the purpose. The point is that when you discover this for yourself and talk about it to others, it creates behavior that others find compelling.

'YOU'LL NEVER GUESS WHAT I'VE FOUND'

One of the most successful leaders I have ever worked with would open with this line when he wanted to tell his people he had found something wrong. If this happened in a traditional command-and-control organization, people might fear for their safety. Yet because he behaved this way, he created an infectious atmosphere for finding things wrong. His view was: 'How can you fix anything if you don't know it's wrong?' The key was how he spent his time: always in the work, always working on method. He created organizations where people who did the work solved problems he did not even know existed. That, for him, was the sign he had succeeded.

There are managers who find it hard to be compelling. They fail to become leaders. I often make the distinction between being 'strong and different' and 'weak and similar.' To illustrate: Suppose you have discovered that measuring your people's activity drives the wrong behavior. You could respond to this by saying: 'It was never management's intention for this to happen, management was and is well intended, there are good reasons why this was done, and we mustn't throw the baby out with the bathwater. It was always my intention that these measures would be used as a guide only.' Alternatively you could say: 'This is clearly dumb. I can see how the measures drive you to do things that don't help us serve our customers, and I have to say the responsibility rests with me as I set the measures we work with. We need to change this, and the change starts with me.' Which do you suppose would get people's attention?

Clients have taught me a lot about leadership. One, for example, has no difficulty behaving in ways that are strong and different. To take an example, many years ago he was running a distribution organization. When he studied his organization as a system, it became apparent that if a customer had a problem it always needed to be escalated to management. Of course, customers learned to bypass the service agents to get what they wanted. In a review with his managers of what had been learned, he decided the right answer was to work with the agents to enable them to solve all customer issues at the point of transaction—effectively to enable them to do whatever the managers would do. The following day he got to work early and locked the managers' offices. He gave them a little time to behave as they might—puzzled, disgruntled, seeking someone to blame and so on—and pulled them all together to ask: 'What did we learn yesterday?' His point was simple: 'We can't achieve what we have agreed to do in our offices.' He and his managers went to work on the floor with agents to address the question: What do the agents need to enable them to handle everything at the point of transaction? In just three weeks they had solved the problem, improving performance and creating a radically different culture. As agents learned to solve more problems they became more proactive, taking greater responsibility. This freed up management time to work on more important things—the things beyond the control of agents that affected the way the system worked. (Just in case it matters to you, he unlocked their offices once he had made the point.)

Just before he died, Taiichi Ohno was asked: 'What are you working on?' His reply was, 'Cutting the time between receipt of an order and getting the money.' How many chief executives would respond in similar fashion? Command-and-control management has led to the development of a method of managing that is remote; our current philosophy even discourages 'interference' with lower ranks of management. We assume top leaders should be concerned with strategy and the lower ranks should be concerned with operations. Yet strategy is inherently linked with operations. Separating the two is often disastrous.

Many service organizations have built service centers that don't provide very good service. I am reminded of a phone call from a long-standing client who, on taking up an appointment to run a help desk, called me to say: 'Help desk is a misnomer. They don't provide help.' He knew that to improve performance he needed to learn how to design the service against demand. The success of the method led to a completely new strategy for the organization. Instead of selling the service on the basis of cost per call, the service is sold at a reduction in cost year by year. In another example from the same sector, IT technicians developed new services for their customers after having studied demand into their system and learned from customers what mattered to them. To solve their customers' problems the technicians worked inside the customer's system. As their understanding of the customer's business grew, they were able to develop solutions that their customers were pleased to buy. Strategy is in operations and understanding demand is critical to developing service operations.

LEARNING TO SEE

The purpose of this chapter is to take you through the steps by which you can learn to see your organization as a system. Although you might not run your organization as a system—and few people do—you can study it as a system. When people learn to see an organization as a system and they talk about what they 'see' with others who do the work, people follow. People follow because what is talked about makes compellingly good sense.

All organizations are systems; they are simply not understood and managed as such. When you learn to look at any traditionally managed organization as a system you find a multitude of forces working against purpose. In service organizations you find excessive costs associated with poor service. For managers this comes as a shock. Some of what you discover seems perverse—people 'do their jobs' but create enormous harm to a system which they are unable to change because it is a shackle imposed and controlled by those who are remote from the work. People do perverse things sometimes without knowledge of the consequences, for these things cannot be seen on management's radar. Sometimes they are aware of dysfunctional consequences and are frustrated at their inability to do something about it. Sometimes managers, in particular, are aware and seek to avoid exposing the problems or acting on them for fear of retribution. If large problems are exposed, someone has to take the blame. It can be far safer to behave as normal and turn a blind eye. Hierarchies don't like bad news.

This indeed is the first hurdle you need to be prepared for. Studying the organization as a system will certainly reveal bad news. Be clear about the fact that you are expecting bad news and you want to know. Many leaders I have worked with use the words, 'at least you know,' as a refrain. It is a useful leadership tactic, making the exposing of bad news good news. 'At least you know' does not mean you have a vague enthusiasm for being open about mistakes (the 'no blame culture'); it means an enthusiasm for getting knowledge as a prerequisite for taking action. Studying the organization as a system provides the means.

Learning to see begins with taking a different perspective. When you think about any organization as a system, you start from the outside in. You think about the purpose of the system in customer terms. As you learn about the system, you find out how and how well it transacts with customers. With this knowledge you can act, with foresight, for improvement.

CREATING URGENCY FOR CHANGE

Studying the organization as a system creates urgency. It gives you knowledge about the 'what and why' of current performance and enables you to see the leverage for change. When you can see for yourself, for example, the waste and causes of waste in work, you are stimulated to address the problems. When you can see how simple the flow ought to be for a customer, you have an enthusiasm for fundamentally redesigning it.

Urgency should come from leaders; unfortunately, more often it comes from events. For Taiichi Ohno, economic stress provided the opportunity to push through his radical agenda at Toyota. In the 1950s, Ohno was making slow progress trying to push his ideas through the organization until a collapse in sales forced the company to cut its workforce. Ohno offered employment guarantees to those who remained, provided they agreed to work in new ways. The oil crisis of 1973 gave Ohno his opportunity to push TPS principles throughout suppliers. Ohno had formed the Operation Management Consulting Group at Toyota in the late 1960s whose purpose was to teach TPS to suppliers, but there had been little progress. The oil crisis provided the imperative.

But you shouldn't wait for the hard times. An alternative way to create urgency is to expose the extent and nature of suboptimization in your current system. It can be alarming—but it is always energizing.

'SEEING' HAPPENS IN 'CHECK'

As shown in Figure 6.1, there are three steps in performance improvement—understanding the 'what and why' of current performance as a system, identifying levers for change and taking direct action on the system. We call the cycle 'check-plan-do.'

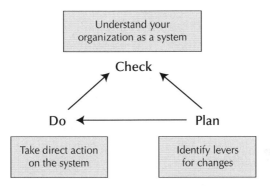

Figure 6.1: Performance improvement through 'check-plan-do'

'Check' asks:
- What is the purpose of this system?
- Demand: What is the nature of customer demand?
- Capability: What is the system predictably achieving?
- Flow: How does the work work?
- System conditions: Why does the system behave this way?

'Plan' asks:
- What needs to change to improve performance against purpose?
- What action could be taken and what would be the predicted consequences?
- Against what measures should action be taken (to ensure learning)?

'Do' consists of:
- Take the planned action and monitor the consequences versus purpose.
- And then you cycle back to '**check**.'

Some followers of Deming are unhappy with this adaptation of his cycle.[35] I believe Deming wrote about 'plan-do-check-act' on the assumption that managers who started at 'plan' were already systems thinkers. He saw 'plan' as 'have an idea based on what you "know;"' 'do' was followed by 'check' to see if the idea was right; finally, 'act' meant 'put it in the line.' His model was built in manufacturing, where changes were tested off-line before translation to the working system. What he 'knew' in his first step was based on working with the organization as a system.

I start at 'check' because managers first need to 'see' things that are currently invisible to them. Often managers will claim that they 'know' of the problems they have, but are unaware that their actions do not lead to sustainable improvement. 'Check' helps managers to 'see' what they may already know to be a problem from a different point of view, a point of view that is more helpful in improving the system. Frequently, it completely reframes their problem.

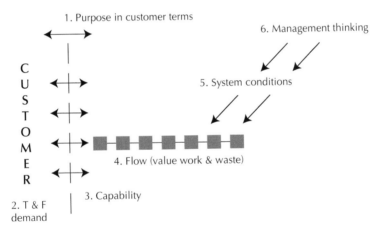

Figure 6.2: The Vanguard model for 'check'

The Vanguard model for 'check' is sequential (see Figure 6.2). You start by considering the purpose of the system from the customer's point of view. Then you study the type and frequency of demands customers make on the system. For every high-frequency, predictable demand you need to know both the capability and predictability of the system's response. Then and only then do you study the work flow. In every work flow there are two kinds of work: value work, the activity required to deliver what matters to the customer, and waste. Having identified the waste, you must look for its causes. These are what we call system conditions: structure, measures, process design, procedures, information technology and management roles that determine how the work is carried out. Now at last you can see how the current thinking about the design and management of work is the root cause of suboptimal performance.

I first developed this model while working with a U.S. organization's subsidiary in the UK. The leaders had been obliged to work with the Baldrige Award—the American equivalent of the EFQM (European Foundation for Quality Management) Excellence Model (about which I have more to say in Chapter 8). A day had been spent looking at each of the Baldrige model's criteria, assessing compliance and scoring. At the end of the day I was extremely disquieted. The following day the leaders were supposed to be planning action. I could see that some of the criteria mattered much more than others and there was the potential for taking actions that might have no bearing on performance.[36] Having expressed my disquiet, I was invited to make proposals the following morning.

I thought about what we had experienced during the day—'leaders' with no understanding of their organization as a system being led through a model by an 'expert' on the model, who had no understanding of their organization: ingredients for an unreliable assessment. I needed to come up with a proposal that would help them ensure they limited their actions to the things that would be important and, at the same time, develop their understanding of their organization as a system. So the Vanguard model for 'check' was born. It has not changed since. Although it began life in this particular circumstance, it has been applied to a wide range of organizational forms with success. Like all models it is bound to have a limit, but I have yet to find it.

Customers can only form their view of an organization from the transactions they have with it, so the model for 'check' starts with identifying those transactions and considering their purpose in customer terms. For example, if you ran a cable TV organization, your first transaction with the customer would be digging up the road.

In a town west of London, local residents still refuse to buy the service from 'those people who dug up the road,' even though that was a long time ago. Atop the management factory, managers were proud of their cost-effective subcontracting of the infrastructure build. The labor worked on piecework; their requirement to make money took priority over the residents' need to get their cars out of their drive.

Subsequent transactions would be: send a marketing pack, send a salesman. If the customer then buys the service, the steps are: install the cable connection, transmit TV programs, send invoices and provide customer service (should the customer make a call).

You need to know what matters to customers at each of these points of transaction. For any point of transaction where the customer makes demands on the system you can learn a lot from understanding the type and frequency of the demands. For example, in the early days of cable TV many customers called customer service because they did not understand their bill. Managers managing remotely from the management factory would see an increase in the volumes of calls and would act to put more resources (people) in place. Of course, the better solution is to send out bills that customers understand.

In some applications of the model for 'check,' the labels need to change. For example, although it makes little sense to treat criminals as customers, it is vital to improving police work to understand the nature and predictability of demand—the types and frequencies of crime and disorder—and the capability of the system in responding to them. Without those measures you cannot design against demand and improve the system. That is the leader's job.

So far, I have concentrated on transactions where customers make demands for service. There is another broad class of transactions (I call them customer-acquisition processes) where the system makes demands on customers. That is their purpose—getting customers, as shown in Figure 6.3.

You may recall in the telecommunications case (Chapter 2) that 'check' revealed that only 1 in 22 of the customers who 'put their hand up' actually became customers. That example was from the late 1980s, yet even today, following years of talk of

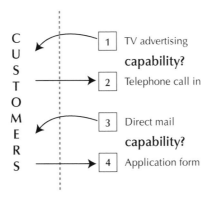

Figure 6.3: Customer-acquisition process

'below-the-line' marketing, there are many organizations that cannot tell you how or how well their marketing processes work—that is, how and how well they 'get customers.'

A financial services organization had four different methods for acquiring customers. 'Check' revealed that the budgeted spend on each of these methods (or processes) remained constant as a proportion of the whole. It was reasonable to assume that the organization was not learning; one would expect to see that as marketing processes were developed, tested and learned from, budgets would change accordingly. Capability data were gathered for each of the processes. It took some time, as management did not normally use them. The figures demonstrated that the best customers came from the lowest-cost process, whereas the highest-cost process was flooding the organization with demand from people who were least likely to buy.

The obvious solution was to spend more on the effective customer-generating processes and stop those that produced waste. Measuring marketing against budget encourages marketers to 'spend the budget' rather than 'learn, predict and improve customer acquisition processes.' When you hear people say: 'Only half of my marketing budget works, the only problem is I don't know which half,' ask: 'How do you know it's half?'

Whether you are learning about customer acquisition or customer-service flows, it is the customers' experience of the transaction that will determine whether they will come back for more. Here is an example of how out of touch managers can be with what happens to their customers. A correspondent wrote:

> *I work in the car business. In my country, car sales grew rapidly but the servicing infrastructure couldn't cope. There were just not enough service agencies. Customers voted with their feet—car sales fell. So what did corporate office do? Sales management ran an incentive program to make more sales! Service management obliged all service agents to register to ISO 9000. Each agent now has a full-time bureaucrat filling in the forms.*

I bet the managers have a slogan or mission statement about how customer-oriented they are. I wonder how long it will take them to wake up. Without being strongly connected to operations, top management can only rely on others telling them if the organization is suffering. Bad news does not travel easily up organizations. People who sit atop such systems cannot be construed as leaders.

FROM DEMAND TO CAPABILITY

The next step in 'check' is to understand capability. I frequently make the point, measure before you map. Often people tell me they are mapping their processes. I ask if they have started with demand; this usually gets a mooted, 'We think so.' Then I ask if they measured before they mapped and, moreover, derived a measure that related to purpose. If you don't measure before you map, how can you know it is worth improving and how will you know you have improved?

Capability measures should be derived from the purpose (in customer terms). I have already given a number of examples. The loss adjusters measured end-to-end time from the customers' point of view, as did the housing-repairs tradesmen. Figure 6.4 illustrates the responses: as a rule of thumb, end-to-end time from the customer' point of view is almost always an essential measure in any 'break–fix' system. The measures also draw our attention to variation and thus invite questions about the causes. When the system is redesigned, these measures—capability measures—become the means for managing.

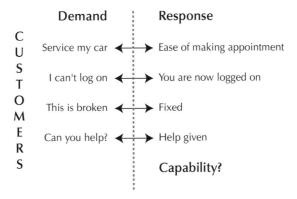

Figure 6.4: How well do we respond?

As shown in Figure 6.5, there are two reasons for conducting 'check' on flow: to understand the causes of failure demand and to see how the work works for value demands. There are only two kinds of activities in a work flow: value work and waste. All the time consumed by dealing with failure demand is waste, and this

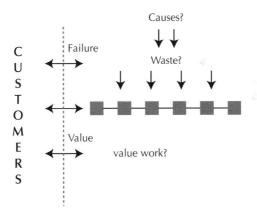

Figure 6.5: Flow, value work, waste and causes

is often the largest single creator of cost. When you look at how the organization responds to value demands, in simple terms, waste is anything and everything that is not 'value work'—the work that needs to be done to meet what matters to the customer. Just as research in manufacturing organizations shows waste can account for as much as 40 percent of productive capacity, you find the same and worse in service organizations.

SYSTEM CONDITIONS

Knowing about waste is not as important as understanding its causes. There are many. I call them system conditions. Structure, policy, procedures, measurement, IT—the factors influencing behavior in organizations are many and complex. Changing them might seem a daunting prospect, but the power of the Vanguard model is that you only tackle the complex from the point of view of how these various elements impact the work (see Figure 6.6).

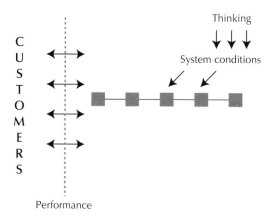

Figure 6.6: Thinking governs performance

System conditions exist because of the way managers think about the design and management of work. For example, managers may believe workers cannot be 'trusted' to do their work accurately, so they build in inspection. Managers believe workers should be motivated and held accountable, so they measure their work activity, offer incentives and appraise them. These are the kinds of management practices that come under scrutiny. Managers, if they are to be leaders, need to learn for themselves just how flawed these ideas are.

A manager of a service center had to choose between working with Vanguard and another consulting organization. I went to look at her organization. At the end of the visit she said that she could understand what the other consultant was offering: his diagnosis was that service agents did not show sufficient 'empathy' with customers, so his solution was training. I was adamant training was not the solution. My solution was to change the system; despite our long discussion of the many things that affected agents' performance in their dealings with customers, she did not understand the concept 'change the system.' Nevertheless I got the work, if only—in her words— because she did not like the other consultant!

This is how she described what she learned from 'check':

We used to take people off the street, train them in the things we thought they should know, not what the customers wanted them to know, make them work to procedures that didn't suit the customer or them, measure them to death so they worried about meeting their activity targets and then we had the audacity to inspect them and tell them where they went wrong. We went wrong.

What she said is exactly what I told her at our first meeting. The point is, she 'got it' only when she did it—in this case, studying the impact of the system on the agents' ability to be empathic with customers.

To take another example:

In a financial services organization where customer complaints could be handled at the point of transaction there were few problems, but an extraordinary number of complaints 'fell off the tracks,' to use the chief executive's description. 'Check' revealed the end-to-end time for dealing with complaints to be extraordinarily long from the customers' point of view. Naturally, this contributed to complaints being 'escalated' and led to high levels of failure demand. The main causes (system conditions) were two. First, departmental specialization had led to the drawing up of rules for which departments had the power to deal with which issues. This meant that complaints had to be passed around, and no one person kept responsibility. Secondly, agents tended to pass complaints elsewhere to avoid losing out on the activity measurement lottery. To deal with the complaint might take time and thus lead to negative consequences for the agent.

The solution required the removal of activity measurement—something that is best done as part of a change to the system—and a change to the rules for handling complaints. Anyone can understand a complaint from the customer's point of view. The agent receiving the complaint was to keep hold of it and 'pull' such specialist expertise as was required from other departments. If the agent could not be persuaded of the adequacy of the answer neither would the customer. The agent was free to 'pull' whatever expertise he or she needed to get a resolution, getting help or guidance from others, experts and managers, as to what was the right thing to do.

When the solution was implemented, end-to-end time fell and the majority of customer complaints were resolved within one day.[37] The cost of handling complaints fell, less compensation was paid, and customer satisfaction went up. It also made the work more interesting and satisfying for the agents.

MEASUREMENT—A SYSTEM CONDITION

Without doubt, the most important system condition affecting performance is measurement. It goes hand in hand with the command-and-control hierarchical structure. Functional measurement is dysfunctional, creating fear, destroying teamwork and encouraging rivalry. It drives short-term performance of functions at the expense of the system. Worst of all, it fosters politics. Political behavior fills the void created by management's detachment from the work. I have said a lot about measurement and little needs to be added here except to emphasize its importance. I shall return to the subject later to describe the kinds of measures that are of value in leading improvement in service centers. But first other common system conditions need to be explored.

When managers are first confronted with the scope and reality of a major system change, their minds leap to the broader consequences. What do we do about pay, appraisal, structure? The answer I always give them is, 'Don't worry about it for now.' This is clearly not likely to be a satisfactory answer from their point of view. But if you give the straight answer, you will offend a deeply held belief and then consume enormous amounts of time and energy discussing theory. What matters at the 'check' stage of an intervention is focusing management attention on the potential benefits of a different way of working. Where there is a lot of emotional and physical investment in the activities that currently constitute the means of management, this will inevitably be a potential block. Talking is not the best way to remove it.

The various things we do to manage are derived from the current philosophy of management. To 'see' how to do things differently requires first an appreciation of the roots of the current idea, which will be in some way to do with the design and management of work. Second, we should consider how the new and different design will function. This is hard to accomplish without actually doing it. Third, we need to return to the idea and ask whether it is actually relevant in the new design, and if so, how it should be dealt with. We will take managing absenteeism as an example.

MANAGING ABSENTEEISM

In many of our service organizations, HR departments have developed procedures for managing absence. Typically, these procedures involve the scoring of absence, allocating points for frequency and duration. Points accumulate. A 'bad score' means the employee will be subjected to a formal interview and a plan drawn up to remedy the situation. As with the operational measures in any command-and-control system, these measures fail to take account of variety. So it becomes possible for someone with a genuine illness to score badly while others who everyone knows are pulling a fast one 'get away with it.' To work on improving the rules is to miss the point—no rules will absorb all the possible variety. Employees learn to optimize their score while maximizing their time off work.[38] It is just another brick in the wall of survival.

If a manager accepts that this is bad news—demoralizing people and not solving the absenteeism problem—and accepts that a review of the rules will always fail, he will usually still want to know 'the right answer.' The right answer is 'change the system.' If you say that, you have a lot of explaining to do. Yet I hope the reader is with me. The point is that the absenteeism problem was part and parcel of the old system: if we change the way we design and manage work, we remove the conditions that created that problem. The work will be inherently more motivating. The people who do the work know who swings the lead and who does not. The closeness of leadership to the work should ensure we all know. All leaders need, if they need anything at all, is a means for managing the few, not a bureaucracy for managing absenteeism across the whole system. So the 'right answer' is: drop the procedures for managing absenteeism as you change the system. The premise is flawed. When the new system is stabilized, return to the question. You will generally find the problem dissolved or reframed.

INCENTIVES

Just as managers will justify their need to control people, they justify their means for motivating them. If you provide incentives, you will have 'winners.' The undeniable fact of 'winners' leads managers to claim this only goes to show how well incentives work. But they don't. Winners create losers. The major causes of variation are in the system. It is demoralizing to lose what is, in effect, a lottery. And it is worse even than that. Psychologists have run a simple experiment: Put two groups of people in two separate rooms and give them the same task. Tell them they are taking part in an experiment, but tell only one of the groups they are doing the task to earn money. After a while call a coffee break. The group that is incentivized stops work, whereas the other carries on. The point is simple—contingent reward[39] ('do this to get that') takes the value out of the task. It is no longer intrinsically interesting. Put this alongside the finding in service centers that agents make no difference to sales (see Chapter 2). You have a system that is a lottery within which agents will, given the scope, nonetheless use their ingenuity to make the incentives. Far from leading to additional sales at no cost to the system, this usually results in a great deal more waste and poor customer service.

Incentives are commonly used to motivate sales forces. In every case I know where the incentive scheme has been scrapped and replaced by salaries, the result has been improvements in cooperation between salespeople, customer service, and, best of all, sales. Moreover, sales force turnover goes down. Under incentive regimes, salespeople play the system by moving between organizations, taking their customers with them, as soon as the incentives move against them. An example:

Junior salesmen in one organization were given 'easy' targets to achieve their bonus (which amounted to around 30 percent of salary). As they progressed, the targets and the bonus as a percentage of salary increased. For the first two years, sales-men would run harder to keep up their earnings, but after three they could get a higher basic salary by moving to a com-petitor. When the salesmen moved, so did the customers.

Suppose you do find a salesman whose sales are reliably better than others. The reason will almost certainly be method—what the sales person does, how he or she spends his or her time. If and when this is the case, it is the leader's job to identify the reasons and adapt the method accordingly; it is part of the system. In all organizational tasks, the major causes of variation in performance are beyond the attributes of individuals. This is the reason people find appraisal so demotivating.

APPRAISAL

I began to wonder about appraisal quite early in my career. I noticed it was something that was revamped and relaunched from time to time—a tell-tale sign of problems. If I asked what the issue was, people would tell me managers were not doing their workers' appraisals. It occurred to me that perhaps managers didn't like doing them. Perhaps they saw them as of no value. Sometimes I was told that the reason managers were not fulfilling their duty to develop people was a lack of know-how. So the answer was more appraisal training for managers. I continued to harbor my doubts.

We see other remedies. Self-appraisal. Let the subordinate drive the process—that might get them to do it. Change the forms, include 360-degree feedback. But what we rarely see is questioning of the very value of the exercise. The truth is that appraisal leaves people bitter, bruised, despondent, dejected, feeling inferior and some severely depressed. Talk to teachers who have been through an inspection. Without prompting, many describe the feeling of emptiness when it is all over. So much work goes into preparing for inspection and the inspection process itself. The inspector has a specification to which he works and any disagreements about variations from the norm as defined by the specification will lead to a more difficult relationship. Talk to people in organizations who have been through appraisal. They tell you how they waited for the 'bad news.' It is psychological torture. In the perennially reinvented courses on how to do an appraisal, managers are told how to deliver bad news—there will always be bad news, because the whole idea is to hold the individual accountable. Some organizations compound the problem by insisting employees are ranked in a normal distribution[40]—you can't have all 'As'; you have to have proportions of each group, including, therefore, some losers. The emotional pain caused by appraisals is incredible, particularly when money is tied to the rating. For substantial periods everyone's emotional energy is consumed by something that is flawed and counterproductive.

I was asked to write an article exposing the problems with performance appraisal for a Sunday newspaper. I submitted my first draft and the editor suggested I should provide balance by talking about what to do instead. My response was that you don't need to find an alternative to doing a bad thing—you should just stop it. He said: 'Call your friends in Japan and find out what they do.' So I did. I asked: 'What do you do about performance appraisal?' The reply was: 'What is that?' I explained. Japanese people tend to be too polite to laugh. In Toyota the HR strategy places emphasis on management's responsibilities. For example, there are no less than 44 questions the manager must address to ensure the employees work in a system that enables them to perform.

Another way to put it is to ask: 'What are all the questions I should address as a leader before I decide I have a "people problem"?' Asking these questions of your system helps you discover how few people problems you have and how much responsibility for performance rests with you—the leader.

SO YOU THINK YOU HAVE A PEOPLE PROBLEM?

To perform well, any individual needs three things:

114

- Information related to the performance required—'What do I have to do?'
- Method—How to use resources, information, equipment, and so on—'By what method?'
- Willingness to do the job—'I like and want to do this.'

Some elements of these requirements are supplied by the system, some by the individual's own repertoire of behavior. Working through the questions that follow will enable you to identify deficiencies in either the system or the individual and take appropriate action. Start at the beginning and work through. To get the maximum value from the exercise, try identifying a person whom you currently label as a 'performance problem,' and keep them in mind as you think about your answer to each question.

Before you read the questions, let me make one other observation. Many managers treat 'people problems' with training 'solutions.' You will discover how far down the list of possible interventions training appears. Despite its popularity, training is rarely the right solution. Many organizations I work with waste enormous resources on training. Sad to say, they rarely evaluate its impact on performance. If they did, perhaps they would waste less of their resources.

Here are the questions to ask about people's performance:

The performer's system

1. Information:

- Does the individual know the accomplishments that are expected and what 'good' looks like in operational terms?
- Are the right things being measured—using measures that relate to purpose—and does the individual get feedback directly from those measures? Consequently, are they informed as quickly as possible and with sufficient frequency how well they are currently performing?
- Are these measures both accurate and easy to understand?
- Do these measures refer to performance over which the individual has genuine control?
- Do these measures tell the individual in what respect they are not performing well?

- Are there adequate guides or job aids to exemplary performance so that memory isn't critical?
- Are these guides or job aids models of simplicity and clarity?
- How certain are you that the individual actually gets this information when needed and in a user-friendly manner?

If information is in any way a problem, it is the responsibility of management to determine the information required and make it available in a usable form.

If information is not the problem, the focus moves to the next consideration.

2. Method:

- Is the system—the way the work works—designed in a way that supports optimal (waste-free) performance? Do the methods, measures, procedures, information technology and so on support optimal performance?
- Could these things be better designed to support optimal performance?

If method is a problem, it is the responsibility of management to ensure workers have the means to work with the best method and the means to work on method for improvement.

If method is not the problem, the focus moves to the next consideration.

3. Nature of motivation:

- Are there 'extrinsic' motivators (incentives, piece rates, awards, etc.) distracting from adequate performance—encouraging people to 'get the reward' rather than 'do the job'?
- Is the individual's job designed such that he/she experiences sufficient 'intrinsic' motivation (from actually doing the work well) to perform to his/her best? Note that intrinsic motivation relies on knowledge of results—how well the individual is performing versus purpose.

If extrinsic forms of motivation are a problem, it is the responsibility of management to remove them and design the system to be intrinsically motivating.

If extrinsic forms of motivation are not the problem, the focus moves to the next consideration.

Personal repertoire of behavior

1. Knowledge:

- Would the individual fail to perform to exemplary standard if their life depended on it—even when they have adequate information, method and intrinsic motivation to do so?
- Does the exemplary performer seem to know something that other people do not know?
- If the answer is 'yes' to either of these questions, training should be considered as a useful strategy.

If knowledge is a problem, it is the responsibility of management to provide it. If there are sustainable differences between individuals, it is the responsibility of management to study the methods of the exemplar and others to transfer method between them.

If knowledge is not the problem, the focus moves to the next consideration.

2. Attributes:

- Is it certain that the person must have special aptitudes, intelligence scores, verbal skills, manual dexterity, and so on, in order to perform in an acceptable, if not exemplary, manner?
- If the answer to this question is 'yes,' you have a selection issue.
- If the answer is 'no,' and all the other prior conditions for adequate performance are in place, then some form of training or education is almost certainly required.

If attributes make a difference, it is the responsibility of management to solve the problem.

If attributes do not make a difference, the focus moves to the last consideration.

3. Willingness:

- Is it impossible or uneconomic to redesign the job to achieve a sufficiently productive 'fit' between the required performance and what the individual would be willing to do?

If the answer to this question is certainly 'yes,' then you have a 'people' problem. This is probably the wrong person for the job.

So ... do you have people problems or management (system) problems?

The majority of performance problems are contained in the system, and the system is management's responsibility. The system disables performance. For most managers this is hard to see. What they see is people 'behaving badly,' which simply reinforces their current view of the world. In this view, the solution is to install control systems to 'manage' the behavior. Appraisal is one type of control system. Another is inspection.

INSPECTION

Quality assurance was developed during the Second World War. People thought inspection would control quality. Nothing could be further from the truth. In manufacturing organizations, quality assurance has come to mean a deluge of figures that tell you how many defective items were produced last month, with comparisons month to month and year to year. Figures like this tell managers how things have been going, but do not point the way to improvement. Improvement always requires different measures—so why don't we use these in the first place? Ohno made the worker the inspector. We need the same solution in service organizations—we need responsibility where it counts.

In service organizations, team leaders are usually given the job of quality control—in other words, inspection. In service centers, they listen to calls to determine whether the agent did the right things. How is 'right' determined? Usually by managers who make up a checklist of things that they think should happen in a call. This leads to much discussion and bad feelings when 'right' is something that is subject to interpretation. Of course, the team leader is just doing his or her job.

I visited a public sector organization's call center. The wallboard showed many customers were waiting. What were the team leaders doing? Listening to tapes of previous calls so they could give their agents feedback. What is the message? Inspection is more important than taking customer calls.

The job of the team leader is to lead and to do that he or she should also be capable of taking calls. To feed the inspection market there are many providers of call-taping technology that enables managers to access agents' calls with ease. The weekly or monthly sampling of agents' calls leads to the dreaded 'one-to-one'—where the team leader sits down with the agent to discuss the agent's performance. As we have seen, this is working on five percent of what governs performance. As such it is waste. In our service centers, inspection is (wrongly) called quality control. There is even a National Vocational Qualification in it. It is a madness. The idea is plausible: inspect people's work and put them right where they are going wrong. But as we have seen, it is the system that governs performance.

To break their belief in inspection, it is usually necessary to help managers through a 're-educative' loop: What are the assumptions behind our current practice, and how well does the method work? What are the causes of failure? What might be a better method? You can't just jump to a better method. You need to get data to answer these questions. If managers don't learn for themselves that inspection does not work, at times of crisis they will do the wrong thing.

One route to re-education is to take the error data found through inspection and put it in a capability chart. In every case where I have done this, the data show errors to be stable and running at a low rate. At this point managers are confronted with the realization that the work they do in inspection and feedback has little or no effect on performance. This leads managers to inspect the inspection. A second exercise can be useful here: Have inspectors rate the same work twice. You will find that inspection is not reliable.

Instead of using inspection, service organizations need to develop preventative systems—to build quality in rather than inspect it out. The solution is to design against demand. One essential strategy is to ensure that training is designed against demand, so that agents only go to work when they can serve the known high-frequency demands. Having been trained against demand, agents are attuned to the nature and variety of customer demands, and this forms the basis for learning on the job. Agents know they are responsible for their own quality and responsible for 'pulling support' as required. Prevention puts responsibility where it belongs: with the managers before work takes place (i.e., in the design of training), and with the workers when working.

FROM 'CHECK' TO 'PLAN'

Training against demand is typical of the kind of solution required to improve performance in service organizations. It typically results in agents being able to handle much more demand than before and with greater confidence in both doing the work and seeking help. In moving from the 'check' to the 'plan' stage of system redesign, leaders should have measures against which they will assess improvement. For training against demand, this means measuring the anticipated increase in agents' abilities to handle demands to completion.

Training against demand is only one component of a plan for change. To illustrate typical issues that arise, I shall return to the example I introduced at the end of Chapter 4. I shall remind you of the design, remind you what 'check' typically reveals and go on to discuss redesign:

> Customer mail arrives in a central location where it is scanned to create an electronic record and allocated to a work queue. The work queues are sent to supervisors who then allocate the queues to agents. The different types of work, defined by the queues they are in, are timed and the timings used to award points. Workers are appraised on their points.

This arrangement appears to be logical. The work is sorted so that it can be allocated to the right skill. Managers also want to ensure people are working on the priorities. Managers measure the workers to ensure each performs as he or she should. Unfortunately, the measures prevent managers from perceiving the failure of the system to absorb variety. This failure is compounded by the way the system then amplifies the problem.

When managers study the work as a system, they discover that the incoming work, all previously treated alike, contains a quantity of failure demand. They realize that the 'sort' step is not very effective: to sort something you have to read it and understand it. Work gets put in the wrong queue and may have different or more requirements than those identified by the queue's label. So a supervisor may then read the work before allocation—which is rework. Sometimes supervisors 'allocate' the work by allocating agents' computers to work queues; the consequence can be agents left idle, because the queues they have been trained to work on are empty. Managers move agents between queues to meet response times. But this is tampering, the consequence of which is to make the work take longer.

Agents learn to do work according to the type classified in the work queue, and they focus on doing this in the specified time. If a customer has a complex demand, or more than one, what matters to the customer can get lost. Taking too long with a predetermined work type attracts unpleasant consequences for the agent. To make their activity numbers, agents learn to do anything to progress the work—pass it to others, place it in pending to wait for further information (if this arrives, will it get attached to the right document?), hold it in his or her personal queue for whatever reason and so on. Agents get points for activity—which is not necessarily the same as doing the work that the customer needs to be done. In such systems, managers discover that a simple piece of work may be handled as many as 12 times.

The next discovery is that agent training does not match customer demand—how can it, when managers have been managing with little or no knowledge of the type and frequency of customer demand? They learn that the labels on the work queues are not representative of demand in customer terms. In short, they discover that the system is unable to cope with the variety in customer demand, is full of waste and the workers are demoralized. They discover it is a design problem.

The purpose of redesign is to create a system that can absorb the variety in demand. The typical solution in such cases is to minimize or even eliminate the sort step and route the work to agents whose responsibility it is to handle it through to completion. This is where the understanding of demand from the customers' point of view is critical. Agents need to be trained against demand, rather than in functional or product specialties, as is normally the case. When training is realigned in this way, agents spend less time being trained and are more productive as a consequence. This is a typical example:

In a customer service center, agents were trained for five weeks before they were put to work, at which point they could handle just 20 percent of customer demands. Following 'check' and redesign of the system, training time was cut to three weeks and agents were able to deal with 80 percent of customer demands.

Imagine the psychological impact of being trained for five weeks and then having to pass on 80 percent of the work. By contrast, the psychological advantage of being trained against demand is that agents are attuned from the outset to think about the work from the customers' point of view—that's what the training is for. They can be put to work safe in the knowledge that if a demand hits them that they cannot handle, they 'put their hand up' and receive immediate support. The rate of learning is fast; the culture is profoundly changed. Instead of agents' 'goodness' or 'badness' being dictated by activity, they are focused on solving more and more customer problems. They appreciate there are two jobs: job one to serve the customer and job two to improve the work. Improving the work might include handling more customer demands at the point of transaction, identifying predictable failure demands and their causes, simplifying forms, improving information and so on.

To support and maintain such a system, leaders must change the measures in use. Instead of managing agents through activity measures, they employ measures of flow, confident in the knowledge that improving flow is the secret to increasing capacity (the amount of work the system does) and persuaded through the work on 'check' that managing with activity measures actually undermines capacity. They know that this means a change in management's role. It stops being 'people management' and becomes leadership. Leaders and agents work on understanding and improving the work, and to achieve that you need good measures.

PERMANENT AND TEMPORARY MEASURES

There are two kinds of measures of use in managing a system: permanent and temporary. Permanent measures, those that are related to purpose, are the guiding measures for all performance improvement work. Temporary measures are those that are useful in ascertaining the nature and size of a problem before action is taken. Once action is taken and checked for improvement, the measure can be discarded. The measures that will be of value should have been established for the first time as part of the work on 'check.' In this kind of system permanent measures might include:

- *Demand volumes and capacity (the amount of work the system does):* These measures remain in use for resource planning purposes but are no longer used for resource management.
- *One-stop capability:* The amount of work that can be handled one-stop.
- *End-to-end time:* How long it takes from the customers' point of view to do the work.
- *Accuracy and value created for customers:* Measures of accuracy and value created for customers are sampled. The a priori assumption is that inaccuracy or failure to create value is more likely to be due to the system than the agent. If the measures show scope for improvement, leaders look firstly at their own responsibilities (for example, job aids and training).
- *Agent capacity.* There may be valuable learning from differences in agent capacity; only capability measures illustrating whether differences between agents are genuine will show if this is so.[41]

Temporary measures might include:

- *Type and frequency of demand.* If demand changes, the system should change. The work completed in 'check' will have given a detailed understanding of demand, and the day-to-day work is now focused on how and how well we respond to demand. If demand changes, agents and their leaders will notice; if it changes sufficiently to warrant a thorough demand analysis, they will know.
- *Type and frequency of 'dirt' in input.* Incomplete forms, insufficient information and the like are examples of this. It is vital to establish whether these things are predictable—if they are, the chances are they are under the organization's control. Remedying the problem may

require changes to forms, letters and other information sent to customers.

• *Type and frequency of waste in flow.* It is vital to identify the causes of waste; what causes more handovers, lost time, rework, errors and the like?

All but one of these permanent and temporary measures pass the test of a good measure: 'Does this help us understand and improve the work?' The exception—the measure of capacity—is a 'rear-view mirror' measure, used to track progress (and plan resources) but not to manage operations. As action is taken against measures of demand, value and flow, the capacity of the system improves. Moreover, because the measures are in the hands of people who do the work and are related to purpose (serve customers and improve the work), the culture changes to one that is engaged, innovative and cooperative.

LEADERSHIP: ACTING ON THE SYSTEM

The new system requires new roles to sustain it. If those who do the work are responsible for serving the customer and improving the work, what do we need managers for?

First-level managers work closely with employees on the quality of today's service. They are concerned with anything and everything that directly affects the system's ability to serve customers. Note that the first-level manager works with people on the work, not on the people. The team and its first-level manager manage all the opportunities for improvement within the team's control. All opportunities for improvement that lie beyond the scope and control of the team are the responsibility of the first-level manager or other managers, whose job it is to eliminate the obstacles that get in the way of service teams serving their customers. In determining these roles, I like to talk to managers about 'toaster processes.'

When conducting 'check' on a chain of roadside restaurants, I learned of a rule that applied when toasters broke down: If the repair cost less than £100 (approximately $187), it would go on the restaurant's budget; if more than £100, it would go on the budget of regional management. You can guess what happened.

Every service delivery team has 'toaster processes'—things they have no control over but which affect their ability to provide service. Every 'toaster process' needs someone to look after and manage it for improvement. For toasters, we need data about the type and frequency, and hence predictability, of breakdowns so that we can work to cut the time from a demand from the restaurants to the provision of a solution and reduce the period between purchasing and deploying toasters. Action on these things will improve the utilization of toasters, cut the costs of toasters and optimize revenue from selling toast.

We have already seen that the systems solution will always require someone working on training against demand—essential to the successful induction of new agents. It is probable that we shall also need roles that work across the organization to remove the causes of failure demand. Often there is a need for roles to build in the expertise required from other parts of the organization to ensure that agents either have the expertise to meet demands or can 'pull' it as required. All management roles are designed from the work 'backwards'—determining what the work requires and designing roles to accomplish that, avoiding the assumption that roles must be designed into a hierarchy. As their new roles are designed, managers learn them by doing—the best and only way.

DEVELOPING LEADERS

You might think developing leaders was a straightforward matter of teaching people suitable material in classrooms. But systems thinking is learned by doing; it is only by doing things that most managers can unlearn—can find out for themselves that their current beliefs about the design and management of work are flawed. This is something that cannot easily happen in a classroom. In classroom presentations, managers often hear things they think they understand. They recognize words like process, flow and demand and fit them to things they already do. More than that, it is hard to persuade managers of the folly of their current measurement and/or inspection methods without data to prove it from their own system. They 'know' the logic of their current methods; it is not easy to dissuade them of their merits. In the detached environment of a classroom, distinctions in understanding and action cannot be easily explored. Presentations of a systems perspective on an organization leads managers to argue, defend, rationalize and do anything to preserve the status quo. It is a natural human response.

Rather than have an abstract dialogue in a classroom, it is vital to have a material dialogue where the work is done. How does the work work? How do current system conditions help or hinder the way the work works? It is only by studying the work as work that managers can assess current methods and use new ones to build better systems. It is only in this environment that one can take a reliable view of what is currently done and with what consequences. That is the purpose of the model for 'check.' It is a framework for getting understanding and knowledge. En route, thinking changes.

Despite my advice, some clients insist that presentations on systems thinking take place as a prerequisite for change. Organizations espouse values like 'buy-in' and 'inclusion.' People translate my advice not to make such presentations as 'exclusion,' whereas it is based on a firm view of when and how to involve people. Well-intentioned as the idea behind it is, making presentations sets hares running. Misunderstandings multiply, making the task of intervention itself more difficult.

Talking about change in a classroom creates resistance which has its associated myths. Managers hear things that were never said. For example, 'no targets' is interpreted to mean 'no measures,' which becomes a block to exploring the dysfunctional consequences of current measures and the importance and value of different ones. Managers hear, 'let the people decide.' It is an emotional reaction to feeling they have been disenfranchised. I would never say, 'let the people decide.' What I would say is: 'If the people who do the work have measures in their hands that help them understand and improve the work, and they know how to act for improvement, then they can decide'—but that's a bit of a mouthful.

Managers object to what they hear as, 'people don't make a difference'—understandably, because we can all point to co-workers who are less good than others. Often we attribute the difference to motivation or ability. But first, consider the extent to which such differences have been created by the system—do measures and other system conditions drive certain behaviors, and do these things have a positive or negative impact on morale? Are people trained in method—do they have measures that help them work on the work? Do some people excel in spite of the system? Or start with current 'poor' performers—can data be used to demonstrate genuine differences in performance and, if so, to what extent is it a management as opposed to a people problem? Is it the system that is creating losers? I never say, 'People don't make a difference.' What I do say is that the major causes of variation in performance are in the system, and once again that is management's responsibility.

Such myths are powerful blocks to learning; they prevent curiosity and questioning of current assumptions about the nature of organization performance. Unlearning—the deconstruction of old assumptions—has to precede the learning of new norms. The change must enable steps through to a change in assumptions. There is no substitute for learning by doing.

When people can discuss the difference between system conditions in a command-and-control world and a systems world, you know they have been converted. This is not a religious conversion; it is a conversion to a common sense that our management practice has obscured. It is hard to take on, and therefore feels like a conversion, because it flies in the face of the things we are brought up to believe. When something goes wrong—as it always has and always will—the first questions should be directed at the system. The questions themselves develop knowledge. For example, leaders ask: Is this a one-off or predictable? Leaders know that to treat the unpredictable as predictable will create the kind of havoc they were all too familiar with in the past.

SOME QUESTIONS FOR LEADERS

If you want to make the transition from command-and-control to systems thinking, you have to ask yourself some fundamental questions:

- Do you want to lead an organization where the people who do the work control and improve the work? It means you will need to devolve decision-making. To do that is not simply to mouth the word 'empowerment,' it is to give up your current conception of management. The people who do the work will manage and control the work with different measures from those you are used to. You yourself will do a different job.

- Are you prepared to change your own role? Could you conceptualize your work as 'working on the system'? Are you prepared to find out just how different this is from what you might currently do?
- Are you prepared to do these things when those above you might not understand it or condone it? When those in higher places choose to dictate the numbers to be obtained, they actually undermine the organization's ability to achieve them. Are you prepared to take this tension on as you investigate and identify better measures for improving the economics of this system? Can you resist managing with these measures downwards?
- And would you want to be the carrier of the news when you find it?

If you can answer yes to all of the above, are prepared to learn by doing (starting at 'check'), and will talk about what you learn, no matter how painful it is, with those who do the work, you'll make an excellent leader.

CHAPTER 7

Customers—people who can pull you away from the competition

A customer services director was accused of cheating by his fellow directors. He had directed his managers to get customers to rate the firm's service one out of ten and visit any customer who rated the service less than eight to find out what it would take to rate it a perfect ten. The board took the view that anyone could improve their service ratings that way. In their view, customer research had to be done professionally; doing as he did was not cricket [i.e., a little shady, not quite honorable]. The director would tell his managers about the other directors' view and say to them: 'I want you to cheat!'

This was the title story of my first book. I repeat it here because in the last 12 years little has changed. Too many managers believe customer research is a 'professional' as opposed to a relationship activity. By professional they mean conducted by specialists. There are some dos and don'ts regarding aspects of customer research, but they can be easily taught. I am firmly of the view that finding out what matters to customers is central to the work of people who serve them—who carry out the core work; that's how to build strong relationships. Instead, we generally find 'customer research' located somewhere in the management factory. And to what effect? The place to start in answering that question is 'check.' I have found the following to be very good questions to start developing an understanding of how and how well an organization uses data about customers to drive operations:

- How much money do we spend on customer research?
- What actions for improvement are taken as a consequence?

In too many organizations, the answers to these questions turn out to be 'quite a lot' and 'not many.' The questions expose the limited usefulness of much common practice in customer research and invite a more detailed exploration of method. As customer research is driven from the management factory, managers typically get involved in specifying, administering and reporting on customer research. Reports are sent down the hierarchy demanding action for improvement. But are actions based on knowledge? Have the right questions been asked?

Mystery shopping is a classic illustration of the underlying issue. Managers specify what they want mystery shoppers (people who pretend to be customers) to look for, and their reports tell the managers whether the prescribed behaviors happened. Whether any of these behaviors reflect what matters to customers is another matter altogether. Better prescriptions will never solve the problem because the locus of control is in the wrong place. The best place from which to make a judgment about what matters to customers is in front of the customer. What matters to the customer is what matters and the people providing the service are the best people to interpret what that means for individual customers. For this very reason, service agents are often able to see straight through mystery shoppers: mystery shoppers don't behave like normal customers, because what matters to mystery shoppers is getting through their checklist.

> Every time I check out of a supermarket the cashier asks me if I want any help. I always say with a smile: 'Do I look as if I need it?' They always tell me they have to ask. Of course, I know this. I say: 'Don't your managers think you can tell who might need some help'?
>
> In many restaurants, staff are told to serve in specific steps: Take customers to table, take drinks order, serve drinks, take food order, offer bread rolls, serve food, offer bread rolls. Mystery shoppers are employed to make sure staff follow the prescribed order.

As an aside, in one case managers ran an incentive scheme for selling bread rolls. I assume they are a high-profit item and can be added to the bill without the customer having seen the price. In one restaurant, the manager gave his staff bread rolls for lunch. How would you feel if your manager had won the prize and you'd had the rolls for lunch? How much sense does it make to treat all customers with the same procedures? Would the nominal value (what matters to the customer) of a family at leisure be the same as a businessman with a laptop?

The same problems—specification and assessment—are found in customer surveys. For example, to ask 'how was it for you?,' as so many organizations do with a post-experience survey, is not necessarily to discover what matters to your customers. I feel irritated when I am sent a customer survey that does not allow me to communicate what matters to me, assuming something does. I have no doubt I am not alone. The survey asks you for your views of things managers want to know about, things they believe they can specify and hence control.

CUSTOMER RELATIONSHIP MANAGEMENT (CRM)

Earlier I distinguished between customer research as a 'professional' and relationship activity. The latest offering in the market, customer relationship management (CRM), purports to combine the two. It is professional in that it requires the services of, not least, information technologists; and it is aimed at building better relationships by establishing computer databases, which in turn will (it is promised) mean better transactions (relationships) with customers.

Is CRM a fad or a critical 'must-have' for a sustainable future? After all, good relations with customers surely lead to loyalty and repeat business. People who get good service tend to come back; when they don't, they go elsewhere. But does CRM improve the quality of the transaction from the customers' point of view and thus build better relationships? It probably depends on what 'CRM' does.[42] We need to explore method—what people actually do in the name of CRM.

CRM AS MORE SOPHISTICATED 'PUSH'

There have been a number of examples of CRM as 'more sophisticated push'—here is one:

A medical business sends out bills that include individually customized newsletters. Using knowledge of the patients' medical history, marketers match the newsletter content with the inferred needs and interests of the individual customer.

This is no more nor less than tailored direct mail. This 'more sophisticated push' works in certain circumstances, in as much as it can demonstrate better return rates than material that is less well tailored. 'More sophisticated push' requires a good customer database and good database management. But in what circumstances might it not work? This is something the CRM vendors don't talk about. To them, the evidence of the particular achieves the status of a generalizable and unassailable truth. If you have more and better customer data, you will give better service, sell more things to your customers and keep your customers for longer. But is this true? When is it not? I copied this from an internet site; I think the writer makes the point well:

Does the customer want to be managed?

I have read numerous articles, talked with several people, and am still trying to find the answer to this question: when I—as an employee of a multinational financial services company in the US—conduct business with my client, I want to know every aspect of their relationship with my organization so that I can customize my product and service offerings to them. However, when I—as a customer—conduct business with an organization, I do not want to have all my information, habits, etc, known to the organization. In fact, I'd like a singular relationship with them, not necessarily a long-term commitment.

Am I alone in this thinking, as it seems ironic that I can be two people at once?

Any 'push' strategy carries with it the costs of intrusion. How many customers will be put off by what they see to be an affront to their privacy or an unwelcome bombardment? The costs of intrusion are 'unknown and unknowable,' to borrow a phrase from Deming.

The central marketing function in a bank was making a major investment in customer databases. The whole plan was based on the proposition that knowing more about customers would

*lead to more 'tailored' offers of products and services. I sug-
gested that rather than invest such a large amount of resources
in something that was, in effect, a 'bet,' it might be more profitable to understand the nature of current transactions between
the bank and its customers. Further, it would help to know the
value created at these points of transaction and then model
changes to what went on at a 'local level' (from the customers'
point of view), to understand what might predictably occur if
such changes were applied universally. I was met with incred-
ulous looks. In essence, the marketing executives were uncomfortable with the idea of working in a local branch and a
service center. After all, they were from the head office.*

If you work in the management factory, it makes sense to
find ways to get data about customers and then engage in new
'push' activities. This kind of thinking goes beyond direct-mail
campaigns. I was working with a telecommunications organization that had brought in strategy consultants to help create a new
'customer-facing' structure. The new structure separated the 'consumer' channel—retail outlets—from the 'corporate' channel—
corporate sales staff. I was working with the director of the retail
operations. Starting, as you should, at 'check,' we found many
small business users being turned away from the retail channel,
because the organization's procedures dictated that demand for
ten phones or more should be to be passed on to corporate sales.
However, corporate sales found such accounts unattractive to
pursue: The numbers of phones per account were small and
would therefore make little contribution to achieving sales targets. Taking the customers' point of view led to a design based on
demand, preventing substantial lost opportunity. As it happened,
small businesses accounted for the most growth.

CRM AS A MEANS OF TRACKING CUSTOMER BEHAVIOR

CRM is sometimes sold as a means of tracking customers' behavior. It is argued this will increase knowledge of what customers
want and thus increase sales.

*One of my team was asked to work with a chain of restau-
rants. Before he went to work he had to attend 'brand school,'*

conducted by the central marketing department. In brand school he listened to a long debate between workers and marketers about what should be done if a customer wanted bacon with pineapple. The marketers believed that the menu was the brand, and hence should be maintained at all costs; their answer was to give bacon and egg without the egg and tell the customer pineapple was available on the salad cart. The workers wanted to give the customer what they asked for. The Vanguard member kept quiet, not wanting to jeopardize his opportunity to get out and do the work.

Starting as we would with what matters to customers and the nature of customer demand, he learned that the majority of customers were local and regular. They liked to have the same tables and had good relationships with their particular waitresses and waiters. The rationale for the menu being the brand was that customers could expect to get the same wherever they stopped at one of these restaurants. Most, however, did not travel the country looking for the brand.

The consultant also learned that the marketers had changed the menu. They had removed ribs as a starter and replaced it with chicken wings. (Chicken wings are cheap and plentiful; there are more of them than people can sell.) Customers who liked ribs as a starter noticed that they were still available as a main course and would ask for a half-portion to start with. Of course, the staff did as they should—they created value for customers. But what happened when the food was entered into the point-of-sale terminal—the means of communication with marketing? The ribs starter was entered as chicken wings, for it was the closest in value. Marketers trumpeted the success of their menu while fridges filled with chicken wings and ribs were 'off' the menu.

Supermarkets also like to measure what is sold, but this is not the same as knowing what the customer wants:

Returning home to an empty house, a customer regularly stops at his supermarket for a ready meal. The choice is limited, so he takes what is available. Over time he realizes that by his behavior—taking things he does not really want but

buys in the absence of anything better—he is maintaining the
system. The only solution is to stop using the supermarket.

Where was the leader? How did this organization find out
what mattered to customers? Just as supermarkets track the
behavior of their customers, e-commerce provides the opportunity to track people's use of internet sites. The CRM gurus tell us
the relationship with the customer has become ever more important in the information age, because relationships are faster to
build and change.

The 'e' world provides many more possibilities. Customers
can go online and find out about organizations and their offerings. Customers might conduct research, buy products and/or get
service. Customers might also want access to their account information and access to information that would make the service
easier for them to use. Customers might also have very good
ideas on potential improvements. But to take initiatives in any of
these areas without knowing about whether and how information would improve the customer experience is potentially disastrous. No investment in new initiatives should be undertaken
without knowledge of the nature of demand from the customer's
point of view. This is not the same as knowing where customers
went on the Web, how long they stayed and what they bought.
Knowing about clicks is not the same as knowing what matters
to customers and what value they are trying to pull from the system. That knowledge can only be found through dialogue.

One CRM guru advocates that organizations should take all
the information they have about customers' current relationships
and make this information easily accessible to the customers
themselves on the net. What information does the guru propose
is used? She talks in general terms about the kind of data available: frequency of contact, type of contact, 'favorite' activities,
things downloaded and so on. Other gurus point to the internet's
ability to let customers create and maintain their personal details,
to help ensure they only get sent what they've asked for and to
allow customers to access their administrative data and information about the products and services they've bought.

Will this information create value for the customer? Who can
know? The value created for customers depends on what happens at the point of transaction. We should not imagine that the

features available to us through e-commerce should dictate how a relationship should work. To take the risk out of new applications and avoid white elephant 'solutions,' these applications should be developed with good knowledge about what matters to customers, what value they are currently trying to pull and then tested and measured for efficacy before large-scale implementation. In the shorter term, the priority is to make today's service better.

CRM AS A SALES TOOL

Some CRM interventions are designed to direct and control the behavior of salespeople. Once the customer database is created, it becomes their job to populate, maintain and use it. Salespeople have resisted systems like this for as long as I can remember.

> In the early days of computing, I recall an organization installing an IT system that required salespeople to record their activity and keep notes on conversations with customers. To the salespeople, it represented further control from management. They complied because they had to, but the data provided about activity was inaccurate and information about customers way incomplete. Of course, the behavior was being driven by the use of targets and ranking tables. Salespeople were focused on making their numbers. This might mean hiding things or moving things around. It certainly meant cheating on activity reports.

To improve sales you need to work on method. To work on method you need capability data to identify and work on the causes of variation. To be able to do this you need to remove the conditions that prevent salespeople cooperating (targets, ranking tables and incentives). The result, in my experience, is always more sales, more cooperation between salespeople and better customer service.

CRM AS RELATIONSHIP BUILDING

Service centers, inevitably, are at the heart of CRM. Heralded by the CRM protagonists as a strategic weapon in the competition for excellence in customer service, they become targets for technology sales. Yet rather than build the relationship with customers, many applications are spoiling it. Customers are frustrated at having to make choices from IVR (interactive voice response) options that bear little or no relation to their problem or need as they see it; they are irritated at having to hang on, repeat their requests, get passed around and so on. In the worst cases, politeness is becoming a substitute for service. Customers want their issue dealt with and they will only put up with so much handling, however customer-friendly the interaction.

The result in such cases—and there are many—may not be strategic advantage, but strategic fumbling; dropping the ball, driving customers to seek services elsewhere. The espoused goal of the service center—improving customer service—is undermined by the methods employed. CRM is often translated into customer event management. More time gets spent managing events than dealing with them.

In many service organizations, customer records are useful in creating value for customers. In the telecommunications case described in Chapter 2, the customer record was crucial to handling customers' queries and solving their problems. It was important to know what equipment the customer had, how it was configured, and so on. And that may be a helpful way to think about CRM—not as relationship management, but record management. It helps us address the same question: When would customer's records help the flow of work from the customers' point of view?

When the first telephone bank was established, a customer record system was (and still is) an essential part of the design. At that time, it was not described as 'CRM'; it was an essential requirement for conducting banking over the phone. Going beyond record-keeping as an aid to creating value and using customer data as means to 'push' sales is often a step too far.

A financial services organization used a computer model of customers to prompt agents to sell to customers while they were answering calls. Often the agent could see that the suggestion was inappropriate for the customer or for the call. There was no data demonstrating the effectiveness of the prompt but plenty of evidence that agents found it a pain to work with; every time the pop-up appeared it required the agent to report on their subsequent action.

The only way to assess the value of the aid was to find out what was predictable about its ability to help or hinder the transaction from the customer's point of view. It required listening to hundreds of calls. It exposed the folly of believing computers are better at relationships than people.

The UK government makes the same mistake in its insistence that local authorities invest in IT to manage relationships with the people they serve.

Managers of a UK local authority invested £2 million (approximately $3.7 million) in a CRM 'strategy.' Every resident's details were entered into a database. The database was made available to those who dealt with customers in the new service centers. The argument was this would improve the way the authority dealt with those who wanted services.

But what did they know about who made demands for services and what those demands were? Most customer demands needed no history or background records to improve the way the organization responded to demand—so service was not improved. Callers who made frequent and sometimes spurious demands were certainly made more visible, but they were already known to those who dealt with them.

The managers had been sold the idea of working with the customers' view of the organization, built up from the transactions they have with it. But at no time did managers develop knowledge about the nature of those transactions; they simply assumed that a customer database would improve relationship building. But it is of no value to know that Mrs. Brown called yesterday about the failure to collect her trash or that she also has a planning application in for a greenhouse. What matters when Mrs. Brown calls is what matters to her. Far from improving service, the application of these 'solutions' in local authorities have led to the institutionalizing of waste, problem management over problem resolution.

All too often, CRM 'solutions' create an internally focused organizational swamp. Persuaded by the consultant's argument that excellent customer relations require a memory, specifications are created for the data to be gathered to constitute the 'memory.' The 'solutions' suck up resources and slow things down. The data provided by the 'solution' feeds the management factory and take up time being 'managed' through meetings and reports. Some CRM 'solutions' can cost a lot of money and cause a great deal of disruption. Do excellent customer relations require a memory? When is this true and when is it not true? When might creating a memory be intrusive to the customer?

There is no CRM solution, to my knowledge, that starts with understanding demand and flow. It wouldn't be as easy to sell to the management factory as promises of bucket loads of plausible data—the stuff of the factory's life.

CRM IS FAILING

Research now suggests that the majority of CRM efforts fail. The researchers don't tell us whether they are comparing apples with apples, and we know their data represents the opinions of those involved. Nevertheless, the results should give cause for concern. The failures lead the proponents to sell yet further services based on the same assumptions. It's the implementation that's faulty. Or CRM consultants blame other parts of the system, offering to align it with organization structure, culture, process design, measures and pay. Although these may indeed be to blame, we have to ask whether the consultants' offerings may be part of the problem rather than the solution. Consultants who see culture as something distinct from the work and, as a corollary, something that can be the subject of an intervention, miss the point. When you change the way work is designed and managed, and make those who do the work the central part of the intervention, the culture changes dramatically as a consequence. By themselves, seminars and workshops on culture generate quagmires of pseudo-intellectual and pseudo-emotional nonsense. Process management that gathers people in a room to talk about how something works, rather than study how it works from a useful (knowledge-creating) point of view, produces little of value at the end of it. Process redesign conducted by experts who then 'cascade' their solution to the workers simply creates resistance. If the consultants' advice on measurement includes notions of targets, standards, service level agreements and the like, you can be sure that the measures will obscure the development of knowledge. If they recommend that compensation include incentives, the system will be suboptimized.

The CRM literature now proclaims the need to worry less about ROI (return on investment) and instead focus on ROC (return on customer). This is a sure signal of the failure. As CRM investments (some massive) fail to produce the goods, the vendors now hope to persuade their customers to continue to invest by implicitly suggesting they would be foolish not to.

The protagonists now assert that CRM should be about creating a culture that engages people across functions in discovering common ground: learning how to cooperate with each other. They say CRM will lower the barriers to the flow of information across the entire organization. They say CRM will break down misunderstandings and stereotypes that functional groups have of each other. They claim CRM will help people discover common ground or a common approach to renewing relationships with customers and that it will create buy-in to that common approach. All plausible, 'why-would-you-not-want-to-do-this' stuff designed to persuade managers to follow the herd. What they fail to realize is that these problems are caused by the way work is designed and managed. Spending vast sums of money on computer systems will not solve this problem; it is more likely to institutionalize and hence exacerbate it. Perhaps managers should ask whether CRM is doing the right thing.

As with all IT interventions, potential CRM customers should beware of the features/benefits trap, something I shall return to in the next chapter. Just because IT can do it (feature), doesn't mean that it will make the work work better (benefit). Understanding how technology will affect work flow can only be understood with knowledge of that flow. This is not achieved through representing the flow by diagrams and data flows in meeting rooms, or in reports or specifications; it can only be achieved in the work flow. And the way the work flow functions will depend in large part on the characteristics of demand.

Some argue that CRM is an attempt to recover some of the traditional values of the service relationship. It is ironic that we are today struggling to harness sophisticated data-mining software to vast consumer databases. We are asking computers to do the very thing they are least good at, and people not to use the quality that they alone possess, the ability to form relationships with others, that is, customers.

FROM 'PUSH' TO 'PULL'—CHANGING THE PARADIGM FOR CRM

To design service from a systems perspective is to think 'pull' rather than 'push.' The object is to understand the nature of customer demand, its variety and predictability, and design optimal responses. Not only is this cheaper for the organization, it improves customer satisfaction; it builds the customer relationship rather than destroying it. The service center can be the eyes and ears of a business; it can be central to relationship management. However, the service center is not an island; it is interdependent with the wider organization. In traditional command-and-control designs, the relationship with customers is specified rather than accommodating. Likewise, the relationships between the service flows and the rest of the organization are specified and controlled functionally, rather than understood and managed as a system.

In Japan, they say the only way to lose your Toyota salesman is to leave the country. It is a long-term relationship based on one-to-one relationships and not limited to the showroom. Incredibly, Toyota has brought marketing into an entirely different relationship with production management. The basic condition of 'pull' thinking is managing demand as part of the system. In command-and-control designs, you find marketing and service managed as different functions, with differing objectives and measures. As a consequence, there is often a problematic relationship between service centers (and for that matter all service flows) and marketing. The way marketing behaves has a major influence on the nature of customer demand. For example, marketing may offer a price which, because of the IT system, will mean service center agents completing information fields in such a way that the customer gets an invoice that is not easily understood. A simpler and astonishingly common example is marketing offering the customer something no one in the call center has knowledge of. Marketing may send out bulk mailings to achieve response rates, but the fluctuations in demand on the service center obviate the system's ability to service prospective customers, to say nothing about the quality of leads generated.

'Pull' thinking goes beyond the creation of product or service to help us look at every transaction between the organization and the customer *from the customers' point of view*. This is a fundamental shift in our thinking about the way we work with customers. The traditional 'make-and-sell' paradigm uses above- and below-the-line 'push' marketing tactics. The shift of interest from 'below-the-line' marketing to CRM masks the fact that there has been no real change in philosophy. Managers invest enormous resources on what is an appealing idea—they have no idea of the potential consequences.

The central issue is: how do we design and manage work to create 'relationships' with customers? If CRM remains no more than a sophisticated 'push' method, it will pass and be remembered as a customer fad of the late 1990s (and perhaps another smash-and-grab raid by the IT industry). If organizations grasp the nettle of 'pull' design and management, the paradigm will have truly changed; and this will be a change from which there is no going back. UK service organizations that are learning to adopt this thinking are growing rapidly in confidence, reinforced by the quick wins achieved through stabilizing demand and designing against it to remove waste.

CUSTOMER-DRIVEN DESIGN—DESIGN VERSUS DEMAND

In the Toyota system, the customer order starts the work flow. Demand drives the system. Without an order there is no production—and therefore no unsold inventory of finished goods, no fields of cars about the countryside. And this is just one form of waste that is avoided. Working on the organization as a customer-driven system also eliminates waste in production. The principle is to design against demand. If the work done is that which is needed to carry out customers' orders and only that, the system will be lean—it will do no work that is not essential and waste will be driven out of the work flows.

This is a key issue for the design and management of service organizations. Because most if not all have been designed on command-and-control principles, work does not flow easily through the organization. So costs are higher and service worse than they need to be. The customer gets the service that has been prescribed and proscribed by those who designed the system management.

The eradication of failure demand leads to improved service and lower costs. Designing against value demand has the same effect. Moreover, both of these activities build the relationship with the customer, for the customers' view of the system can only be formed from the transactions they have with it.

Engineers providing 'break–fix' support to customers with enterprise systems (big computers) went out to listen to what mattered to their customers. When the customers got over the shock (their perception of the organization was one of arrogance) they talked of how painful it was for them to have to explain their problem to first-level call loggers, who knew nothing about computers, then explain it again to people who had less knowledge than they did, and explain it again once they got to someone who spoke their language. It became obvious that the best people to pick up the call would be the expert engineers, for they were most like their customers and could speedily understand the customers' problems. Not only did this result in an immediate improvement of service and a lowering of costs through increased capacity, the relationships built with customers led to better understanding of how customers were using the computers and the kinds of service they were providing to their own organizations. As the relationship developed, so did the opportunity to offer new services based on a good appreciation of need.

These things could never be dreamed up in the marketing suite. Marketers are interested in markets; these new services were developed with and for customers.

In a computer services organization fixing breaks on a customer's IT system, the engineers took the view that the client's e-mail system was not "man enough" for the job. The customer said he could live with the problem for the time being, but when the engineers pointed out that it was a problem affecting customers as well as internal personnel and supported their argument with data from the customer's system, the customer was pleased to ask for help.

While supporting an application in a retail environment, engineers became aware of their client's plan to add financial services to its offering to customers. Taking the time to find out what the new service would mean for the equipment in use, the engineers discovered sales transactions for financial services would mean extra demand on the printers and were able to alert the client to the issue before a problem occurred.

Many other examples could be cited. In the computer services organization I am describing it is part of the normal work to spend time in the customers' system to understand the customer's work; how and how well the customer is able to serve their end customer. The service people who work there often find themselves advising the customer to change requests for tenders, because they have greater knowledge of the work than their clients. Helping the client see things that are transparent to them can be a powerful reinforcement of a good relationship. I say 'reinforcement' because the work didn't start there; it started off with designing the service against demand. This provided the legitimacy—some would say earned them the right—to gain greater access to the client's operations.

Having redesigned its manufacturing operations from a batch ('push') to a 'pull' (make-to-order) system, a fireplace manufacturer set about finding out what mattered to its customers. Customers were segmented by value (profit) and type (retail, wholesale, catalogue). It uncovered a category of customers that had been largely ignored by the sales force: those concerned primarily with speed of delivery and quality. Salespeople spent their time identifying new customers most of whom bought on price alone, so to get their business sales were heavily discounted. As the company now only made to order, end-to-end manufacturing time had fallen from months to days. So there was now an opportunity to work more closely with customers who wanted speed and quality because this was part of its everyday offer.

Segmenting customers empirically by value, as the company did in this example, is not the same as dictating segmentation by value, as many consultants recommend. There may well be a case for treating your most profitable customers differently. Knowing how much the customer spends could be important. But could a focus on high-value customers lead to strategies and tactics that dissuade low-value customers from doing business? Is this good for an enterprise? How many low-value customers are latent high-value customers? How many low-value customers talk to people who are high-value customers? To provide high-value customers with better service may ignore the fact that the current service is bad simply because it is badly designed, and redesigning it could mean better service for all.

The ultimate in designing to handle variety is in effect segmentation at the individual customer level. In the computer services examples, the implication is that every demand will dictate its own flow. This represents a move away from selling a 'menu' of services, which in practice means differentiated response times. It is a beneficial move for both parties, because the contractual arrangements provided by the 'menu' choice always fail to fit with customers' demands; there are times when a slow service fits the bill and others when fast service is critical. Selling from a menu will always cause suboptimization.

A leasing organization set about finding out what mattered to its customers. The object was to make administrative systems easy for the customers to deal with. In the course of their conversations, the leasing people discovered a new business opportunity. It was normal practice to auction nearly new equipment that had become available through default. Auction prices were poor. The customers had a market for nearly new equipment and together the organizations made arrangements to exploit it.

Finding out what matters to your customers is a relationship-building activity. It does not start with writing a survey. The most common problem with customer surveys is that the wrong people write the items—customers should write them, not managers or research professionals. The first step in good quality customer research is to go 'naked' to customers and ask them directly about what matters to them. It is a vital qualitative research step that precedes writing the surveys. But often you find you don't need to go to the next step in conducting research—writing items for a quantitative survey—because you discover things you should take action on straight away.

> *A financial services organization wanted to know what mat-*
> *tered to people who had sought to buy one of its products.*
> *Before talking to them, it segmented them into buyers and*
> *non-buyers. The most important thing it learned was that*
> *many of the would-be customers who did not buy found the*
> *application form confusing and threw it away. This added to*
> *evidence provided by previous work on demand—many cus-*
> *tomers called in with problems completing the application*
> *forms. Now managers knew that the application forms not*
> *only generated failure demand, they lost the company sales.*

This example demonstrates the order in which to do things. There is no point doing customer research if you have not first studied demand in customer terms and found out how and how well you create value for them at the point of transaction. Failure to do that is likely to confront you with findings you should already be aware of—not a great way to build a relationship. Customers might well feel that they had told you most of what you needed to know through their querying and progress-chasing.

Working against demand provides the greatest leverage for improvement. Working against demand is something only people can do—computers cannot be used for what is essentially a relationship task. Of course, computers may usefully record and count the things you are concerned with; used in this way, how-ever, they support rather than dominate a service agent's work. When people have the measures and methods for working against demand, the system becomes naturally adaptable—as demand changes, so the work is changed by the people who do the work. This is to capitalize on the very thing that people are good at and computers are not.

THE CUSTOMER-DRIVEN ADAPTIVE SYSTEM

Imagine an organization that is designed against demand. It will be *customer-driven* because the customer is central to the design of the organization—the fundamental design would be outside-

146

in (from the customer inwards) rather than top-down. The organization will be managed from the customers' point of view. The relationship with customers will be central to operations; a continuous understanding of the nature of customers' demands will drive the way the system is conceived and managed. Customer acceptance will dictate the longevity of the enterprise.

It will be *adaptive*, because it can respond naturally to changes in customer demands. Success will depend on the ability to learn about the 'what and why' of current performance in ways that lead to knowledge and, hence, predictable improvements. Measures and methods will be central to learning. The capacity to learn will have been designed in.

It will be a *system*, because the point is to manage with understanding and knowledge of how the parts work together. This will mean a different way of designing and managing the work. Management will be directed at the interactions of the parts in pursuit of the organization's purpose, not the way the parts behave on their own. Their role will be to act on the system.

Working on the system, the way the work works, will be the mindset of everyone who works in the organization. People will think like this because of the way their roles and associated measures are designed. The result will be continuous application of useful knowledge.

The customer-driven adaptive system will have the following characteristics:

- An unambiguous sense of purpose that permeates the organization. Purpose is thought about in customer terms. It is known and understood by everyone, and the measures and methods in use reinforce that perspective. It is the universal way of thinking about all decisions and tasks, and it is focused on finding better ways to achieve the organization's purpose.
- Strategic and operational plans that support each other. Strategy is informed by operations. Decision-makers understand how their roles contribute to the whole. Day-to-day operational decision-making is in the hands of those who do the work. Management and worker roles alike are designed to improve understanding, control and improvement of the system. The ethos change from status

to contribution. And last but not least, people have a sense of freedom. Freedom to act, learn, experiment, challenge—and build relationships with customers. Becoming a customer-driven learning system requires freedom, not command and control.

CHAPTER 8

Do these hold water?

CRM is just one of the many management fads (fad: 'an intense but short-lived fashion,' according to my dictionary). Organizations represent markets for performance improvement 'solutions,' and managers like products. So we see solutions being sold under labels—CRM, Total Quality Management (TQM), Business Process Re-engineering (BPR), European Foundation for Quality Management (EFQM) and so on. As I observed in the discussion of CRM, what happens, what the label means in any particular application, can vary enormously. There is little doubt that each fad—perhaps with the exception of ISO 9000—did something for someone somewhere. But can they deliver for all in all circumstances? To have any chance of doing so they would need to be based on sound theory.

It is always the same. Each new fad is launched with dramatic claims. A few years later, there are equally spectacular reports of failure ('80 percent of BPR efforts fail,' '80 percent of CRM efforts fail'—it always seems to be around 80 percent), accompanied by a litany of reasons. The debate is always after the event, never before. Management ought to be about prediction. But managers can only predict the results of applying a given fad if they have knowledge about the 'what and why' of their organization's current performance and knowledge of the fad's theory and method. Sadly, both are invariably lacking. Perhaps inevitably, managers place trust in the fads' promoters. If managers were more knowledgeable about such things, there would be fewer fads.

I have been a frequent critic of fads. My criticisms are based on what I have seen; it could only be thus. I say this, because when a fad fails the response is always, 'it's because you're doing it wrong; it works if you do it right.' But I don't see many examples of fads being 'done right.' I see fads creating activity more than substance. I do find some good things, but a lot more rationalization. I find top quality marketing materials, I find plausible arguments offered by people who behave as though the fads represent certain truths, but I find little substance. I feel compelled to explore theory and method when I come across fads in organizations.

If you have followed the argument in this book, you will accept what follows as a systems thinker's view of some recent fads. I fully acknowledge that at some stage, many fads may have contained a 'grain of truth'—but are the results capable of being generalized? Are they, and can they be shown to be, attributable to method? In many applications of fads, the requirement to report success up the hierarchy takes precedence over the need to evaluate the program's methods.

I shall discuss some of the better-known fads in the approximate chronology of their appearance, beginning with the one that drives me crazy: ISO 9000.

ISO 9000: A BAD THEORY FOR THE CONTROL OF OUTPUT

When Margaret Thatcher came to power in 1979, she recognized that public limited companies (plc) in the UK had a problem. Comparisons with other economies showed the UK to be falling down in ranking; there was (and still is) a consensus that British management had to improve. Something had to be done ('this is something . . . let's do this'). Thatcher was persuaded to push the button on the promulgation of BS 5750—a so-called quality standard. Who could not be pro-quality? In 1987, BS 5750 was adopted by the International Standards Organization as ISO 9000, despite there being no evidence of its benefits and plenty of discontent among those obliged to work with it.

More than 20 years later, the most recent report on ISO 9000's impact begins with the following paragraph:

> *The notion of improving the UK's industrial competitiveness through enhancing product and service quality has been a feature of government industrial policy for more than two decades. Central to this has been the formulation and implementation of initiatives aimed at increasing quality awareness and achieving better performance, for example, the Quality Enterprise Initiative of the '80s, etc. Despite this effort, the UK has slipped down the competitive*

*tables although this country is by far the main user of one
of the initiatives, quality management standards, based on
ISO 9000.[43]*

The report cannot actually be considered to reflect the 'true'
effectiveness of quality-related initiatives, because it is an opinion study among executives. That it chose executives as its
source of opinion is at least an improvement over asking the
views of the quality community—which of course has a direct
interest in a positive result. But to assess the true effectiveness,
one would need to research cases and determine what the standard led them to do, as I reported in my book on the subject.[44]
This, however, is only the most recent in a long series of reports
casting doubt on ISO 9000. And what happens when such
doubts surface? We carry on exactly as before. Despite all the
evidence suggesting that ISO 9000 has a negligible or negative
impact on economic performance, supplier organizations continue to be coerced into using it—'you comply or we won't buy'
drives its take-up around the world. Evidence cannot dismantle
its infrastructure.

What happened was that the standard's champions con-
vinced Mrs. Thatcher that it held the secret of the 'Japanese miracle,' which was much in the news in the 1970s. But nothing
could be further from the truth. The standard had nothing to do
with quality; it was and is no more than a poor method for the
control of output. In thousands of organizations around the
world, procedures for work and its management have been documented and inspected for compliance. It was and is anathema
to what was happening in Toyota, where control was and is in
the line.

Despite numerous revisions, ISO 9000 still promotes the idea
that you should control work by controlling procedures. Worse, it
encourages the idea that design should be separated from
process—a revealing testimony to the standard-writers' thinking
about the design and management of work. If design is separated
from process, work becomes a prescription, something that will
inevitably cause waste, and more so in service organizations.
Even in manufacturing, focusing on compliance is no substitute
for focusing on achieving. The successive revisions of the standard represent the ISO 9000 community's attempts to reach a

consensus about the true nature of quality and its role in the performance of organizations. The revisions have shown nervousness about treating quality simply as the way the whole organization works; it betrays the protagonists' origins as quality managers—that is, their role is assuring quality—not managers full stop. The fact of the matter is that what revolutionized Japanese manufacturing was not quality assurance. The Japanese were concerned to build quality in, not inspect for it afterwards. Their approach was to change the system—the way work was designed and managed. Toyota led the way.

As a matter of record, Toyota experimented with ISO 9000 in its Shimoyama manufacturing plant and decided it added no value to the system. Toyota's public doubts might have been expected to put a brake on the phenomenon, but the institutions surrounding ISO 9000 now have their own momentum. As elsewhere, take-up is driven by pressure from higher up the supply chain. Again, as elsewhere, we now see Japanese reports casting doubt on the value of the standard. 'Upgrading' to the 'new' standard, a requirement of the 2000 revision, means a lot more work, which managers may be unwilling to undertake given growing scepticism about its operational value. At the time of writing, registrations to ISO 9000 in the UK, France and Germany are in decline (21 percent down compared to last year). However, the 'new economies'—for example, Russia, China, Romania—are showing massive growth in registrations. Organizations in the new economies are being coerced to register to ISO 9000. It is seen as a ticket to world trade. The assessing organizations sit on the institutional committees that promulgate the standard. There is no one responsible for determining whether ISO 9000 works. It is an economic disease for which the UK should be ashamed.

THE 'EXCELLENCE MODEL'

The second quality model to be promulgated among managers began life in the United States as the Baldrige Award. Malcolm Baldrige was a close friend and political colleague of Ronald Reagan. He was also a horse rider. According to accounts from American correspondents, the Baldrige Award was precipitated by Baldrige's death—he had been riding in a bucking-bronco competition and fell off his horse. Commentators who were concerned about the need for American managers to change their ways had written a specification for a better way of managing and seized the opportunity by suggesting the President honor his friend with the creation of an award in his name. It is what I like to call a 'yes-able proposition.' When the Baldrige model came to Europe with organizations like IBM and ATT, European managers took the view they should develop their own. It fascinates me that they did not first ask for evidence that Baldrige worked, but just as with quality, you don't want to be seen to question excellence.

When what was originally called the 'Business Excellence Model' (now the EFQM Excellence Model) came to hand, British government ministers were not in the same position to make it a requirement for doing business ('you comply or we won't buy') as they had been with ISO 9000. This was something that the business community had created; government was supportive, rather than driving. The 'excellence model' received public funding, and organizations were encouraged to adopt it. However, in the public sector, where British government ministers had more managerial control, the model was encouraged more forcibly. In the late 1980s, 'Next Steps' agencies, the separated parts of government that were to stand alone as businesses, were obliged to use the excellence model as part of their plans. Later, much the same happened with hospitals that wanted to become trusts—showing that they planned to undertake one of the prescriptions—'excellence,' ISO 9000, Investors in People (IiP), the Charter Mark award, could only help their cause. Today the ability to parade the certificates and 'gongs' helps towards what is described as 'light-touch' inspection in the public sector.

Disaffection with the excellence model set in quite early in the private sector. I recall many senior managers complaining that ISO 9000 and excellence were mostly plaques and flags. Despite the lack of perceived value, however, they continued to espouse the models for fear of sending the wrong signal to customers. As the debate grew, defenders declared (as they always do) that failures were the result of poor execution (try harder!)—companies were failing to take the model seriously enough or giving up too soon. My own view is that people experience a 'honeymoon' with the excellence model—in the first two years there is much positive energy and activity. People score themselves and determine projects for action. After a while, however, doubts begin to set in. Managers, especially top managers, begin to ask: 'Does it hold water?' The argument that the model requires a long-term perspective raises the question, 'How long does it take to change?'

The real problem is that the use of the model drives the wrong actions.

The excellence model has two 'areas for improvement' (to use its language)—content and method. The method begins with managers scoring their organization against the model's criteria. But comparing your organization with anything is not the right place to start change. It will lead to unreliable conclusions and inappropriate or irrelevant actions. The right place to start change, if you want to improve, is to understand the 'what and why' of your current performance as a system.

The content problem is that the wording of the criteria betrays, implicitly or sometimes explicitly, command-and-control thinking.[45] Leaders are supposed to show they have a vision, mission and subscribe to values. I think they need to lead learning by working on the work. There is no assertion or guidance in terms of management's responsibility to act on the system. Unlike ISO 9000, the excellence model is not supposed to be prescriptive. The areas to address are described as elements you 'may' include. As such, you can choose to interpret the model in any way you like. For this reason I wrote a guide to the model taking a systems interpretation for those who are obliged to use it and don't want to suffer the disadvantages, but its users face the hurdle of explaining what they have done to their inspectors. Many protagonists claim the model itself is a representation of the organization as a system. But it is nothing of the sort. It is a set of ideas, not a proven framework for understanding and improving performance.

I have yet to find examples where use of the model has led to improved performance; in every case I study, I find reasons why the model has led managers astray. For example, the model provides little guidance on how to think about processes (outside-in, measure against purpose before mapping processes, etc.) and much that encourages managers to do the wrong things—begin by establishing procedures, standards and targets and so on. The model promotes the use of staff surveys, customer surveys, communications and many other activities that are considered standard practice. But staff surveys generate data about symptoms—you cannot act for improvement if you know nothing about causes. Customer surveys typically have the weaknesses I discussed in Chapter 7. In short, assessing themselves against the model, managers will draw conclusions that are not based on knowledge about the 'what and why' of performance and will plan actions (to 'improve their score') that will have negligible or even negative impact on performance.

Like ISO 9000, the excellence model has momentum. Institutions exist to promote its use and offer awards. Many organizations set up teams of people whose sole purpose is writing reports to win awards. Some even hire specialized experts to write award submissions. The focus is on winning the prize. The perennial problem for the awards business is: Who can we find that is worthy of an award? Without winners, no awards dinner. The desire to run an awards program is not the same as the desire to improve quality or excellence in UK plc (public limited companies). I have made a habit of visiting award winners. In all cases, I found things they did that made them worse and things they could have been doing that would have made them better. As with ISO 9000, the momentum is slowing. I predict the demise will be speedier as the excellence model does not have the same marketplace coercion.

INVESTORS IN PEOPLE (IIP)

By the time IiP arrived, I was well known for being a critic of models and standards. I chose to leave IiP alone. IiP did not impress me; I knew that because people's behavior is driven by the system, logically we should 'invest in the system' rather than the people. But I had been widely misinterpreted in my criticisms of other models, and I felt it would be damaging to be labelled as 'anti-people.'

IiP came into being in the 1980s in what was then the Manpower Services Commission, a British government organization responsible for employment. At the time, the British government minister responsible for employment was wrestling with the problem of how to improve the competitiveness of UK public limited companies. Getting organizations to invest in their people seemed to be the answer. It appears to be logical. People are our most important asset; if they are well trained, performance will improve. IiP was originally administered through the education department, but as a result of the 'increase in demand,' it was felt that the standard needed its own organization to 'protect its integrity' and promote and develop it. In 1993, IiP UK was born.

To create a standard, you need to write a specification. In this case, if we boil it down to its essentials, the specification asks:

- Are people trained enough for their jobs?
- Are people communicated with enough?
- Do people know where the organization is going?

What do you suppose the answers to these questions are in any organization? Because the questions have framed the analysis, the interventions that follow are concerned with objective-setting, training and communications. In my experience, these are rarely the major causes of performance problems. Objective-setting is firmly rooted in the 'people make a difference and people need targets' world; they are better off with measures that help them control and improve the work. Measures should be derived from the work, not aimed at the people. Most training in our organizations is of doubtful value; we invest in a host of courses that have no bearing on how work is done. Where training is job-related, the specification of the content shows no understanding of the reality of the work. And communications is a hardy perennial; it could always be improved—I doubt that anyone could honestly claim otherwise.

Of course, training is essential to improving performance. A Harvard professor once famously said: 'If you think training is expensive, try ignorance.' But if you go through the lists of training courses offered within and to organizations, you find essentially the same list of things we have been doing to people for many years with no discernable effect on performance. You may have undertaken training courses yourself. How often did the learning transfer from the classroom to your real work? It is the thesis of this book that we should provide training on what I like to call 'how work works.' The Japanese miracle had at its heart the training of the workforce to work on the work, not just do the work. When we look at the commonly used training for how to work on the work, we see content on making presentations, working in teams, reading accounts, managing people, getting a deeper understanding of yourself, among many others. These are more to do with how to get on rather than how to improve the work.

The IiP assessment produces evidence of the current state (versus the specification) and an associated action plan. All is written down and executed; progress on actions is documented. These documents and interviews with staff provide the inspectors with their raw material. The actions generated and the processes of assessment and inspection add significant cost to the enterprise. So we ought to ask: 'Does IiP work? Do organizations become more competitive?' An IiP spokesperson once told a journalist the standard 'has to have an effect on the bottom line somewhere.' Revealingly, she didn't specify where. More importantly, she didn't say why.

I know why it *wouldn't* have much effect on the bottom line—performance is governed by the system. To change the system, you have to change thinking. Paradoxically, if you take the systems approach to organizational change, you meet the aims of IiP—motivated people who know what to do to improve the work. But IiP appeals to traditional thinkers who think the people are the problem. It is just a variant on, 'how do we get them to do it?' The standard was developed to encourage training. Appealing, but flawed. Instead of 'investing in people,' we should be investing in the re-education of management and providing help on how work works to those who are in the best position to use it.

THE UK "CHARTER MARK" AWARD

The Citizen's Charter was UK Prime Minister John Major's 'big idea.' The initiative was supposed to ensure that public services put the customer first; the citizen should be treated as a customer. To encourage organizations to do this, some ideas were borrowed from the private sector—from those, you may recall, who also were in need of having their performance improved. Charter Mark, an award, is the badge of evidence that a public service is compliant with these aims. To gain the Charter Mark, an organization has to set service standards, publicize them and monitor them. It is not an approach that fosters knowledge. It is an approach that fosters a dysfunctional bureaucracy—established in the name of improvement.

> *In the early days of the Charter Mark, I had occasion to visit a government agency that was one of the first to receive the award. Part of its submission included evidence that it responded to customer phone calls within 20 seconds. What was not disclosed was that the organization used a computer to limit the volume of incoming calls to those that could be picked up within the specified time—other callers received an engaged tone. I pointed out that this was hardly thinking about the organization from the customers' point of view. I was asked to keep what I learned to myself. This organization still has a Charter Mark, is notoriously difficult to get through to and has a poor reputation for service. The first step to improvement would be to understand the nature of customer demand, something it has still not learned to do. This is not surprising. After all, Charter Mark does not specify it.*

Charter Mark effectively mandates waste in specifying, monitoring and reporting of service standards. Whenever I visit a public sector organization that boasts Charter Mark, I find bucket-loads of failure demand, indicating dissatisfied customers and inefficient or badly designed service processes. I also observe demoralized staff—after all, their job is to survive in the lousy service design and fill in the forms that feed the specification bureaucracy. And finally, you usually find proud but sadly ignorant managers—they are proud to have achieved the standard but they do not know what it is doing to their service operations.

> *In another government agency, a new customer help desk had been awarded the Charter Mark. It was seen as an innovation in customer service. The help desk had set service standards, done customer care training, written procedures manuals and had all of the detailed documentation required to meet the specifications. When one of my team studied that help desk, he found a massive level of failure demand and plenty of evidence that customers found the organization extremely difficult and frustrating to deal with. Managers had no idea that*

this was the case. Only the occasional noise from customers would appear on their desks as a complaint. They knew nothing about how their organization worked from their customers' point of view. What would you imagine would be the customers' view of the Charter Mark?

The purpose of Charter Mark is to 'provide a quality improvement tool that improves service delivery, places its user at the center, and drives continuous improvement.' But it does not have a method that will achieve this aim. To set standards and monitor will only lead to argument and retribution when times are hard, and leads to setting 'soft' standards precisely to prevent times being hard. It teaches nothing about the nature of customers' demands on a system, the capability of the system to respond to those demands and the extent and causes of waste— all essential knowledge if you want to improve.

The real causes of poor service delivery are not made visible to management when they adopt the Charter Mark; on the contrary, the intervention makes opportunities for improvement yet more invisible. Measurement is critical to any change for improvement. Charter Mark, by specifying the need for standards, causes managers to use measures that do not aid understanding and improvement. These measures are at best misleading and, at worst, causes of waste. The reporting bureaucracy is also waste pure and simple.

The foregoing fads have featured strongly in attempts to improve public and private sector performance in the UK. But despite the promulgation of ISO 9000, excellence, IiP and Charter Mark, our public sector organizations in particular are not improving (the record is not much better among companies). I shall return to a discussion of public sector performance improvement in the Appendix, for these interventions were nothing compared to what was to come next.

THE BALANCED SCORECARD

The idea of the balanced scorecard surfaced in 1992 in a much-noticed article in the *Harvard Business Review*.[46] A multi-organization study group[47] was concerned with measuring performance in 'the organization of the future.' The study group had as its

starting point the recognition that existing (financial) performance measures were becoming obsolete; the group believed that
reliance on financial performance measures was hindering
organizations' abilities to create future economic value.

One member of the study group was using what he called a
'corporate scorecard.' This was a collection of measures—financial, customer delivery times, quality and cycle times in manufacturing and the effectiveness of new product development.
Attracted by the approach, the study group christened it the
'balanced scorecard.' In doing so, an idea achieved the status of
knowledge; it became the basis for generalization. The group
proposed that the balanced scorecard should be organized
around four perspectives: financial, customer, internal and
innovation and learning. The argument went on that 'balance'
should be sought between: short and long term, financial
and non-financial, lagging and leading and external and internal
measures.

What was missing was a discussion of the theoretical framework for determining measures—how could anyone be sure that
the measures chosen could help users understand and improve
the work? Following the initial impact, the leaders of the move-
ment reported that although some organizations were using the
ideas to improve existing processes—lowering costs, improving
quality, speeding up responses—many were not identifying
processes that were 'truly strategic'—those that had to be performed well for the organization's strategy to succeed. It was the
first evidence that the balanced score card was not holding water.

But, as so often seems to happen, as the market began to
express these uncertainties, the promoters moved on to the next
version. So, in 1996, the balanced scorecard became a 'strategic
management system.' This system, it was reported, should
include individual and team goals, compensation, resource allocation, budgeting and planning and strategic feedback and learning. Now we were in trouble. Deming would have described this
as 'rule 4,' getting right away from the point.[48] The proposed
measures were all abstractions from the work, classical command-and-control measures. Again appealing and again flawed.
Managers like the idea of the balanced scorecard if it fits with
their view of the world, but this view of the world will not produce a set of measures that hold water.

Here are three examples of the balanced scorecard in use:

1. The telecom company. The telecom firm I described in Chapter 2 was a proud early adopter of the balanced scorecard. You might want to reread the case. All the measures of the work managers used in the original design—time to answer the phone, total work volumes, work states (backlogs), work activity and aged debt—were brought together with measures of staff and customer satisfaction to form the scorecard. Managers believed themselves to be up to date—thoroughly modern management, they thought—but it left them completely out of touch with their operations. Their measures ensured that they were in the dark.

2 The healthcare company. The head office of a health insurance group dictated its requirements for a balanced scorecard to its subsidiaries. In all the customer service organizations, the requirement was to report measures of incoming post and telephone calls, outstanding post ('backlog') and the usual call-center measures—service level (percent of calls answered within 20 seconds), abandoned calls and calls taken per person per day. In the subsidiary in which I was working, the backlog was removed by working on cleaning the flow. You might think this would receive the attention of the head office and that best practice might be shared, but that, unlikely as it is because of the nature of organizations, is to miss the point. The backlog was removed, not by throwing more resources at the problem, but by understanding its nature—that is, understanding demand, value and flow. These are the measures that should have been employed in the balanced scorecard. But as managers had no guidance on how to establish measures, the usual measures were brought to hand. As I have shown in this book, these measures not only hide the means for improvement, they suboptimize performance.

3 The components company. The head office of a components manufacturer specified the balanced-scorecard measures to be reported by the various parts of the organization. The customer measures chosen were:

products delivered by manufacturing and delivery versus commitment in sales. The manufacturing measure was a measure of when the parts left the factory—hardly a measure of delivery from the customers' point of view; worse, salespeople would regularly recommit orders to customers to distort the delivery versus commitment measure. One enlightened manager had established a better measure—orders delivered to customers as and when the customer wanted them. Of course, this showed how bad performance really was. But at least he knew— a position from which it was possible to improve.

I have yet to see an example of the balanced scorecard using metrics that pass the test of a good measure (see Chapter 3). In every case, I have seen traditional financial measures complemented by other command-and-control abstractions. It is no surprise that senior managers find the idea of the balanced scorecard attractive and junior managers do everything they always have done to satisfy the requirements of the hierarchy, regardless of the impact on performance. To get to measures that have value in understanding and improving the work first requires some hard thinking about the nature and value of measurement.

KNOWLEDGE MANAGEMENT

The value of knowledge is its use, not its collection.

The pressing problem that suppliers of knowledge management 'solutions' want to help you solve is: How should you capture and use knowledge in your organization? It is an attractive idea and one that managers are motivated to explore, especially as it scratches an itch—what if we are losing precious knowledge, what might be the awful consequences? And, of course, we can all think of anecdotal examples of our organizations dissipating knowledge, having to reinvent the wheel and so on.

Instead of being preoccupied with how we should capture and manage knowledge, I think we should be concerned with asking: What role does knowledge serve in decision making and performance improvement? Rather than exploring this question, knowledge management vendors treat it as a given. Ackoff[49] observed that sometimes it is useful to 'dissolve' a problem rather than solve it. I think we should dissolve the knowledge problem by asking a different question: What stops organizations from capturing and using knowledge?

Deming often asserted that knowledge should not be thought of as experience. He observed that you could have years of experience but no knowledge. An oft-told joke among lean manufacturers is that of a Japanese guru who visited a UK manufacturer. The guru asked the managing director: 'How long have you been working here?' The answer was: 'Twenty years.' The guru observed: 'It looks as though you have only been here twenty weeks.' Twenty years of experience, twenty weeks of knowledge.

So what prevents the development of knowledge? I have given examples throughout the book: the separation of measures from work, focusing workers on adherence to procedures, designing work in functional specialties and assuming knowledge is associated with hierarchy: all features of command-and-control systems. My contention is that these conditions should be reversed. The principles for the development of knowledge are: integrating measures with work, focusing on purpose, designing work in flow rather than functions and assuming knowledge is associated with work. If these principles were employed, how would we expect a 'knowledge worker' to behave? He or she would be clear about the purpose of the work, would have measures related to purpose, would be knowledgeable about the end-to-end work flow and would as a result be in a position to understand and improve the work.

I was asked to work with an organization that was considering buying a 'knowledge management solution' (in essence computers). The firm, which supplied services to the oil industry, had a problem. On the one hand, it had registered to ISO 9000 because its customers demanded it; but on the other, adherence to standardized procedures was problematic because everything it did for its customers was a one-off. The workers, generally highly skilled, were hugely demotivated. It was also concerned that because it was failing to capture learning from its projects it was prone to reinventing the wheel. Hence the lure of the knowledge management solution: what could be more plausible than to capture the knowledge held in the heads of workers on computer and store it for future use? But would this have worked?

The more likely result would have been the destruction of knowledge at work. Instead of jumping to a solution and purchasing computers to 'manage' knowledge, I encouraged managers to start at 'check.' They took all the previous year's projects and studied them, asking: 'What can we learn about the type and frequency of demands from our customers: How many broad types of demands do we get and how many of each? For each of the major types, how well did each deliver from the customers' point of view and how do we know?' Having looked at demand and capability, they then asked: 'What were the major steps for any piece of work, and do the different types of customer demands require us to do different things?'

What they learned was interesting. Although they dealt with an enormous variety of demands from their customers, every demand, no matter how large or small, how complex or simple, went through four stages of work: understand what matters to the customer, determine by what method the work would be done, do the work, and review it against the original purpose (what mattered to the customer).

Although all work, whether done well or badly, went through these four stages, the various types of work needed quite different methods at each of the stages. For example, being clear about what mattered to the customer differed according to what was being done, as did method, and so on. Furthermore, where things had gone wrong, they could now begin to see at what stage it had happened and how, as ever, something not done right at an early stage became a much larger problem later. Although the core flow was standard, the organization had to be designed to cope with variety. The people set about brainstorming the different methods they used and might use at each of the four stages. They designed an organizational template describing the four core steps and all the possible tools and methods available for dealing with any particular customer demand for each of the steps. Having learned the kinds of things that predictably went wrong, they were able to see the value of using these tools and methods to prevent failure and improve quality.

They set to work with this new template. It was the basis for their quality manual and hence also registration to ISO 9000. Like all innovators, they had to explain the system to their ISO 9000 assessor. The assessor had to learn to assess by asking questions, not following detailed documentation. The assessor would ask: Who is the project manager for a piece of work, what stage is it at, what tools or methods had the project manager chosen for each or any of the stages and how was the project manager monitoring progress against purpose? Instead of all demand being subjected to the same procedures, each demand had its own procedures, as determined by the project manager. It put control where it should be—with those who did the work.

The motivational impact was significant. People saw the value of keeping information about tools and methods. They began to create their own ways of doing so and signposting their availability to others. Being technical, they had no difficulty in creating their own systems for capturing and signposting information. They built their own knowledge management system. Would the result have been the same if senior managers had bought someone else's 'solution'?

SIX SIGMA—TQM ON STEROIDS

In the mid-1980s, I learned a lot from studying TQM programs that failed to make an impact on performance. TQM usually meant some kind of analysis across the organization, the establishment of projects and lots of training in quality tools. I learned that the implicit theory in the toolbox was diametrically opposed to the operating theory in the organization—you can't easily improve flow in a functional design. Six Sigma is an attempt to do the same better. Rather than a few days training, Six Sigma offers many weeks of training. Rather than a few tools, Six Sigma offers a basketful.

I have never felt the need to train tools. If people need a tool, they will beat a path to the cupboard door to get it. In my experience, the most needed tool is the means to create a capability chart, but I have never taught anyone how to do it. They do it for themselves. My job is teaching the need, teaching people how to think. I am sure Ishikawa drew his famous fishbone diagram to illustrate cause and effect.[50] We need managers to think cause and effect; we don't want managers out looking for things to try out their cause-and-effect tool on.

The Six Sigma training and accreditation process provides healthy revenue for the providers and it results in a plethora of people trained to different levels, the ultimate being the 'black belt.'[51] Many who have gone through the training observe that most of the tools never get used; most organizational problems don't need weeks of training to solve. I am with them—the problems solved in the examples in this book illustrate the simplicity of solutions if an analysis is based on sound method. Although Six Sigma has vast amounts of training in tools, there is little content on how to study work.

> *In a presentation of Six Sigma's application to a service center, I saw no appreciation of the importance of understanding demand. Rather, the 'solution' contained the mistakes that I described in Chapter 2: treating all demand as units of production and assuming the workers can be held accountable for the work they do. The 'solution' missed the greatest leverage for improvement. Instead it focused on one of management's current preoccupations: how to get people to do more, which in Six-Sigma terms meant how to reduce variation between the workers. There was no appreciation of the system, no methods for understanding the work. Instead, the solution, if successful, would hide the means for learning and improvement—the causes of variation, which are in the system.*

In many Six-Sigma interventions, the analysis of the current state is conducted by interviewing managers—something that is common to many consulting interventions.[52] This is not the same as studying the work.

> *A Vanguard consultant had the privilege of watching the start of a Six-Sigma program in a client whose system he knew. The initiative had been sent down by the head office. It began with the training of many 'black belts.' Three weeks of training on tools for improving performance. Then, five consultants interviewed managers for four weeks (imagine the cost) about their problems and ideas for improvement. The results were brought to a decision-making forum of consultants and managers, the priorities identified and managers sent forth to apply their new tools. To add to the sheer dishonesty of the intervention, the consultants then established a reporting structure for projects and their progress.*

So now the managers were responsible for executing what the consultants had helped them to come up with. But how had they conceptualized their problems? From their current (traditional) point of view Six Sigma had not changed their thinking about the design and management of work. The tools would not do much for them. They needed to think about their business from a different point of view—as a system. The consultants didn't help them do that, but will ensure that whatever gets done is subject to strong project management. It appeals to the command-and-control mindset. It is another device to 'get them to do it.'

The reporting structure associated with Six Sigma ensures positive results are reported. No doubt some are genuine. But it is not hard to find examples of reports of success that meet the requirement to report rather than reflecting the value of the intervention.

I received the following from a correspondent by e-mail:

I was talking to a woman engineer yesterday who used to work in an organization well known for promoting Six Sigma. She told me that many employees hate Six-Sigma because:

1. It targets cost reduction exclusively and more and more cost reduction, year on year, is being demanded from all departments. If you fire a member of your staff this year, the savings goes into your pot and you must therefore further increase your cost reduction next year.

2. It is elitist. Only 'specialists' (black and green belts) can do it.

3. These specialists run around saying: 'Look at all this training I have received.' Others respond with: 'How much of it have you actually used?'

4. If you want to get something done, you have to call it Six Sigma.

I have never yet seen a Six Sigma intervention present a challenge to management thinking. Rather than starting with 'this means you too,' Six Sigma represents an appealing bureaucracy for directing and controlling improvement efforts. Jack Welch, chief executive of GE for 20 years, is often quoted as a management hero and advocate of Six Sigma. Will Hutton[53] writes that

Welch's priority was cost reduction, which he achieved by massive redundancies and allowing the R&D spending to dwindle everything was subordinated to ensuring that profits grew smoothly quarter by quarter. Six Sigma was employed as a means to project manage cost reduction activities.

By his own admission[54] Jack had little idea what Six Sigma was. He was attracted by the practical examples shown to him by the consultant. Jack is not alone.

> I gave a presentation to a senior management group in a major bank. The quality director told me he was going to introduce Six Sigma. I asked him what he knew about the theory of variation. His blank look said it all.

I never cease to be amazed that managers buy things knowing nothing about them. But Six Sigma provides the things that are important to the command-and-control manager: focus and reporting. It has associated with it all the distortions and elegances well known to command-and-control systems, which is the most important criticism of Six Sigma: There is no requirement for management to change the way it thinks.

DOES I.T. COMPUTE?

In many organizations, IT suppliers have a stranglehold on operations, rendering it impossible to make major changes to the business without further and often substantial investment. Naturally, managers become cautious about never-ending investment in IT. They have heard the horror stories of soaring costs and limited or no delivery. To take an example from the public sector: The Audit Commission reported that the unit cost of passport processing rose by 30 percent following installation of a new IT system. The costs have been passed on to the public in higher charges for passports.

The IT industry continually reinvents itself. The major players have moved from promoting 'mainframe solutions' to 'distributed solutions' to 'server solutions' to 'groupware;' applications such as work flow[55] and knowledge management are also sold as 'solutions.' But are these 'solutions' really designed to improve your organization, or is their purpose just to sell more boxes? Research on the effectiveness of IT makes sobering reading. Many IT projects never reach completion, the costs of implementation generally vastly overshoot what was planned, implementation often fails to deliver the expected financial benefits and sometimes result in higher rather than lower costs. In short, IT is frequently not the savior it is claimed to be.[56]

Beyond failing to deliver or delivering at higher than expected cost, IT sometimes 'entraps' rather than 'enables' the way people work. When IT providers sell what they describe as 'office productivity tools,' they neglect to tell proud purchasers that they may be swamped with e-mail, overloaded with and misled by spreadsheets and subjected to 'death by presentations.' 'Productivity' tools can result in more time preparing for and conducting meetings than getting things done.

FEATURES VERSUS BENEFITS

Often, IT 'solutions' create worse service and higher costs. Managers forget that features are not the same as benefits. Many IT features appeal to managers because they fit with the command-and-control mind-set. Managers like the idea of being able to track all work and monitor all workers. They like the idea of giving everyone access to the organization's repository of knowledge. These are features, but they are not necessarily benefits.

Without information technology, there would be no service centers. Call routing (a feature) is the prerequisite to establishing a service center. But we need to ask: 'When is call routing not a benefit?' One answer is, when continuity is required. To solve the continuity problem, managers may invest in customer record systems so that any agent can see the history of the customer's contacts. But what records should be kept? That can only be answered by first understanding the nature of demands from the customer's point of view. In one extraordinary example, managers of a service center invested in 'caller line identification' (CLI) that routed customers calling back within 24 hours to the same agent. Nobody, least of all the IT consultants, asked what the probability was of the same agent being available when the call came through. The investment was a write-off.

Although managers are attracted by features such as up- and cross-selling provided by tools like computer telephony integration (CTI), there is no way of knowing if they will provide benefits without understanding why customers call in. Only if they understand why they call in from their point of view can they predict the ability of these tools to increase sales.

In a financial services organization, agents received screen prompts telling them to approach customers with offers of sales. The prompts were often impossible to follow—it is hard to sell home insurance to a customer who is asking for an account balance—but the IT system required the agent to complete the prompt screen before he or she could get on with serving the customer and/or completing the call. The prompts made no difference to sales, but consumed resources in IT spend and management factory behavior, not to mention irritating the hell out of customers and agents.

Whenever I work with an organization using IVR (interactive voice response), I investigate how many customers 'drop out' or misroute themselves. It happens with alarming frequency and it is easy to see why. IVR only makes sense when you can predict why customers call in *from their point of view*. If the IVR doesn't use language that customers can relate to, customers are bound to have difficulties. Managers like IVR because it passes some or all of the costs of service provision to the customer; it fits with their current view of the world. Customers, on the other hand, hate them like poison.

Many organizations use IT to record incoming work, sort it, scan it, route it, record how long people took to do it and to archive it. It is the 'command-and-control' manager's dream. Managers can tell you where everything is, how much work is being done by which person, what work is coming in, going out and in backlog. When you look at the work from the customers' point of view, however, you regularly find it is impossible to predict how long it will take to deal with any individual customer demand. In other words, you have no knowledge about the system's ability to 'make and meet' commitments—first base in being customer-driven. Moreover, when you study the value work—the work that matters to customers—it is often a minuscule proportion of the total work. The IT system drives the sorting, scanning, batching, counting, routing and recording of work under the misguided assumption that this is helping the work get done. The customer couldn't care less about these processes—except when, as always happens with sorting, batching and queuing of work, errors are introduced. If that is not bad enough, the IT system itself consumes further resources because all of these applications needed maintaining. As more documents are scanned into the system, more memory is needed, which in turn demands more storage and more maintenance. The waste in these circumstances is inextricably linked to the IT system. Managers are sold a dream that in fact becomes a nightmare.

In summary, managers make investments in IT without knowledge of their impact on the work. All too often, the result is to make service provision more complicated for the customer and more costly for the organization.

IMPROVE FIRST, THEN 'PULL' I.T.

The problems with IT begin with the way we approach it. The normal way is for managers to start by writing a specification. The IT provider then takes the specification, creates its own version of the same thing and then delivers against it. When it fails, as it so often does, the supplier blames the managers, who after all wrote the original specification. Even more incredibly, having failed to deliver benefits, the supplier will often succeed in selling more 'implementation consultancy' to put matters right. Perhaps only in IT do failures in service provision lead to more sales. It is a good indication of the stranglehold in which purchasers find themselves.

There is a better way to approach the use of IT. It goes like this: Understand and improve—then ask if IT can further improve.

- *Understand.* Ignore IT. Do not even assume you have an IT problem or that you need an IT solution. Instead, work first to understand the 'what and why' of current performance as a system. To recap, this means looking outside-in and end to end; and learning about demand, capability, flow, waste and the causes of waste.
- *Improve.* Improve performance without using IT. If the current work uses IT, leave it in place, work without it or,

if necessary, treat it as a constraint. But don't do anything to change the IT.

- *Ask, 'Can IT further improve this process or system?'* Now and only now should you consider the use of, or changes to, IT. Only at this stage can you address the potential benefits from a position of knowledge about the work and therefore predict the benefits IT solutions will bring. The result is always less investment in IT and much more value from it. IT is 'pulled' into the work rather than dictating the way work works.

If and when IT has been used to further improve the way the work works, a fourth step is: measure improvement resulting from the use of IT. This, of course, is measured using operational performance data. This is quite different from the normal way of measuring IT, which is more often measured by 'delivery against project plan and budget'—a metric that has no necessary connection with operational improvement.

Working in this way ensures that decisions about the use of IT are only taken from a position of knowing the 'what and why' of current performance as a system. Traditional IT implementation leaves 'knowledge of the work' to a mixture of business analysis (provided by IT specialists) and managers' views—both usually reflecting a command-and-control perspective. The traditional approach to IT implementation is 'push'—here is the new IT system, now how do we get people to use it. In the alternative approach, IT is 'pulled'—the people doing the work understand the 'what and why' of the work and 'pull' IT applications in to parts of the work knowing what to expect. The traditional problems of implementation—incomprehension and resistance to change—simply do not exist.

OTHER APPROACHES TO SYSTEMS THINKING

The approach to systems thinking I describe in this book is different from others. Most other systems thinkers take a nonlinear approach. One, who advises the UK government, suggests systems thinking means that, when determining how to act, managers should 'try things out and see what works.' I can't see any manager buying that. I would prefer that managers see systems thinking as a means to obtain knowledge. The implication is they should be able to act with prediction and confidence of improvement.

The Vanguard approach to systems thinking is linear and inductive—it is certainly logical. It is, of course, a completely different logic to command and control. There are many other systems theorists.[57] Although all systems thinkers agree that a system is a sum of its parts and the parts must be managed as one, the Vanguard approach is unique in that it starts and ends with the work.

In the early 1990s, Peter Senge wrote *The Fifth Discipline*.[58] It was an important book, making a cogent case for the system's influence on behavior and performance, bringing systems thinking to the attention of many managers for the first time. In this book, Senge described what has come to be known as 'the beer game,' a simulation in which all players, regardless of organizational background or level, always arrive at the same result. It is a powerful demonstration of how the system governs performance.

The beer game requires three types of players: retailer, wholesaler and a factory. The retailers are selling a product ('lover's beer'). Each player is told to maximize his own profit. The game is triggered by a doubling of demand for lover's beer at the retail outlet. The 'trick' in the game is that the time from order to delivery is four weeks. What happens is that the retailers begin to panic as their stocks run low and the orders they have placed have yet to come through. They over-order. Once the lag of inventory starts to come through, the system is flooded with product, so orders cease and the factory goes out of business. It happens every time; it is a consequence of the way the system is set up.

In his book, Senge offers two solutions to the beer game: 'take two aspirins and wait' (be patient, wait on the inventory already in the pipeline) and 'only order what you've sold.' I remember reading this with a feeling of disquiet. I regarded them as 'victim' solutions; you cannot control the system but you must take account of it in your behavior. I think most managers are like me; they want a solution, not a palliative. They want to be in control.

It wasn't until years later when I reread the beer game that it occurred to me that Taiichi Ohno would have had a quite different solution. He would have run the demand data in the factory and had all players in the system work to reduce time between sales and production. Everybody would win.

Recently, a client who was working with other approaches to systems thinking told me how Vanguard's work was different. He described two essential distinctions. The first was: 'When you ask the consultant when you should stop adding interdependencies to your system picture, the answer is: when you think you have exhausted the major interdependencies. That question does not occur with the Vanguard approach, because the analysis of the system starts with the work and only looks at successively wider influences from that point of view, their impact on operational performance.' The second was: 'When you ask the consultant how we should go about taking action, he tells you to get a team together, develop a vision, make a plan, establish milestones and so on. By contrast, the Vanguard approach leaves you in no doubt as to the scope and means for improvement, because you have studied the work in an operational way.'

My concern is that some approaches to systems thinking will turn managers off the most important subject on the management curriculum. If managers try 'systems thinking' and get no value from it, they may not be inclined to try again.

Although we may recognize the systemic nature of the world, and would agree when challenged that something we normally think of as an entity is actually a system, our culture does not propound this insight as particularly interesting or profitable to contemplate.[59]

When, following Ohno, systems thinking is applied to the design and management of work, and that is set as the boundary for the activity, it is both interesting and profitable. The Vanguard approach sets a boundary. Other approaches to systems thinking might be interesting but not, in my experience, profitable.

The Vanguard approach is *interesting* and *profitable*. Interesting, because it provides a method for developing relevant knowledge and, consequently, achieving the ideals all managers would aspire to: a learning, improving, innovative, adaptive and energized organization. Profitable, because it provides the means to develop a customer-driven, adaptive organization; an organization that behaves and learns according to what matters to customers. If the system is to have viable economics, it could only be understood and developed from this point of view.

The Vanguard approach to systems thinking is a methodology for change and improvement that *engages* the organization. Any change is based on an understanding of demand from an 'outside-in' or customer perspective, identification of the value work, adoption of relevant measures and then designing out the waste within key processes. People who do the work must be engaged in these activities. The results: better service, reduced costs and improved morale.

What is especially interesting is that the Vanguard approach cuts costs as service improves—increasing profits. Most managers equate improvements in service with additions to cost. It is because they have been conditioned to think this way. They cannot 'see' where their costs really are. When managers learn to see their organization as a system, they see the scope for improvement and the means to achieve it.

Few organizations have achieved this level of competence. Many parts of organizations, some of which comprise the case material in this book, have learned what it means in practice. The results have always been significant, sometimes extraordinary.

Despite these results, some organizations that were early adopters of these methods have reverted to the command-and-control philosophy. In every case, these organizations have been taken over by managers who do not understand and share the new philosophy. The newcomers impose what they know—command-and-control norms. Usually they reimpose the very measures and methods that their predecessors had taken out. When command-and-control thinkers listen to systems thinkers, they hear the words but don't appreciate their meaning. If systems thinkers point out the value of working outside-in, command-and-control thinkers just treat it as an example of what management should be doing in any event. When systems thinkers point out benefits achieved by measuring different things, command-and-control thinkers treat it as something else to be reported. Should systems thinkers point out that traditional, command-and-control measures were part of the problem and should not be reintroduced, the command-and-control thinkers will insist such measures to be the fundamental stuff of management.

When the old doctrine is reintroduced, a fog descends on the organization. Managers can no longer see. In the sense that people can't know what they don't know and the methods they reintroduce are natural to them, you can only blame them so far. Managers who have learned the principles and practices of systems thinking leave. They can no longer put up with practices they know are wrong and dysfunctional. The transformation in thinking is personal and is maintained by those who have 'got it' as they go on to other jobs in different organizations.

CHAPTER 9

Watch out for the toolheads

Many management fads appeal to managers because of the means of intervention; managers like to think of change as something you do with training and projects. I gained an antipathy to change by tools training and projects in the early 1980s while studying TQM programs that failed. Of course, people do get improvements with tools, but they are insignificant when compared to the benefits from changing the system. I took the view that it is better to teach perspective—how to think—and if tools help, people will 'beat a path' to the door. For example, it is more important to teach the value, importance and issues associated with managing flow than teaching how to map a flow. I am still of that view. What's more, teaching tools very rarely results in a change to the system.

It is a problem of intervention. If the object of a change is to change the system, tools can, at best, be only an aid. It is a common fallacy to believe that change is no more than a matter of education. This was the fallacy of TQM programs and today is the fallacy behind the promotion of the Toyota System as a set of tools. Managers are being told that tools such as 5S, takt time, Poke Yoka, and Value Stream Mapping are the means by which they can emulate Toyota. The purpose of this chapter is to explore how these tools got developed and assess their suitability for making effective change in service organizations.

TOOLS—THE CODIFICATION OF METHOD

With an ever-greater interest in the Toyota phenomenon, it is perhaps inevitable that 'lean manufacturing tools' emerged. People assume that writing the method down will facilitate its adoption by others. The Toyota Production System was labelled 'lean' by Womack, Roos and Jones when they wrote *The Machine That Changed the World*.[60] The word represented the ideas of economy of effort, minimizing waste and thinking in terms of working hand-in-hand with suppliers to manage flow; the consequences were low cost, low inventory and fitness for purpose. Taiichi Ohno did not call it 'lean.' Creating the label 'lean' (what it is), leads naturally to the notion of tools (how you do it), obscuring the importance of perspective (how to think about it). Obscuring the importance of perspective leads to a failure to appreciate that Ohno's ideas represent a philosophy for the design and management of work that is diametrically opposed to today's norms. The codification of method misses this important issue: thinking. Although the tools are accurate descriptions of what happens in terms of method, it is the context that is more important.

To Ohno, the approach was intuitive; a way of behaving when faced with problems that needed solving. It was both conceptual—for example, focus primarily on flow, not function—and behavioral—if you found a problem, it was normal to talk about it, get data about it, share it with colleagues and experts, learn the right way to fix it and then apply the solution in a way that was focused on this 'learning.' It was based on both knowledge and empiricism. When another problem cropped up, the same principles would be applied. It was what we might call a learning and knowledge culture.

From codifying methods it is a short step to choosing those 'tools' that appear to be making the big difference and describing them as a series of tasks or steps to be undertaken. Codification itself suits the command-and-control culture. Tools could be taught and directed at problems (as defined in the current view), and reporting on progress could be institutionalized through the hierarchy. Thus we have a stark contrast in leadership: learning and method through active involvement versus tools training and projects with involvement limited to specifying (the wrong) problems (or specifying them wrongly) and receiving reports on progress.

AN ESSENTIAL GUIDE TO THE LEAN MANUFACTURING TOOLS

To understand the dangers of trying to introduce change via tools, I shall describe the lean manufacturing tools being promoted as 'solutions' to service organizations, illustrating how they are used in manufacturing. For each tool I address the questions:

- What is it?
- How does it work?
- What benefit does it bring to manufacturing?

Subsequently, I will assess their suitability for application in service organizations.

Five S

What is 5S?

5S is a tool that is used to provide a standard workplace environment, enabling standardized work and helping to remove waste. 5S provides visualization of the work and waste; it enables you to see flow. 5S involves employees in maintaining an organized, efficient, safe and clean workplace. 5S is known as many things: 5S, 5C, Cando, Work Place Organization (WPO), illustrating the fact that codification often results in a struggle properly and accurately to describe the purpose. Below are translations and pronunciations for the steps in 5S, with a brief description of each:

Seiri	'Say-ree'	Sort	Instant disposal of unnecessary things, arrangement or reorganization
Saiton	'Say-ton'	Set in order	Put things in order
Seiso	'Say-soo'	Shine	Clean to original condition, do clean work positively
Seiketsu	'Say-kit-sue'	Systemize, standardize	Clean, pure, untainted workplace. Free from bad habits
Shitsuke	'Shit-zuk-ay'	Sustain	Be well mannered, use polite behavior, be disciplined. Maintain what has been achieved

The philosophy behind 5S is: order, organization, discipline, elimination of bad habits and wasted effort.

Looking at 5S this way illustrates the link between the language, the meaning of the words and their application. These words are inherent in the Japanese language. For example, three of the four words above contain the word sei, which means 'to arrange, to create sequence.' The Japanese word for production is seizou, meaning organizing into a whole. In this sense, 5S is an intuitive aspect of the approach to working. Command-and-control thinkers would say they too are concerned with organizing into a whole, but in practice their methods and measures are concerned with the management of parts, not the whole.

How does 5S work?

The idea is that through a systematic approach, people will feel more ownership of the workplace. This encourages self-discipline and the improvement of the quality and safety of the working environment. It also ensures the workplace is well organized and the workflow can be easily seen.

The 5S or 5C activities are as follows:

Sort	Clearout and classify	Throw out what you don't need— free-up space. If not sure, use a red tag—ask: Who owns it? Can we throw it out?
		Store other things not needed
		Often short blitz sessions
Set in order	Configure	Set in order—a place for everything and everything in its place, e.g., shadow boards/fixed capacity-shaped shelves
		Order what is remaining according to frequency of use
		Create a standard layout—easy to see if everything is in its place
Shine	Clean and check	Ensure equipment is fit for purpose
Standardize	Conformity	Establish best way to do things and format. Make this the standard and communicate it
Sustain and Improve	Custom and practice	Make it a habit and review frequently

What benefit does 5S bring in manufacturing?

Standardization and 5S go hand in hand. In manufacturing, 5S is a solution to problems of organization, order and safety in the workplace. By enabling you to see flow clearly, it helps to improve visual management in the workplace. Seeing and standardizing flow are essential prerequisites for improving manufacturing operations. For this reason 5S is generally something you do first.

Takt time

What is takt time?

Takt time is the demand (units of production ordered by customers) divided by the time available to produce them. It is an essential method for understanding at what rate parts need to flow to meet the requirement of the whole, and the requirement of the whole is driven by the rate of customer demand. In simple terms, takt time is mathematics for managing flow throughout the system at the rate of demand.

In German, 'takt' means 'heartbeat' or 'rhythm.' It is not a Japanese word. In the 1950s, Ohno had a problem. Toyota's trucks and tractors were in high demand because of the Korean war, but because of the war it was difficult to bring in raw materials. As a result, Ohno found he often ended up trying to complete a month's production in the final two weeks of the month.

Ohno set out to deal with this problem by seeking to understand what the system would need to do in order to meet demand. He took the expected demand over a given time and divided it by the time available to meet that demand. This gave him the 'takt' time, which allowed him to understand if the system was producing enough or too much at any given time and in any place. Ohno did not use the label 'takt time.' He saw the 'heartbeat' as a way to manage production.

How does takt time work?

An example will illustrate:

Bottled Water Co.

The number of bottles of water a shop sells will vary enormously.

A large supermarket will sell much more than a corner shop.

What will affect sales?

The weather—if it's a hot day the shops will sell more
Promotions
Health scares . . . etc.

How does a bottled water company deal with this variation in demand? Hold stock. In this case, costs rise with inventory and warehousing. Forecasting.

The problem is variation in demand, which will lead to variation in production and thus inefficiencies. If you make too much, it costs you in raw materials and storage; and lost profit if you use promotions to get rid of the excess. If you make too little, it costs you in lost business and, possibly, penalties with major customers.

Take a typical summer period when we expect the demand to be about 25 million bottles:

The period is 16 weeks

The company works a six-day week, using the other day for cleaning and maintenance, on a 24-hour shift pattern

$16 \times 6 \times 24 = 2304$ hrs available

Demand / time available: 25,000,000 divided by 2304 = 18,851 bottles per hour

18,851 bottles per hour is the what the heartbeat or rhythm of the whole system needs to be; it is the primary guide for production.

Now that we have this figure, suppose it rains? What happens if a machine stops? What about variation? The answer is that the takt time is varied to react to changes as required. The production must be a stable, standardized flow, otherwise takt time will be irrelevant. Takt time works like a faster/slower control on the system, allowing you to produce in accordance with variation in demand. The system is, therefore, flexible and responsive. Without takt time, other problems within the process and the demand would be hidden by production variation and tampering by the managers. With takt time, bottlenecks within and outside the process can be understood and managed.

What benefit does takt time bring in manufacturing?
Takt time gives you a volume control for the management of production against demand. It is essential in managing flow against demand. The benefits in manufacturing are the ability to produce to demand with better control and predictability. Like so much of

the Toyota Production System, its effect is to clear away the chaff of management's 'created variation' so that the real causes of variation can be addressed.

Poke Yoka

What is Poke Yoka?

Poke Yoka is a tool for error prevention and mistake proofing. The idea is to design products and processes to detect errors before they become defects, thereby improving productivity and reliability.

Poke Yoka is the label used generally, but if you look at Ohno's written work he describes the idea as Baka Yoka. Changing Baka to Poke was driven by a combination of political correctness and Western interpretation. Baka is a mild word for 'chump/idiot/fool' and Yokeru means 'to avoid bad situations', or 'move out of the way to avoid being in danger.' Translated into English, Baka Yoka literally means 'fool proofing.' It would appear that this was not palatable, so a similar word was used which translates as 'mistake proofing.'

How does Poke Yoka work?

A machine will have a built-in automated stopping device to prevent it from doing the wrong thing. One consequence is one operator can man several machines, because the machines will signal when someone is required to fix a problem. Making problems loud, visible and obvious guarantees that they are dealt with. The flow of production is halted until the error is corrected.

In command-and-control designs, we build in inspection (which only leads to more errors), whereas in Baka Yoka the next process is inherently a quality check. If there is a fault, the process stops; the problem then gets rectified at source and never returns. Examples of the application of Poke Yoka include gauges where everything but the 'OK' reading is blanked off: if you can't see the needle on the gauge, there is a problem.

What benefit does Poke Yoka bring in manufacturing?

Poke Yoka prevents errors moving forward in the production line. In this way it is a method for controlling and improving the flow of production. Note that the control is designed into the work, sending a signal to the worker to act.

Value stream mapping

What is value stream mapping?

Value stream mapping (VSM) is a method for visualizing and thus understanding a flow, end to end. In many manufacturing environments, the end-to-end flow is difficult to see. In their book *Lean Thinking*,[61] Womack and Jones define five key steps for going 'lean': Identify the value stream, understand value, flow, pull, perfection. VSM is primarily concerned with the second and third steps: understanding value and flow. Without managing value work through a flow, it is difficult if not impossible to make any real steps towards a true 'pull' (make-to-order) system. The ability to identify key product flows and understand them from end to end is central to the improvement of manufacturing flows. VSM can be used to illustrate problems and trigger solutions or to build information required to redesign a manufacturing flow entirely.

How does VSM work?

VSM requires gathering the following data:

- Inputs
- Processing times
- Waiting times
- Batch sizes
- Value-adding time
- Waste

The idea is that you build the whole picture before you decide where to act.

Figure 9.1 is an example of a value stream map.

In building a value stream map, the first step is to map the physical process, described in the rectangles running horizontally through the middle of the map. The hexagonal shapes within the rectangles detail the cycle time for each process. Below this, you add information relating to batch sizes of incoming goods, machines speeds, downtime and uptime percentages for machines and so on. This information gives a detailed insight into what is actually happening on the shop floor.

The next important rows are the 'Qs' and triangles above the physical process. These detail the quality check points and the typical inventory found between each process. Above this are

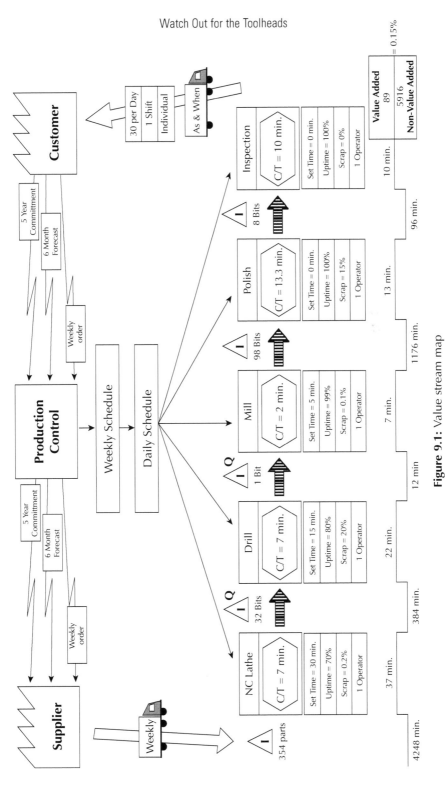

Figure 9.1: Value stream map

the management activities, describing the nature of control within the organization, planning methods and frequencies both at shop floor level and above. It also contains information about the frequency of customer orders and typical order characteristics. The current method of planning and communication is also detailed here, with different styles of lines for electronic or non-electronic approaches.

The final and perhaps most important detail is the value-adding ratio, found at the bottom of the map. This is the ratio of time spent on value-adding to non-value-adding activities. It should be remembered that typical manufacturers struggle to achieve better than 5 percent value-add; world leaders such as Toyota operate at around 20 percent. It should be understood that the value-add ratio is never an impressive figure.

What benefit does VSM bring in manufacturing?

VSM can be used to identify and target some or all of the seven kinds of waste:

- Output quality/defects
- Overproduction
- Inventory
- Transportation
- Motion
- Waiting/delays
- Processing time

By visualizing the process with this level of detail and quantity of information, tackling problems becomes substantially easier. Any activities undertaken will be from an end-to-end (systems) perspective rather than specific to activities, so there will be no downstream negative impacts of local solutions. That is, solutions will be undertaken in terms of impact on flow, rather than activity improvements for their own sake. Merely building this map would give a sufficient understanding of the flow to trigger some improvements. But VSM also provides the opportunity to redesign the whole flow. The understanding gained from this exercise can be used to build a future-state map, based on optimizing end-to-end flow.

To do this, the map is analyzed to identify where bottleneck activities are, that is, processes that have slower cycle times than the rest and/or are less reliable or are subject to other restrictions. From this the flow capability can be compared to the takt time for demand. If the activities globally take longer than the available takt time, then there is a capacity issue. If not, the activities will have to be balanced around the takt time.

VSM makes it possible to redesign the manufacturing process to optimize flow. Without establishing and managing flow, it is impossible to achieve sufficient balance and control to implement a pull system: a system that makes to order.

TOOLS SOLVE PROBLEMS

The tools that have resulted from the codification of Ohno's methods have valuable uses and can certainly solve problems in manufacturing. But it is the philosophy behind the tools—how managers think about the design and management of work—that is the key.

The methods developed in the Toyota Production System were responses to identified and understood problems. The methods were developed to eliminate these problems permanently. The choice of method was based on an understanding of the problem.

The danger with codifying method as tools is that by ignoring the all-important context it obviates the first requirement to understand the problem, and, more importantly, to understand and articulate the problem from a systems perspective. The problems managers articulate from a command-and-control perspective are often different (and wrong) ones.

All of the methods (tools) described above were developed to solve problems associated with managing the flow of manufacturing at the rate of demand. 5S gets things in order and enables you to see flow; takt time is an essential measure for managing the components of a flow such that they work in harmony; Poke Yoka prevents errors moving forward in a flow; and VSM enables a detailed overview of the end-to-end flow in order to determine where to act.

ONE PHILOSOPHY—TWO METHODS

When the Vanguard team first discovered Taiichi Ohno's work, we recognized the challenge to translate his ideas for service systems. We knew that service differed from manufacturing in several important respects:

Nothing is 'stored' in the way products can be stored.
Service is not 'made' by physical (making things) means.

Service happens at the points of transaction (we used to call these 'moments of truth').

The service agent is part of the service delivery.
The customer is involved in the service delivery.

In Chapter 3 (Purpose, measures, method) I introduced the idea that in service organizations, it is the customer who sets the nominal value. So to design an effective and efficient service organization, we first need to understand the nature of customer demand. Ohno's 'demand problem' was, 'which model?' 'which color?' and 'how many?' The demand problem in service organizations is quite different.

THE VANGUARD METHOD

Because the customer is 'involved in production,' in service organizations we need to understand the variety of customer demands and then design the system to absorb that variety. Although the methods we developed in Vanguard are entirely consistent with Ohno's philosophy, they are completely different from the methods developed in manufacturing, because they are designed to solve different problems. As I have illustrated throughout the case material in this book, this involves:

- Studying customer demand in customer terms
- Distinguishing between 'value' and 'failure' demand
- Understanding whether demand is predictable or unpredictable
- Redesigning services against customer demands
- Changing the system (measures, roles and other 'system conditions') to remove the dysfunctional aspects of command-and-control thinking and replace them with the requirements for managing the work as a system

It will serve as a summary of the material already covered to briefly emphasize the importance of each of the steps in the Vanguard Method.

Studying customer demand in customer terms

If you want customers to 'pull value' from the system, you need to know the nature of demands customers place on it. If you don't know this, you risk giving poor service at high cost.

Distinguishing between 'value' and 'failure' demand

Value demands are those you want customers to place on the system. Failure demands are those you don't want. Failure demands are caused by a failure to do something or do something right for the customer. It follows that failure demand is entirely under the organization's control. Turning off the causes of failure demand is one of the greatest economic levers available to managers.

Understanding whether demand is predictable or unpredictable

Before managers act on demand, it is critical to determine whether demand is predictable or unpredictable. The secret to effective design is the knowledge of demand and its predictability.

Redesigning services against customer demands

When failure demand falls, customers experience better service and costs fall. When service flows are designed against customers' (nominal) value demands, service improves as costs decline.

Changing the system

Measures, roles and other 'system conditions' need to be changed to remove the dysfunctional aspects of command-and-control thinking and replace them with the requirements for managing the work as a system.

It is the system that delivers performance. To manage the organization as a system requires the removal of harmful practices and the establishment of helpful practices. Just as Ohno set out to understand and manage the whole manufacturing process as a system, the Vanguard Method does the same for service organizations. Ohno's methods were developed to solve problems associated with managing flow at the rate of demand. Vanguard's methods were developed to change the characteristics of demand and absorb the inherent variety in customer demand.

TOOLHEAD EXCESSES

Unthinking toolheads promote their tools to the detriment of the system. Instead of being focused on what questions to ask and how to think about problems, the toolheads do as they have been taught. They apply the tools in an unthinking way. Here are some examples of wrong-headed application for each of the tools I have introduced:

Five S

5S is generally thought of as the way to start. Here is an example:

A local authority appointed a consultant to help it implement 5S. He instituted 'black-bag Friday,' that is, he got people to clean up the office and put things in their correct place. Although every Friday was 'black-bag day,' after the initial purge there was not much trash to be collected and files were neatly arranged. After the 5S completion, some senior managers were not convinced that anything had changed. They asked our advice. We told them that as a result of 5S there was not much mess, but that didn't mean there was no waste. There was lots of it—much of it now sitting in computers where it was even harder to see.

5S in service organizations may give the impression of doing something, but nothing really changes.

A typical 5S office solution might be a row of box files on a shelf with a readily identifiable pattern drawn across their spines to indicate the order in which they belong. If someone removes a file, it is thus immediately evident where it needs to go back. This raises the questions: When might this help? Are the resources available in the files important, and does accessing them constitute value work? In other words, marking up the files for the sake of an exercise in tidiness could be failing to ask the important questions. It is to return to the theme: What is the problem you are trying to solve?

Behind 5S is the idea that 'everything has its place.' The idea is a good one and may be important in sorting out a manufacturing line, but it is less so in an office where the same considerations of safety and routine do not apply. We have seen instances where in the cause of 5S workers have been required to mark out their desks with defined spaces for scissors, stapler, paper clips, tape, and other office supplies. Can you imagine the impact on morale when people are told to do this? In service organizations, keeping yourself or your desk a bit tidier will have little impact on the system.

Is 5S the place to start? No, the place to start in service organizations is studying demand. The question you need to address is: 'To what extent does the current system absorb variety?' To solve this problem, you need to study demand in customer terms and the capability of the system to meet it. The people who should do this work are those who work with customers every day; they find it motivational to think about their work from the customers' point of view.

Applying 5S in service organizations is solving the wrong problem. Indeed, rather than solving problems, it can actually create them.

Standardize first?

The toolheads often start with 5S, quoting Ohno as saying you cannot improve without first standardizing work. That may be true in manufacturing, but it is wholly wrong in service organizations. Indeed, the impact of standardization in service organizations is to damage the system's ability to absorb variety.

Standardization in the Toyota Production System is essential—it is a manufacturing system. Ohno valued standardization, but not for itself. He and his workers valued standardization as a means for learning and improvement. For example, if something 'nonstandard' occurs, both the worker and manager would assume there was something that needed attention in the work. Command-and-control thinkers value standardization for different reasons. First of all, if something 'nonstandard' happens, the manager assumes there is something wrong with the worker; it is axiomatic in command-and-control thinking that the workers should be held responsible for variation in performance. Further, command-and-control thinkers value standardization because it helps them in the bulk of their work, planning and resource management tasks. They are unaware of the need to separate their planning and operations management activities.

In service organizations, there are countless examples of this error. Service 'work queues' have standard times; workers have requirements to meet standard work measures (targets). Variation in work content is ignored in terms of its value in the pursuit of improvement and causes managers to behave in unhelpful ways as illustrated throughout this book. Managers miss the obvious and exacerbate the situation, making learning even more inaccessible. These and other 'system conditions' have the unintended consequences of driving waste into the system and making it hard, if not impossible, to see.

Just as Ohno used standardization to learn and improve, in service organizations it is vital to use actual data (for example, time taken to execute tasks, volumes of tasks done) for learning and improvement, not arbitrary data (which is what standard times become because they do not accommodate variation). Moreover, these more useful measures must be used by those who do the work to understand and improve the work. The consequences are not only improved service at reduced cost; morale is transformed. If you start 'improvement' with standardization in service organizations, you risk making service worse, driving costs up and driving morale down.

Takt time

Takt time is essential if you want to manage flow at the rate of demand in manufacturing. But does it have a place in service organizations?

A recent article in a prominent management journal contains a classic example of the misuse of takt time. The example concerns improving the processing of new business. Following the principles established for takt time in manufacturing, the author takes the volume of new business cases coming in to the organization and divides this number by the available resource (manpower hours). The author then determines that to accommodate demand, each application would need to be dealt with in the resulting time. This is completely arbitrary. The consequence is management of the workers with an arbitrary measure that is unrelated to the needs of the work. This is pure command-and-control thinking, having nothing in common with Ohno's philosophy.

To improve new business processing, you would want to understand the following:

- End-to-end times for new business processing, from first contact by the customer to completion, showing capability and variation
- Proportion of applicants who complete the transaction (become customers), over time, showing capability and variation
- Waste and causes of waste and hence variation in the flow: 'dirt' in input, failure demand, process design, measures, management behavior, IT and so on

You would then redesign the flow against the value work as defined by the customer. You would use the measures identified above to track improvement, relegating the 'old' ('lagging') measures to keeping score. In this way, you remove the causes of failure demand, increase capacity (faster processing), make more sales (less customers 'drop out' or give up); thus happier customers and happier workers.

Poke Yoka

The most common application of Poke Yoka in service organizations is 'forcing' a service agent to complete a field in a computer screen. Unless the field has a value or entry, the agent cannot advance to the next screen. Because service agents are (wrongly) targeted on time taken to complete tasks, they frequently enter any value that will allow the process to move on. Typically, they will use a code or entry they can most easily remember, especially when there are many such codes and finding the right one would take time. The consequence, of course, is dirt in the system.

This kind of rule violates the principle that the worker should be in control. In manufacturing, Poke Yoka is used to send a signal from the work to the worker. In service designs, because of the inherent variety in demand, the worker needs to be able to control the 'cleanliness' of the work (the input to the next step in the flow). Any rule set by managers from above is likely to make the system less able to absorb the variety inherent in customer demands. The information required to make clean flow—provide the service efficiently to the customer—should be the focus of any agent's work in a service design. If the system is designed in such a way that the agent's role is to both provide service to the customers and improve that service, he or she will be much more likely to ensure that any information gathered is correct and useable. In a service design, the agent must be responsible for mistake proofing.

Value Stream Mapping (VSM)

VSM is of little value in service organizations. The mapping work starts with the machines and worker activities in a physical manufacturing flow. The constraint of machinery is not relevant to a service flow; treating work functions as proxies for machinery assumes de facto that they are necessary functions/activities. In services, the flow is understood by working from outside in—core flows are dictated by customer demands.

Everything that is analyzed in respect of the value-adding ratio (cycle time, waiting time, downtime, etc.) requires prior standardization of work. As I have said, this is an inappropriate intervention in service design, driving up costs by making the system less able to absorb variety.

The analysis of flow in service is concerned with matters such as preceding activities supplying information fit for purpose, rather than levels of inventory in front of processes. To measure inventory in service organizations in this way is to make a fundamental error.

In manufacturing applications of VSM, there is a strong focus on the management activities associated with the interface with the customer. In service designs, it is far more effective to have the person supplying the service, at the interface with the customer, to be the means of control.

WATCH OUT FOR THE TOOLHEADS

Labelling Ohno's work as 'lean' led to the codification of method. The methods developed in manufacturing have value there, but solving the problems of service organizations requires a different approach because the context is different: Service differs from manufacturing in important respects.

Much of the growth of interest in 'lean' for service organizations has been due to manufacturing organizations moving their 'lean tools' off the shop floor and in to what they call 'back-office' activities. Many of these activities may need to operate in synchrony with the manufacturing plant, and the tools may have value in clarifying and improving processes. But before we jump to the conclusion that the tools will work in any service organization, we had best first study the systems.

It is also worth noting that whenever I have listened to a presentation by a lean manufacturer of its use of lean tools in the back office, I am interested to find out whether their use of lean tools has changed the system in the core manufacturing operations. The best question to ask is: 'Have you taken the measure of "revenue out of the factory gate" off the factories?' If the answer is 'no,' manufacturing cannot be working as a pull system. To manufacture to revenue targets causes inventory and other forms of waste. Such manufacturing organizations are employing 'lean' tools as they employed TQM, as training and projects focused on process improvement. With the size of investment they get a return, but is it the kind of return they would achieve by transforming the system?

Many of the manufacturing companies using lean tools openly claim to be engaged in cost-reduction exercise. Although cost reduction is a natural consequence of 'lean,' it is not its purpose. The purpose of 'lean' is to increase capacity by designing a system that optimally responds to customer demand.

Today our service organizations (and their customers) suffer high cost and poor quality service. Like manufacturers, they have the opportunity to increase capacity by ridding the system of waste (the natural consequence of a command-and-control design) and deliver better service at lower cost. The opportunity will only be realized by changing the system.

Watch out for the toolheads. They risk wasting the opportunity to improve our service organizations—and they may make it more difficult to do so in the future.

Think about it . . .

Ohno insisted we should not codify method.

Why?

Revisiting Taylorism

The management philosophy that underpins command-and-control thinking is Taylorism, named after the American engineer who developed a theory of scientific management. His work led to the growth of organization and methods and industrial engineering departments, the hallmark of which is time-and-motion studies. The consequences in our organizations were production quotas with associated pay systems. His methods worked. Many workers were taken to levels of achievement well above the then-accepted norms. Workers typically doubled or tripled their previous output and increased their wages, albeit by a lesser multiple.

BACKGROUND ON TAYLOR'S IDEAS

In his book, Taylor made clear his belief that any worker must be trained by someone better educated than himself and that this trainer or expert should base his work on what he called the laws of science. Today, the consequence of separating decision making from work is often described as 'leaving your brain at the door,' perhaps illustrating how much our organization cultures have changed over the last century.

The first reported worker to leave his brain at the door was a man called Schmidt. Taylor uses the example as the first case in his book. Handling pig iron is very simple work. The pig-iron carrier picks up a pig (i.e., the crude iron casting) weighing about 92 pounds, walks for a short distance and empties it. Taylor studied the workers and chose one he thought would be physically able to do significantly more work. Taylor's first words to Schmidt are famous: 'Are you a high-priced man?' he asked. In the dialogue Taylor recounts in his book, it is clear Schmidt did not understand what he was being asked. Taylor explained that he wanted to know if Schmidt was happy with his earnings or whether he was keen to earn more, describing those people who were happy to stay at the usual rate as 'cheap fellows.'

Responding to criticism that he was rough towards Schmidt, Taylor said that for the 'mentally sluggish type' his attitude was appropriate and not unkind, because it focused Schmidt's attention on the possibility of making more money and away from the task that Schmidt would be asked to perform, which in isolation he might consider impossible.

Schmidt was told to do exactly as instructed. When he was told to pick up a pig and walk, he would do so; when he was told to sit down and rest, he sat down. He was told not to talk back, just to do as he was told. Taylor made it clear that high-priced men did just that. Schmidt succeeded. He increased his productivity almost fourfold; his wages rose from $1.15 to $1.85 a day. One by one, all the pig handlers were trained by industrial engineers; all improved to a similar level. It worked. Taylor gave the workers a better method. He provided the brains.

Taylor gave the world a systematic way of tackling method— how the work works. But he could not foresee that the way he did it had what would become a systemic weakness. He made the separation of decision making from work the defining relationship between manager and worker. As in the quote by Konosuke Matsushita at the beginning of this book, management was assumed to have the good ideas and the worker's role was to carry them out. This was acceptable in the organizational cultures of early-20th-century America, especially at a time when many workers spoke no English. And it was a real step forward. Taylor's methods boosted jobs and wages and increased industrial output.

TAYLORISM IS THE BEDROCK OF COMMAND-AND-CONTROL THINKING

Because Taylorism worked, making mass production possible, it dominated approaches to the design and management of work. It still does. It is the bedrock of command-and-control thinking. It is institutionalized in the private sector and in the process of being institutionalized in public sector organizations. In the private sector, we still have 'organization and methods' and 'industrial engineering' departments; today they are often called by more modern names, but they fulfill the same function: specification. In the public sector, we have a massive and growing variety of forms of specification. Common to both private and public sectors, however, is the fact that the specifiers who govern organizational life have moved away from Taylor's idea that their specifications should be based on a scientific approach. Today specifiers are appointed on the basis of experience. Deming knew what this meant. He wrote: 'Without theory, experience has no meaning. Without theory, one has no questions to ask. Hence without theory there is no learning.'

As time-and-motion departments have become less popular, there has been a similar drift away from Taylor's requirement to be scientific. The methods employed in service organizations are based on rudimentary concepts that are flawed. Industry associations and government organizations promulgate 'best practice' ideas, assessment tools and methods, specifications and regulations, none of which is based in theory and knowledge. Ultimately, all are based on opinion. Rather than being catalysts to increased productivity, these 'methods' often stifle and obviate improvement.

Perhaps the fall in popularity of the time-and-motion expert was caused by association: these specialists were often required to support management as they battled with unions over wages, incentives, work methods, job specialization and measurement systems. The evidence presented in this book could well form the basis of new versions of the same battles. There are already instances where the application of the ideas in this book has led to union representatives encouraging managers to adopt the ideas on a wider scale.

Today's managers will tell you that they encourage and indeed incentivize people to show initiative. They want people to bring their brains to work. They expect those who have to carry tasks to 'find ways' of doing them better. But they do not behave as though it is method that is paramount.

Although we might not lament the passing of the industrial engineer, we should lament the subsequent lack of emphasis on knowledge. Of course, industrial engineering is not dead yet, and many would now argue that the industrial engineer no longer sees the worker as an extension of a machine and instead recognizes them as capable of being involved in the design of work.

Many of the industrial engineer's techniques are of value to all: flowcharting, measurement and so on are essential to understanding and improving performance. Some of the techniques, however, still cause industrial strife. For example, work quotas have become a major cause of suboptimization in service centers.

The value of theory was Taylor's contribution. That we needed and benefited from a focus on method is unquestionable. But the legacy of Taylorism was the separation of roles.

BREAKING TAYLOR'S MODEL

When Deming first presented his ideas to American business leaders after World War II, their view was they could get away with the costs of poor quality in an ever-growing market. Otherwise, how could manufacturing have survived over the last century? Taiichi Ohno broke the mold in manufacturing. The ideas represented in this book break the mold in the design and management of service organizations. The case for integrating decision making with work is even more important for service organizations because it is the only means by which they can absorb the variety of demand. To do that, people need method. The method that Taylor created needs to be brought back to life, but this time where the work is done.

Taylor provides evidence that Schmidt wasn't so dumb. In his interviews when selecting Schmidt, Taylor learned that with his meager wages Schmidt had bought a small plot of ground and was building his own house. What might Schmidts achieve if they have in their hands the means for improvement? What are the potential costs of not giving Schmidts the means? Although Schmidt certainly became a high-priced man, perhaps he could have become something else.

APPENDIX

The better way to improve public services

In the summer of 2003, the British Prime Minister Tony Blair acknowledged that perhaps British government ministers had been too 'managerial' and 'technocratic' in their approach to public sector improvement. Other spokespeople for his government said the emphasis on targets and 'delivery' should be balanced with the Labour party's values. What this means is unclear, but what is sure is that the British government knows its public sector is not improving.

Asked about their achievements in public sector reform, British government ministers point to increases in investment. More money for employing more people resources—teachers, policemen and social workers. More money for specific projects, particularly IT. At the same time, ministers are uneasily aware that the investments are not being matched by results. For this, they blame everyone but themselves. They argue that the public sector is dominated by what they call 'producer interests' that are 'unresponsive to the needs of the consumer.' British government ministers think of public sector managers as needing to be 'shaken up,' inducing motivation to avoid failure—being ranked at the bottom, for example. Ministers and their agents also prescribe actions and threaten that if public sector managers don't act, officials will decide for them.[62]

Demonstrating their unquestioning belief in command and control, British government ministers believe that public sector managers need to have 'buttons pressed' and 'levers pulled' by those who know better in the center; they believe they need to make public sector managers do what they otherwise would not do. Talking of his frustration in trying to modernize the public sector, Tony Blair famously declared: 'I have learned the limits of government.' He talked of his scars from dealing with public sector reform. What he fails to realize is that it is a problem of method—successful change by foisting opinion-based initiatives on people through an upward-facing hierarchy is logically and practically impossible. Those who need to be the agents of change look only to satisfying their masters. The focus of their effort should be in the other direction, on the work.

Aware that change by command and control from the center is failing, British government ministers are currently introducing the idea of giving greater latitude and flexibility to 'high performers' who will determine for themselves how outcomes are achieved. But this is not a substantial change. To achieve what ministers now call 'earned autonomy', public sector organizations must first demonstrate compliance with specifications that themselves hinder performance. Public sector managers have to 'cheat' to be free. This is no kind of freedom at all.

Government will be held directly responsible for the state of public services—indeed British government ministers have asked the electorate to judge them on this basis. But they are in a bind. They cannot let go of outcomes, nor will they let go of close monitoring of achievement. They are in a bind that is insoluble if they remain within their current paradigm. Illustrative of their dilemma is that British government ministers now tie themselves in knots trying to reconcile centrally set standards with 'empowerment' of those charged with delivery on the front line. In effect, they are saying: 'You are empowered unless of course you are not.' The standards themselves are part of the problem. Just like command-and-control managers in the private sector, they cannot see that the block to empowerment is the very regime they enforce.

TARGETS JUST DON'T WORK

In 2003, a British Parliamentary select committee carried out a review of the impact of targets on public sector performance improvement.[63] Perhaps because I had been banging on British government ministers' doors, I was asked to give evidence. I was the only person submitting evidence who recommended that targets should be abolished. Nearly everyone gave evidence underlining the shortcomings of targets, but they stopped short of the logical conclusion, that they should be got rid of, because they believed like Margaret Thatcher in another context that 'there is no alternative.' They are obliged to repeat (we know the mantra by now) that targets would work if they were 'done right'—that is, they were 'realistic' and involved those who were to achieve them. In neither case, of course, is there anything about method or knowledge.

When asked for evidence of distortions to the system caused by targets, those who gave evidence from the front line gave copious examples and those representing the top of the various hierarchies claimed they were minimal and controlled. At my own hearing, a police chief told the committee how his organization audited crime information to ensure there was no 'cheating.' He was decent enough to accept that in my terms the auditing was waste, but he remained unaware of the distortions present in his own system. By chance I met one of his officers the next day. I said I'd been with his chief; he asked why, I explained what the select committee was about, and he said: 'So I guess the chief was there to talk about the scams.' And out they all tumbled. The one I liked the most was: report a 'domestic' (husband and wife fighting) as two assaults—each on the other—and record them as detected with no further proceedings. Apparently it does wonders for the detection rate.

People who work in public services want to focus on their purpose. Police want to prevent and detect crime; doctors and nurses want to treat patients. They need help with measures and means, not cajoling to focus on arbitrary activities through hierarchical dictates. Managers in our public services describe themselves as being on 'P 45[64] warnings' should they fail to meet their targets. As a consequence, they drive their workers crazy. (A P 45 is the form British workers receive when they leave an employer.) Their purpose has become 'serve the hierarchy' and 'meet the targets,' rather than 'improve the work.' This is why public sector workers get disheartened, demoralized and sometimes obstructive. But it is nothing to do with 'producer interests.' People are prevented from focusing on purpose by the requirement to concentrate on what the hierarchy has decided is important.

SUBOPTIMIZING LOCAL-AUTHORITY SERVICES

I showed how targets suboptimized performance in housing repairs in Chapter 5. It is the same with all local authority and housing services. Local authorities have a wide range of discrete services, each of which is subject to its own targets regime. The consequences are distortions of purpose that suboptimize performance of every service. Take planning. The British government target is that 80 percent of domestic planning applications should be determined in eight weeks. To ensure compliance, many planning departments simply refuse applications rather than work with applicants to draw up an application that would pass. This frustrates citizens and adds to costs (a second or third application is failure demand). Using the methods described in this book, all planning applications can be dealt with in much less time than the government targets, satisfying applicants and lowering the costs of administration (satisfying citizens again). But the targets and reporting regime casts a fog that makes the 'seeing' of such solutions impossible. Only courageous local authority managers employ these methods, because it means, first, putting aside the inappropriate measures, then studying the work, establishing measures that help in understanding and improving the work, making the changes—and finally, explaining all of this to an inspector who will be looking for something else.

In Chapter 8, I described the way a series of initiatives—ISO 9000, Excellence, IiP and Charter Mark—have been foisted on the public sector. They had (and have) no beneficial impact, but they were nothing compared to the terror of the targets regime. The plethora of targets came as part of what is called the 'Best Value' regime. Best Value was policy created on the fly; when a British government minister was asked what was to replace compulsory competitive tendering, the reply was 'best value.' When it all started, I wrote about Best Value as having bad measures and no method.[65] Best Value is enshrined in legislation; it is a statutory duty for all public services to review performance in accordance with the Best Value specifications. This has meant the creating of a measurement and reporting bureaucracy and a burdensome inspection regime. None of this effort is of value; it represents waste on a massive scale.

Most pernicious of all, many government targets specify method—how work will be carried out. For example, the 'Best Value' target to have '100 percent of legally permissible services e-enabled by 2005' should concern us all. It is a specification driven by opinion, not knowledge. It has led all local authorities to spend large amounts of money on call centers and computers. The majority of calls into local government call centers are failure demand. The British government's strategy results in the institutionalization of waste by moving failure demand to a call center and treating this as 'normal' work. The consequences are high costs, poor services and tremendous obstacles to future service improvement. The better way is to begin by improving the service—planning, housing, road repairs—to remove or at least greatly reduce the failure demand. Then and only then is it appropriate to investigate whether the remaining (value) demand is best handled centrally or by specialist service. The dreadful irony is that local authorities that take this route will improve service and reduce costs—but risk being punished for not meeting the government specification.

Managers conducting Best Value reviews almost always conclude that 'more resources are needed.' This simply demonstrates lack of method. Every public service I know has significant scope for improvement with no extra resources. The services are full of waste that has been designed in. Public sector managers need help with method for seeing it and designing it out.

Benefits processing is an example of bad design. Moreover, it is a good (i.e., shocking) illustration of the way in which government specifications of work method actually prevent improvement.

Requirements for managing benefits are detailed in manuals produced by the Department of Work and Pensions (DWP). In conformance with chancellor Gordon Brown's insistence that there shall be no investment without reform, they lay down centrally specified alterations to the way benefits processing is managed. In return, the chancellor has made available more than £200 million (approximately $387 million) for investment, mainly in IT. I am confident he will not get a return. The specification makes the work worse, as I shall illustrate.

Benefits processing is a system with three high-level elements: a front office, where claimants are dealt with; a back office, where the benefits are calculated and paid; and a means to connect them. This is usually electronic, in the form of a document image processor,[66] through which documents are scanned and passed to a central database where they are stored. As with all specifications, those who write them think of things they can measure which seem consistent with doing things properly. Although there is a massive number of standards and targets in the specification (all of which need establishing and monitoring, creating a bureaucracy), here are the essential few that suboptimize the system:

- Front office: the front office is measured on time to see claimants and time to respond to correspondence
- Back office: the percentage of claims paid in a certain time

Why should they be so damaging? They seem reasonable things to focus on. Yet, as in every public service I have studied, such measures actually create disorder. When staff study benefits processing as a system, they discover that there is a high level of front-office failure demand consisting of progress-chasing and, more importantly, waste ('dirty input'): applicants failing to produce all the documentation needed to settle a claim. At this point, to meet their service requirements, front-office staff send the incomplete documentation for scanning and instruct the applicant to return with the missing paper. Document image processors—'scanners'—require that work be sorted and batched into like work types—driver's licenses must be scanned as a batch, bank statements likewise and so on. This means applicants' information is separated and thus needs to be reconnected later electronically. Inevitably, documents are poorly scanned, duplicated, lost or wrongly sorted; applicants are frequently asked to bring in things they have already been provided. In the back office, the clock for the performance measure begins when all of the required information is to hand. Achieving this is hampered by the way work is designed and managed.

To open up these problems, you need to start by looking at the end-to-end time for processing benefits from the applicants' point of view, establishing a measure of capability. Figure A1 is the capability chart for one local authority.

The capability measure shows that under present system conditions it could take up to 134 days to process a benefit from the applicants' point of view. Anything from 1 day to 134 days can be expected from this system. The causes of variation are in the way the work is designed and managed, in other words, the Department of Work and Pensions specification.

The local authority whose data is reported above redesigned benefits payment processing using the principles described

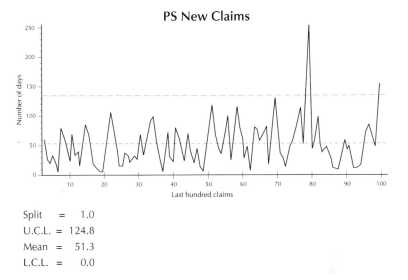

Split   =   1.0
U.C.L. = 124.8
Mean   =   51.3
L.C.L. =   0.0

Figure A1: End-to-end time to manage benefits

in this book, removing all major causes of variation. It now processes all benefits in 8 days, against a reported national average of 60 days. As with planning applications, the essence of the solution is to control the work at the start of the flow. If planning and benefits applications arrive 'clean,' they flow easily and time is reduced. As a consequence, quality and capacity improve. Nothing in the DWP specification could have helped people to make these improvements; following the specification obviates improvement. As with all government specifications, the focus is on activity measurement. Managing activity always suboptimizes flow.

SUBOPTIMIZING POLICING

Like local authorities, British police forces now have centralized call centers—'call receipt units'—to take calls. As with local authorities, these are a British government-inspired 'solution.' And as with local authorities again, when you study the call centers as part of an end-to-end system, you discover high levels of failure demand caused by the way the work is designed. As we have come to expect, the focus is on activity and targets—response times, call handling capacity and the like. Not surprisingly, the flow of work is atrocious. I once recommended that the Home Secretary, who is responsible for policing in the UK, go out with a 'response officer' (one who deals with 'non-emergency' events). He did not take up my suggestion. If he had, he would have found, as I have, that much of the officer's time is wasted doing things he should not be doing.

The problems all start at the front of the system, where demand is handled—as with call centers in the private sector—as 'units of production.' To maximize 'efficiency,' British government ministers had the idea that 'non-police' work should be done by civilians. The result in many police forces is a fragmented work flow, many handovers and, tragically, a loss of intelligence about what is going on on the ground.

Although intelligence is lost in response operations, the 'national intelligence system' ensures it is dissipated on a wider front. The system is designed to keep intelligence *out* of operations; it is located in the management factory, where those responsible specify how police officers on the beat should behave. If the directives don't make sense to the police officer, too bad. The job is to do as you are told.

Although policemen and women are convinced that their time is not being employed in the most productive way, the focus of the system is on meeting government targets. Response times and detections/arrests (for particular crimes) are the priorities, so people's ingenuity is engaged in making those numbers. Currently in some forces there is an emphasis on community policing. However, there are no measures or targets applying to community policing, so when overtime is under pressure or a target needs to be met, community police are given other duties. In some police forces, community police spend as little as 20 percent of their time on their intended duties. Because of the focus on meeting targets, police systems create records of crimes and incidents. In many forces there is no systematic attention given to offenders. Yet this is the kind of preventative work that could cut crime and make people feel safer.

I heard from a man who got a job as a reserve policeman. His force doesn't work by tying all of the relevant information about criminals and their activities together—it responds to incidents. So he decided to set up his own database to track offenders. Because he is lowest of the low, he is not allowed to access data or contribute to it; he can only send in reports. Like many others, his police force has a 'drive' on 'visibility.' Policemen and women record the hours they spend being visible. The same occurred many years ago in a police force in the south. A survey among the community showed people wanted to see police out and about—at the train station in the morning, at the school gate, when out shopping and so on. Unbelievable as it may seem, the force bussed policemen around to the different locations. It didn't take long to demoralize everyone. The British government-inspired practice of seeking feedback from communities and acting on it has led to similar nonsenses in all public services. What matters to the public is how they get treated when they transact with these services. If you call the police for whatever reason and get a lousy experience, you talk about it. When you study how police systems respond to demand, it is no surprise that people have lost confidence in their police. Although British government ministers trumpet 'localism,' they have dictated a centralist, remote design.

Just as with other public services, to improve performance police need to learn how to design their system against demand—demands from the public and demands in terms of crime and disorder. It is of no value to know about the achievement of arbitrary targets, but it would be of immense value to know about the predictability of crime and disorder (demand) by time and geography. Such measures can be used to determine how to design the work and used to track improvement. Successful prevention or detection work should show through in changes in demand data. Instead of sucking data up to 'intelligence' units in the management factory, data about the work (reducing crime and disorder) should be used where the work is done. You would have thought that the police, above all, would have understood that intelligence is most needed on the beat.

Most police officers I have met would rather their job had a sense of purpose. Doctors have the same problem.

SUBOPTIMIZING HEALTH

In his parting address to the British Medical Association in July 2003, chairman Dr. Ian Bogle made a scathing attack on the British government's attempts to improve the health service. He described the 'creeping morale-sapping erosion of doctor's clinical autonomy brought about by micromanagement from Whitehall.' (Whitehall is where the British government's chief offices are located.) His argument was that centralization stifles innovation through audits and dictates. He is right. He complained about 'guidelines and protocols' because they stop doctors doing what is right for patients. He said: 'If you remove responsibility, you remove the job.' Who wants their doctor to 'leave his/her brain at the door'?

Dr. Bogle described the health service as being management 'by spreadsheets and tick-boxes' (i.e., checklists) full of 'target-setting and production-line values.' His complaint was that the interventions were not evidence-based; that satisfying the regime distorted its priorities. Only weeks before Dr. Bogle's address, reports showed how hospitals distorted their systems to meet accident and emergency (A&E) targets—extra staff were brought in to meet the targets during the week government officials were measuring them. This resulted in delays to other services, cancellation of treatments and operations; never mind, the hospitals met their targets.

The target for A&E departments is that they should deal with 90 percent of patients within four hours of arrival. British government ministers say this is 'putting the patient first.' Yet there are many patients that need to spend more than four hours in A&E: asthma patients and suspected heart-attack patients need observation and tests that require extra time. To comply with targets, patients can be sent home and be put at risk. Hospitals will admit patients into other wards rather than waiting to discharge them, so many patients are referred up the line to wait somewhere else in the hospital. Inappropriate admissions create bottlenecks in the wards. All such distortions (and more) are caused by targets. Targets ensure the patient is not put first.

Dr. Bogle charged that the investments were not impacting service. He noted that the Commission for Health Improvement (now subsumed into the Healthcare Commission) and the Audit Commission had found the same. The Audit Commission found inaccuracies in waiting-list data from one-third of hospitals. Other reports claim more. Most inaccuracies involve inventive ways of disguising the true number of patients waiting for an operation. If a hospital fails to meet its targets, it may be downgraded in its 'star rating,'[67] affecting morale and weakening bargaining power with health officials. Dr. Bogle asserted that targets make people dishonest. It is easy to see why. He said doctors had refused the then 'new deal' offered to them because the extra work envisaged was to meet targets: The work did not have a rationale in clinical evidence. Dr. Bogle's pleas for a return to rational behavior fell on deaf ears. The very next day, the Prime Minister's office made it clear targets were here to stay.

I have not worked in the NHS (the National Health Service, the UK's free public health service) in the sense of studying the work and helping people to change its design. I have held two 'master classes' for NHS people, both of which came to the same conclusions. When you think about the NHS as a system, it has four high-level components, shown in Figure A2.

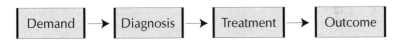

Figure A2: Healthcare as a (high-level) system

In the master classes, I discovered that there were no data for boxes one and four: the type and frequency of demand and clinical outcome. Such data may exist in projects conducted in the management factory, but they are certainly not in evidence where the work is done. At the same time, there is plenty of evidence of the government regime interfering with the way the work works in boxes two and three, diagnosis and treatment.

The same is true for the ambulance service, where I was given an opportunity to visit and study for two days. I am going to describe what I learned, but I do so with the reservation that this is the only case material in the book that is not from an organization that has been changed; my assessment in two days may not be reliable. Nevertheless, it is in line with the purpose of this book to raise questions to which there are not yet answers (to my knowledge) in the health service.

The first time the ambulance service came to my notice was some years ago when I overheard a journalist talking to an ambulance chief on TV. The ambulance chief had made significant improvements in response times by moving the ambulances to geographic locations where patients were most likely to make demands. Excellent, I thought, design against demand: if demand is predictable by geography, move the ambulances to meet it. The journalist then went to another ambulance chief and asked why he didn't do the same thing. 'It wouldn't work here,' was the reply. I have told this story to leaders and asked: 'How would a good leader respond to the journalist's question?' The answer is: 'Where is our demand data? Do we have it by geography? If we don't have any, get it.' And to the journalist: 'Good question. I'll be back in a week.' Some leaders seem to think they shouldn't be tough about such things. I like leaders who are tough about getting data and knowledge.

Years later, in the summer of 2003 when I visited the ambulance service, I found only two or three services were employing this simple practice. I thought it was a no-brainer. It obviously didn't strike the other services in the same way. In their defense, *their* leaders—British government ministers—were not asking the question I would have asked. They were not asking for data about demand—they were asking for data about targets and their achievement. Unfortunately, targets have little relation to real performance. Instead, they drive dysfunctional behavior among managers and subvert the system's ability to achieve its purpose.

The national target is for ambulances to arrive at 'Category A' (the most critical) incidents[68] within eight minutes in 75 percent of cases. Why 75 percent? There is no rational reason. When the target was first set, ambulance managers argued that the clock should only start ticking when the work was under their control. Understandable, but wrong. The process should be measured end-to-end from the patient's point of view. But rather than become embroiled in when to start the clock, managers should have been questioning the usefulness of the measure.

What is the purpose of the ambulance service? I think it is to save lives or otherwise solve the problems that cause people to dial 999 (the UK equivalent of 911). The purpose is not to answer every call in eight minutes. Before even considering time as a measure, it is necessary to think about the nature of the work.

The eight-minute target was set because thousands of people who experience cardiac arrest could be saved if they were reached and treated quickly. I asked: 'What is the demand for cardiac arrest?' the answer was around 1 to 2 percent. It seems strange to me to design a whole system around 1 or 2 percent of its demand. I asked: 'Are there other life-threatening conditions where time is critical?' Different people had different views—estimates varied between 8 and 20 percent. The important point, however, is that no one knows, because the service does not study the type and frequency of demand. A time measure should only be used where time is critical to the purpose. Even then the time measure should be subordinate to the primary measure—in this case, clinical outcome—because it makes no sense to para-medics to have 'succeeded' because they got there in 8 minutes and the patient died and 'failed' when they got there after 8 min-utes and the patient was saved.

Successive consumer reports[69] have shown that the chances of survival for cardiac-arrest patients are poor throughout the UK. The service is not improving. Publicity over slow response prompted British government ministers to put pressure on man-agers to deliver a faster service. As a consequence, managers behave in dysfunctional ways. The UK Commission for Health Improvement reported evidence of inaccurate reporting or infor-mation, bullying by managers and the dubious use of financial incentives to improve 'staff performance.' Like the government, whose philosophy they share, ambulance managers see the prob-lem as staff performance. But it's not: it is a system problem.

As the new regime went on, the Department of Health proudly announced that more services had hit the 75 percent tar-get. The statistics said one thing, but the reality was another. A *Which?* report[70] revealed that 'eight minutes' meant different things to different services. A response recorded as eight minutes could take as long as nine, ten, eleven minutes or longer. The report also provided data on clinical performance, showing huge variation between health services. This is to be expected as the predictable result of tampering. Unfortunately, managers don't know it. They would only find out if they ran true end-to-end times in a capability chart.

The *Which?* findings were backed up by the Commission for Health Improvement, which decided that start times were so inconsistent that it couldn't compare response times between trusts. Yet the department makes such comparisons every year. The reviews also found that 'cheating' (or 'gaming' as they term it in the health service) was ubiquitous. The minister denied it, as British government ministers always do: having demanded results that they can qualify as 'improvements,' they then deny the existence of, and their responsibility for, the adverse consequences of the tampering that results.

There are more important problems with response-time targets than cheating. Any demand for an ambulance has to be classified at the point of transaction. When you talk to paramedics and ask: 'Do you attend "Category B" incidents that should have been "Category A" and vice versa?,' sure enough—they do. This is the inevitable result of force-fitting a wide variety of demands into three categories and making the choice by machine or low-cost operator. We do not know whether the incidents that 'fail' the 75 percent target are the same or different to those that 'passed'—only a capability chart would help distinguish between the two. When managers (and government ministers) intervene without this knowledge, they are likely to make the system less stable, not more.

To add to all the other problems, the British government has saddled the ambulance service with a management factory of outstanding proportions. In my short visit I noticed the following 'specification and inspection' organizations sitting above it: the Commission for Health Improvement, the Health and Safety Executive, the Clinical Negligence Scheme for Trusts, the Risk-Pooling Scheme for Trusts, the Audit Commission ('value for money' auditing), Control Assurance Standards, Patient Focus (for general practitioner and patient views), the Workforce Development Confederation ('improving working lives') . . . and I'm sure I didn't find them all.

It makes me wonder: How many people in the ambulance service actually do the work (solving people's problems) and how many others are doing what else and to what ends? How many people and how much of their time is consumed by the management factory? How and how well does the work of the management factory help (or hinder) the system? I think you would find that most of management's time is eaten up by activities in the management factory. It should be spent working on the work with those who do it.

A correspondent put it this way:

We spend all our time preparing for or responding to inspections because our bosses' corporate managerialism requires

*that we chase the next 'badge' to put on the trust letterhead.
I shall leave you to imagine who gets the blame when these
awards are not achieved, and where patient care is on the list
of priorities.*

I went out with an ambulance crew. In this service, ambulances
were assigned to geographic 'hot spots.' This might be sensible
from one point of view, but to the crew it just came as an instruc-
tion to go and sit in a filling station. For them, the prospect was two
hours doing nothing—and without the comforts of the station to
boot. They were despondent. They told me that the study of
demand was a purely management factory project that had taken
place a couple of years before. Even on brief acquaintance it was
clear that the demand data should have been current and running
in the front line where it could be used for learning and improvement. Even sitting in a gas station would be bearable if it was
learning to solve problems rather than just doing as you were told.

Talking to the crew, I soon learned that their training bore
no relation to their daily routine. Like service center workers,
they were not trained against demand. Few of the calls they
answered required life-critical paramedic skills. The system's
response to demand was effectively specified: two specialists in
a fully equipped vehicle attended every incident. It was easy to
see that, judged against demand, the response was usually
overspecified. Some ambulance services are experimenting with
'rapid-response' vehicles, but without good data about demand
and outcome it is hard to see what can reliably be learned from
such experiments.

And, just as Dr. Bogle had described, I found clinical protocols interfering with patient care. When you ask paramedics, 'Do
you ever find the protocol does not really match what is best for
the patient?' the answer is 'yes.' All medical personnel face the
same problem. It is little different from the 'schedule of rates'
dilemma in housing repairs (Chapter 5); any attempt to specify
every action is doomed. If you could achieve it, the manual would
be so large it would be unworkable. The inherent variety in
demand requires the system to be designed to absorb it, not force
it through pre-specified routines. Ambulance staff are judged by
adherence to protocols; deviating from a specification requires a
report to justify it. We can agree with Dr. Bogle that this is

morale-sapping. Instead of talking with patients to agree to the best course of action, medical personnel are first concerned to follow the protocol; not to do so could invite a claim. It is no surprise that claims on the health service are rising—the system might be designed to attract them.

While I was travelling with the ambulance crew, I discussed with them probable causes of variation in response times. The volume of demand, availability of vehicles, location of demand (and hence distance), road and traffic conditions, and the clarity of information taken from the caller are all likely candidates. If demand by geography is predictable, moving the ambulances is one of the few things under the service's control. The point is, assigning blame, as these organizations do, with forms, meetings and reports, is pointless and demoralizing where the means for improvement are not in the workers' control. As with so many other examples, the bureaucracy around targets does nothing to improve the system; it makes it worse.

Any leader in the ambulance service ought to be passionately interested in the type and frequency of demand. As in all systems, the greatest leverage will be had from understanding demand and designing the system to meet it. In the short time I had I saw demands that might be better served by a completely different response. Understanding demand would also open the window on creating 'joined-up' (i.e., integrated) services, something the government talks about but has no method for. Ambulance services get demands that reflect failures of other services. Some demands cut across organizational boundaries. Only by understanding the 'what and why' of current performance against purpose for all major demands can you get to a position of knowledge and subsequent improvement.

For all major demands, leaders would then need capability data about achievement of purpose. For all demands, this means data about outcome, for some it will mean time. Leaders should not wait for or specify a computer system to gather these data; they should find whatever practical means they have to do so. The data should be tested for usability: Do the metrics pass the test of a good measure? Leaders and their workers should begin experimenting with method—whom to send, with what, and so on, focusing on clinical outcome as the primary criterion of success and improvement. It would restore morale and improve the system.

There is, alas, little chance of this happening. Change of any significance is controlled by the top of the management factory, the Department of Health. To get anything done requires persuading those who have power but no knowledge. Moreover, a change of this order would disenfranchise the various specification and inspection organizations. The inertia for continuing suboptimization is designed in. The management factory is healthy and growing as the health service sickens.

We now read reports that hospital doctors are being forced to slash the time they spend with patients as health-service managers resort to stopwatch techniques to deliver targets.[71] This is the embodiment of what Dr. Bogle called 'production-line values.' There are now allegedly more managers than beds in the health service. As the management community grows, we can expect to see more 'managerialism.' Here is just one example:

Researchers at Manchester University analyzed 15 studies on medical errors in primary care, including unpublished work by the Medical Protection Society that found 63 percent of all medical legal action arose from GP errors. Errors occurred in 0.8 percent of consultations, whereas errors in diagnosis and subsequent prescription resulted in up to 78 percent of all problems. The UK government[72] is to introduce a system of aviation-style near-miss reports for family doctors in an attempt to reduce medical errors. GPs will be expected to report mistakes to the National Patient Safety Agency.

Mayor Lakhani, of the Royal College of General Practitioners, said that he was concerned about the level of error. 'With healthcare becoming more complex, with the fragmentation of services, errors will become an even more important issue.'

He should have said that with the fragmentation of services, the occurrence of errors will be more likely. The risk of error increases as managerialism takes hold. And as risk increases, British government ministers introduce risk management as a mandatory exercise for all public sector organizations (and those in the private sector which are subject to regulation).

A correspondent wrote:

In a meeting of health-service managers, a representative of the NHS Modernization Agency made it clear he understood how damaging targets could be. I suggested that measures of demand would be a better starting place. He told me the NHS always looks at 'activity' data, and virtually never at 'demand' data, and he asked all in the room to keep his comments confidential.

Even those charged with helping with improvement are shackled, emotionally and intellectually, to the mad regime. The good people will leave.

What would Taiichi Ohno have made of the government's approach to improving the health service? British government ministers say that capacity needs to be increased and so are investing significant extra resources. Ohno taught that capacity equals work plus waste. By adding more resources, the government intends the system to 'do more work,' in Ohno's formula. But he would insist that the better way is to remove waste; adding resources to a wasteful system just compounds inefficiency.

But 'waste-busting' initiatives won't help in a system that is managed and measured with targets. The targets are themselves a major cause of waste, consuming people's time in artificial activity and, worse, deflecting their attention from what they ought to be doing. Ohno's insight is that waste can only be removed when managers learn to manage the overall flow of work rather than functions within it. This comes as no surprise to the people who do the work—some health authorities have radically improved the way they respond to patients' conditions by redesigning their processes to cut out multiple visits and waiting. Simply, patients get what they need more quickly. To the surprise of traditionally minded 'production' managers—who assume that putting expertise at the point of transaction will increase costs—this results in lower costs and improved service. Similar results have been achieved in a variety of local-authority services. But to get to results like these means ignoring targets, which are functional and activity-related, and instead measuring flow in terms that matter to customers. These kinds of initiatives will not show up in the government's measures because they are based on flow, not measures of individual functions like numbers of operations cancelled or appointments met within specified times—the things being targeted. To concentrate on function always impedes flow, a paradox that managers find difficult to come to terms with.

The British government promises it will pay attention to 'the customers' experience' of the health service. Patients would prefer that they paid attention to how well the service treats and prevents disease. Patients and staff do not need charters, visions, values or, for that matter, any of the rest of the 'modern' management ideas being promulgated by the UK government.

When he took over as secretary of state for health, John Reid said the patient must come first and that the patient should be the basis for all measures. In which case he and other ministers should review their measures, for in every example I have experience of government targets are . . . [distorting, etc.]. In every example I know, British government targets are distorting the system and damaging the delivery of service. Furthermore, UK government-inspired specifications like e-enabled services in local authorities, benefits standards, clinical protocols in health care, dumb down the service providers, impede the flow of work—making service worse and cost higher—and damage relations between the service provider and those being served. The measures the government has introduced are producing the exact opposite effect of that intended.

SUBOPTIMIZATION THROUGH SPECIFICATIONS AND MONITORING

British government ministers make change through specifications (commands) and monitoring (controls). Money follows the specifications. This is a major source of irritation to the consultants who work with the Vanguard methods. Can you imagine, for example, knowing how to improve service and reduce costs in a local authority and being confronted with the reality that the funding for any 'improvement' initiative is specifically tied to purchasing information and telephone technologies—things that will add to cost and worsen service if implemented without first changing the nature of demand? The money doesn't follow improvement, it follows specifications; the two are not the same.

Because the money follows specifications, the expenditure and activities need to be reported and accounted for.

The Guardian (UK newspaper) reported[73] how a man running a Drug Action Team (DAT)—whose purpose is to deal with drug problems—quit because he could no longer stand the waste and bureaucracy. His work was dictated by 44 different funding streams, each with its own detailed guidance and micro-targets from the center. Each required a detailed business plan and quarterly reports back to the center. He was obliged to sign endless service agreements with every local provider, which had its own micro-targets and was obliged to send quarterly reports back to him so he could collate them and pass them back to the center. He was to follow 9 planning grids with 82 objectives. The funding was always announced too late for planning, handed over too late to be spent on the right things, and finally spent for spending's sake to prevent it being reclaimed by the center. Staff were hired and trained and then suddenly fired when funding or targets were switched by the center (or they just quit because they couldn't stand it any more). He estimated he and his staff spent only 40 percent of their time organizing services for drug users— the rest of their time was consumed by producing paper plans and reports for Whitehall (i.e., the British government).

Talking about the government, he said: 'They don't know very much about drugs but they do know about management and monitoring and data collection. So that's what they do.' Actually they know nothing (of use) about management. They know about specifying, monitoring and data collection.

I have yet to find a British government-inspired specification that is based on knowledge. They are all based on opinion. The implementation of these opinions makes performance worse, not better.

Take money laundering as another revealing, if depressing, example. British government ministers believed that the best chance of catching serious criminals was at the point when they tried to launder the proceeds of, or means for, their evil deeds. Accordingly, the UK Proceeds of Crime Act (2002) makes staff in financial services organizations personally responsible for reporting suspicious transactions to the national criminal intelligence service. As a result, the British police are receiving more and more such reports—60,000 in 2002—the volume increasing threefold over the last two years. It is expected to increase further as the regulations take hold.

Unfortunately, the Inland Revenue department (the UK equivalent of the IRS) says that these money-laundering procedures are more likely to catch tax evaders than terrorists. Terrorists take care not to use the complex and unusual transactions that financial services firms are urged to bring to police notice. For their part, managers have no idea whether anything is done with the information they pass on, or if it has any useful effect. Figures show that just 4 percent of their reports turn into investigations and there have only been 129 prosecutions and 50 convictions over the past year. Meanwhile, the regulator is making up for the failure of the Act to trap international criminals by fining financial organizations for non-compliance with the ineffective law. It is only a matter of time before individual employees are charged with a criminal offense.

It is a similar story with benefits payments. Current procedures were drawn up in response to significant fraud. Real fraudsters evade them with ease, but they are quite good at 'catching' old people who forgot to disclose modest savings on previous applications. There is now a significant increase in people turning to Citizen's Advice Bureaus (i.e., UK government services providing the public with legal and financial advice) because they have been disenfranchised by this legislation. People without passports and driver's licenses cannot get service from the financial system. Social exclusion is an unintended consequence of the legislation.

SPECIFICATION AND INSPECTION AS WASTE

When he took over as chairman of the Audit Commission, James Strachan noted that the UK is the most regulated public sector in Europe but not by a long way the best performing. I was hoping he would see the connection. He openly admits that targets are not working, but his remedy is simply to have fewer. This is not a logical position. In his evidence to the British Parliamentary committee investigating targets, Strachan observed that it was normal for managers in the private sector not to achieve all of their targets. Yet for many public service managers, failing to meet targets is viewed as a firing offense.

The growth of the targets and specifications regime has an associated growth in employment of specifiers and inspectors—a vast administrative bureaucracy to monitor it by gathering, collating and reporting information. It is the most pernicious form of waste, consuming enormous resources but adding no value.

Moreover, inspectees are acutely aware that it is the inspectors who hold the whip hand in the relationship. The inspected regularly express concern about the quality of the inspectors and the vulnerability of the process to personal interpretation and error. It is no surprise. It reminds me of a cynical comment about ISO 9000 in the early days: 'People who have little idea can now pontificate on how to run your business.' Current inspector training emphasizes something called 'triangulation.' The idea is that an inspector should not rely on one piece of evidence, but should get it confirmed by two further corroborative observations. In effect, three opinions make a fact.

WHO IS ACCOUNTABLE?

The new 'accountability' regime that has swamped the British public sector is, in truth, a regime of detailed centralized control. The specifications—regulations, instructions, funding-linked initiatives and targets—and inspection, with their internal and external bureaucracies, serve to obstruct the achievement of purpose. Having ensured conformity, record keeping and standardized information provision, government casts the other side of the 'accountability' coin: complaint handling. This, too, requires its own bureaucracy of reporting and monitoring. In addition, it features blame allocation and compensation. The government rationale is the interests of citizens. Paradoxically, the regime undermines the public sector's ability to serve citizens' interests and ensures that more waste is attached to any failure. Fear is a two-edged sword: fear of failing to meet specifications and fear of being blamed for failure.

The government's intention was to make public services accountable to the electorate. Yet the culture of 'accountability' distorts the systems providing services by making them accountable to British government ministers. People who work in them are driven to act in ways that they know are against their real purpose, and when the evidence becomes public knowledge it undermines trust and confidence. British government ministers blame the managers, yet they are the architects of the system.

In July 2003, 14 heads of state, including Tony Blair, met at a 'Progressive Governance Summit' in London. The final communiqué committed the leaders to freedom, justice, fairness, mutual responsibility, protecting people against risk, empowering men and women, growth, equity, innovation, entrepreneurship, public services that put the citizen first, safety, social cohesion, democracy, full employment and children. It believed in tackling causes as well as symptoms and in using evidence of what works instead of dogma. There is no evidence that the UK government, signatory to the communiqué, knows anything about 'by what method' and is unwittingly working against its stated aim.

Of course, many people in government departments and 'improvement' institutions are aware that all is not well. But over time these institutions have naturally become self-serving. If and when they review their impact on economic life, they ask: How should we do what we do better? They do not ask whether they should be doing it at all. To borrow Ackoff's phrase again, this is doing the wrong thing righter, rather than doing the right thing. We now face a very challenging task: the dismantling of the culture and institutions of specification and inspection. It is challenging because we cannot expect those with a vested interest to put a brake on their own activities.

THE FUTURE OF THE SPECIFICATIONS AND INSPECTION REGIME

I recommended to the Public Administration Select Committee that all targets should be removed and recent legislation associated with the 'Best Value' regime be suspended. We should have only one requirement of public sector organizations: that they establish measures that, in their view, help them understand and improve performance. If and when they are inspected they would be required to demonstrate how they have satisfied the requirement and to what effect. The principal advantage of this approach is that it places the locus of control where it needs to be—with those who need to change. It will therefore be more likely to foster innovation than the current regime, which fosters compliance. It will also remove the need to comply with requirements that undermine improvement.

The vast numbers of specification organizations should cease to impose their opinions of 'what good looks like,' and we should ensure managers in the public sector have the means to develop knowledge about operations within their control. British government ministers have recognized the waste associated with serving the demands of the specifiers, but their solution has been to create more bureaucracy by adding a 'filter' whose purpose is to reduce duplication of demands from specifiers to the inspected. It is, to use the phrase once more, to do the wrong thing righter. It is no solution, merely further evidence of the problem.

Getting rid of the specifications and inspection industry is necessary not only because the specifications themselves are faulty, but also because the method of intervention represents a deeper problem; not just what to change, but how to change. If you want managers to change—and surely we all do—would you put the specification as to the nature of that change in the hands of a third party and then employ inspectors to assess whether the managers are compliant? Of course not. There is no guarantee the compliance leads to learning. If managers are to change, the locus of control in that change should be with the learner—the manager and the people who do the work.

The savings associated with the removal of the specification and inspection bureaucracies will be immense. A far smaller budget could be allocated to management education, guidance and support, for it remains the case that public sector management is poor. The current regime only exacerbates this problem. Setting targets cannot and does not magically educate managers about method.

Finally, this change will provide a framework of legitimacy for much of the current improvement work that goes unrecognized in the current regime. I am astonished at the frequency with which I come across good work being done that is not recognized because it does not fit within the specifier's or inspector's framework. The dedicated public sector people who manage to improve their services despite all the obstacles deserve a system that encourages rather than obviates improvement. That is the responsibility of government.

Endnotes

Introduction: There is a better way

1 With acknowledgment to Russell Ackoff for the use of this phrase. For a summary of his work, see: Russell Ackoff, *Ackoff's Best* (John Wiley, 1999).

2 Deming was the first Westerner to question management norms. His seminal work *Out of the Crisis* (Cambridge University Press, 1982) describes the problems caused by command and control.

3 After Frederick Winslow Taylor (1856–1915), the American industrial engineer and author of *The Principles of Scientific Management*, published in 1911. For more on Taylor's legacy, see the Conclusion of this book.

4 Konosuke Matsushita, founder of the Japanese electronics group that includes Panasonic, JVC and Technics, quoted by Richard Pascale in *Managing on the Edge* (Penguin, 1990).

5 The use of the phrase 'systems thinking' should not be confused with others' ideas about organizations as systems. A discussion of other approaches to systems thinking can be found in Chapter 8.

Chapter 1: Once upon a time in manufacturing

6 His seminal work is: Taiichi Ohno, *The Toyota Production System* (Productivity Press, 1988).

7 James Womack, D. Jones and D. Roos, *The Machine That Changed the World* (Macmillan, 1990).

8 Thomas Johnson and Anders Broms, *Profit Beyond Measure* (Nicholas Brealey Publishing, 2000).

9 Johnson and Broms report Ohno as spending time at the River Rouge plant. My sources tell me it was the Highland Park plant that Ohno referred to. The River Rouge plant was the first attempt by Ford to mass-produce variety—my sources tell me the 'flow' there was like spaghetti.

10 *Sensei* is the name given to experts trained in Taiichi Ohno's methods.

11 In *The Machine That Changed the World*.

Chapter 2: The customer service center as a system

12 It is a tragedy that most of the money invested in team-leader training in service centers is spent on 'people management.'

13 For a more detailed explanation of the theory of variation and the use of control charts, see 'The Vanguard Guide to Creating and Using Capability Charts', available at www.lean-service.com.

14 I return to this in Chapter 4.

15 It is difficult to change a mindset through argument. Managers who went to study the flow saw for themselves how sales simply 'dropped out' of the flow through poor design from the customers' point of view. Touching the reality makes it easier to change your point of view.

16 Stability and predictability are important concerns when managing flow. The nature and use of measures for establishing stability and predictability are discussed in Chapter 3.

Chapter 3: Purpose, measures, methods

17 I shall say a lot more about system conditions in Chapter 6.

18 An example of this phenomenon is included at the end of Chapter 4.

19 Taguchi, a Japanese engineer, won the Deming Prize for his work on raising quality and reducing costs in engineering. His quality loss function shows how value to the customer falls as quality declines.

Chapter 4: Better measures, better thinking

20 In defense of accountants, I find most of them take quickly to the ideas in this book, as they are more aware than managers of the flaws in management accounting.

21 Frederick Hertzberg, 'One More Time: How Do You Motivate Employees?,' *Harvard Business Review*, Vol 81, No 1, Jan 2003 (reprinted).

22 This is a favorite argument among government ministers in the UK.

23 'Realistic, Achievable, Worthwhile'

24 Deming was the first person to describe this phenomenon.

Chapter 5: The 'break–fix' archetype

25 The UK government has mandated that all services should be 'e-enabled,' meaning available by electronic or telephony means by 2005. It is a tragic example of a target causing suboptimization. I return to this in the Addendum.

26 In other cases failure demand has been found to run as high as 80 percent.

27 The solution is particular to this example. Other housing repair departments have developed variations on the theme. Method

can and should vary according to local circumstances—design is against demand. The constant is that all measurement is against purpose.

28 You cannot illustrate systems thinking without case material. The reader should not mock the palpable nonsense exposed by taking a systems view. The managers are to be praised, for at least now they know and are able to act with knowledge for improvement.

29 The UK government has itself in much the same position with regulation. It is easy to create a regulation and terribly hard to remove it. What politician would want to be seen to be 'relaxing' something that was set up to prevent something going wrong?

30 This remains a fundamental flaw in ISO 9000 despite the year 2000 revisions.

31 This is a common problem. Managers first need to appreciate systems thinking before they can see alternatives to their current practice. I return to this phenomenon at the end of Chapter 6.

32 The difficulty experienced in getting good data about system performance is indicative of the gap between command-and-control and systems thinking.

33 We borrowed the idea of a clean room from Taiichi Ohno. He taught that when a manufacturing facility was in a total mess it was preferable to start again and learn how to make one unit cleanly. The same method can be applied in service organizations.

34 Rather than 'roll out' the redesign achieved in the clean room, the clean room is expanded as the 'old' system is closed down. New entrants to the clean room need to go through a reeducational loop, helping them see the badness of the 'old' design and the rationale for the clean room. This is important to prevent people taking with them the bad habits inculcated by the 'old' system.

Chapter 6: Learning to see, learning to read

35 Deming preferred 'plan-do-**study**-act.'

36 This is a general problem with management models, which I discuss in Chapter 8.

37 Avoiding the need for documentation. The Financial Services Authority requires documentation of all complaints taking longer than one day to resolve. It reflects an assumption that those that take longer are more important to know about. Not true.

38 In one case service agents would trade their result on the absence score against making their incentive: if they took a week off, their target would be 'pro-rata.' Thus if they had made

75 per cent of their target by week three, the only way to ensure they got the incentive was to take a week off.

39 See: Alfie Kohn, *Punished by Rewards* (Houghton Mifflin, 1993).

40 The normal distribution or Gaussian curve is a convenience dreamed up by statisticians to enable them to use parametric statistics. Few if any human characteristics are normally distributed.

41 Be warned against assuming either that there are real differences between agents or that if they exist they can be attributed to the individuals. As we know, the major causes of variation are in the system—that is, they are management's responsibility. Differences between agents usually points to method.

Chapter 7: Customers—people who can pull you away from the competition

42 It is an interesting feature of fads—people do a variety of things under the same label.

Chapter 8: Do these hold water?

43 Engineering Quality Forum, *The true effectiveness of quality related initiatives in the UK* (2002).

44 For a full discussion of the problems of ISO 9000, see: John Seddon, *The Case Against ISO 9000* (Oak Tree Press, 2000). Also available at www.lean-service.com.

45 For a full discussion of the elements of the excellence model and a comparison of traditional versus systems interpretations, see: 'The Vanguard Guide to Business Excellence', available at www.lean-service.com.

46 Robert Kaplan and David Norton, 'The Balanced Scorecard: Measures That Drive Performance', *Harvard Business Review*, Jan–Feb 1992.

47 The details of this working group are reported in Kaplan and Norton, *The Balanced Scorecard*, (Harvard Business School Press, 1996).

48 'Rule 4' is from Deming's famous funnel experiment. In simple terms it means getting further and further away from what was intended. 'Off on the milky way', is how Deming put it.

49 *Ackoff* (1999) Ibid.

50 Kaoru Ishikawa developed the cause-and-effect diagram as a quality-management process at Kawasaki shipyards. It is a means of systematically exploring all the real and potential causes that result in a single effect. When drawn out it looks like a fishbone—hence its other name.

51 'Black belt' is a clever form of marketing. Who would not be excited at the prospect of becoming one or having many of them?

52 Something I never do. I always assume managers are part of the problem (but not that it is their fault). It is of much greater value to study the work.

53 Will Hutton, *The World We're In* (Abacus, 2003).

54 Jack Welch, *Jack* (Headline, 2001).

55 'Work flow' is a misnomer. Most often work-flow systems create work rather than improve the flow of work.

56 Outcomes from IT investments: 80–90 percent do not meet their performance goals; 80 percent are late and over budget; 40 percent of developments fail or are abandoned; fewer than 25 percent integrate business and technology objectives; just 10–20 percent meet all their success criteria. See: OASIG, Institute of Work Psychology, *Failing to deliver: the IT performance gap* (University of Sheffield 1995).

57 Robert Flood, *Rethinking the Fifth Discipline* (Routledge, 1999), gives a good summary of the other systems theorists.

58 Peter Senge, *The Fifth Discipline* (Random House, 1993).

59 Stafford Beer, *Designing Freedom* (John Wiley, 1974).

Chapter 9: Watch out for the toolheads

60 Womack, Jones and Roos, *The Machine That Changed the World* (Macmillan 1990).

61 James P. Womack and Daniel T. Jones, *Lean Thinking* (Simon & Schuster 1996).

Appendix: The better way to improve public services

62 For example, it was reported to me that at a meeting of local authorities, called to decide courses of action to meet the government's target for e-enabled services, representatives of the Office of the Deputy Prime Minister made it plain that if a decision was not reached the officials would do it for them.

63 House of Commons Public Administration Committee, Fifth Report, *On Target? Government By Measurement*, 22 July 2003, HC 62-I, ISBN 0 21 501204 6. For the UK government's response, see the Committee's Sixth Report of 11 November 2003, HC 1264, ISBN 0 21 501377 8.

64 P45 is the form you are given when you leave employment.

65 A more detailed criticism of Best Value is published on the Vanguard web site: www.lean-service.com.

66 The DWP guidance provided a field day for IT suppliers selling scanning equipment.

67 Hospitals are rated on a number of criteria by stars ranging from 0 to 3. Three-star trusts are supposed to be subject to 'lighter-touch' regulation, whereas zero-rated trusts are singled out for central attention.

68 All incidents are classified in three categories, A, B and C, in descending order of priority.

69 *Health Which?*, 2002 to 2003.

70 *Health Which?*, April 2002.

71 *The Observer* (UK newspaper), 20 April 2003.

72 *The Times* (UK newspaper), 21 May 2003.

73 *The Guardian* (UK newspaper), 22 May 2003.

Further reading

Ackoff, Russell. *Ackoff's Best*. John Wiley, 1999

Beer, Stafford. *Designing Freedom*. John Wiley, 1974

Deming, W. Edwards. *Out of the Crisis*. Cambridge University Press, 1982

Engineering Quality Forum. *The true effectiveness of quality related initiatives in the UK*. Engineering Quality Forum, 2002

Flood, Robert. *Rethinking the Fifth Discipline*. Routledge, 1999

House of Commons Public Administration Committee, Fifth Report. *On Target? Government By Measurement*. HC 62-I, ISBN 0 21 501204 6, 22 July 2003

House of Commons Public Administration Committee, Sixth Report, *On Target? Government By Measurement*. HC 1264, ISBN 0 21 501377 8, 11 November 2003 [government's reply].

Hutton, Will. *The World We're In*. Abacus, 2003

Johnson T. and A. Broms. *Profit Beyond Measure*. Nicholas Brealey Publishing, 2000

Kohn, Alfie. *Punished by Rewards*. Houghton Mifflin, 1993

OASIG, Institute of Work Psychology. *Failing to deliver: the IT performance gap*. University of Sheffield 1995

Ohno, Taiichi. *The Toyota Production System*. Productivity Press, 1988

Pascale, Richard. *Managing on the Edge*. Penguin, 1990

Seddon, John. *I want you to cheat.* Vanguard Education 1992.

Seddon, John. *The Case Against ISO 9000*. Oak Tree Press, 2000. Also www.lean-service.com

Senge, Peter. *The Fifth Discipline*. Random House, 1993

Taylor, Frederick Winslow. *The Principles of Scientific Management*. Kessinger Publishing Co, 2004

Vanguard. 'The Vanguard Guide to Business Excellence.' www.lean-service.com

Vanguard. 'The Vanguard Guide to Creating and Using Capability Charts.' Available at www.lean-service.com

Welch, Jack. *Jack*. Headline, 2001

Womack J., D. Jones and D. Roos. *The Machine That Changed the World*. Macmillan, 1990

Womack J. P. and Daniel T. Jones. *Lean Thinking*. Simon & Schuster 1996

Other publications by the author

"I Want You to Cheat: the unreasonable guide to service and quality in organizations" First published in 1992

"The Case Against ISO9000" First published in 1996, revised to include the ISO9000 revisions in 2000.

Vanguard has published a series of practical guides and manuals. These publications can be found on the Vanguard website: www.lean-service.com

Index

Page numbers in *italics* indicate illustrations. Page numbers in **bold** indicate charts.

About the author

John Seddon is an occupational psychologist and management thinker. In the early part of his career he studied programs of change that failed and, as a consequence, has developed his own methods, which he describes as a combination of systems thinking—how the work works—and intervention theory—how to change it.

John leads the Vanguard organizations. Vanguard consultants reject normal consulting practices—sending in 'the suits' to conduct an analysis, writing reports and making changes through training, projects and communications. Instead they work with workers and managers to help them make the change from a command-and-control design to a systems design, building expertise in to the organization.

John has been a vocal critic of management fads, arguing they don't challenge the fundamentals of management thinking. He is well known for his antipathy towards ISO 9000, and he has been a regular critic of government intervention in the public sector.